To Walt Whitman, America

The

University

of North

Carolina

Press

Chapel Hill

& London

To Walt Whitman, America

KENNETH M. PRICE

Set in Cycles and Copperplate
by Tseng Information Systems
Manufactured in the
United States of America
The paper in this book meets
the guidelines for permanence
and durability of the Committee
on Production Guidelines for
Book Longevity of the Council
on Library Resources.
Library of Congress
Cataloging-in-Publication Data
Price, Kenneth M.
To Walt Whitman, America / by
Kenneth M. Price.
    p. cm.
Includes bibliographical references and
index.
ISBN 0-8078-2849-1 (alk. paper) —
ISBN 0-8078-5518-9 (pbk. : alk. paper)
1. Whitman, Walt, 1819–1892 —
Criticism and interpretation — History.
2. Whitman, Walt, 1819–1892 —
Appreciation — United States.
3. Whitman, Walt, 1819–1892 —
Knowledge — United States.
4. National characteristics, American,
in literature. 5. United States — In
literature. I. Title.
PS3237.4.U6 P75   2004
811'.3 — dc22   2003020181

Portions of this work have been
previously published, in somewhat
different form, in Robert K. Nelson
and Kenneth M. Price, "Debating
Manliness: Thomas Wentworth
Higginson, William Sloane Kennedy,
and the Question of Whitman,"
American Literature 73 (September
2001): 497–524; "The Mediating
'Whitman': Edith Wharton, Morton
Fullerton, and the Problem of Com-
radeship," *Texas Studies in Literature and
Language* 36 (Winter 1994): 380–402;
"Whitman, Dos Passos, and 'Our Story
Book Democracy,'" in *Walt Whitman:
The Centennial Essays*, ed. Ed Folsom
(Iowa City: University of Iowa Press,
1994), 217–25; and "Walt Whitman at
the Movies: Cultural Memory and the
Politics of Desire," *Whitman East and
West: New Contexts for Reading Walt
Whitman*, ed. Ed Folsom (Iowa City:
University of Iowa Press, 2002),
36–70, and are reprinted here with
permission.

cloth   08 07 06 05 04   5 4 3 2 1
paper   08 07 06 05 04   5 4 3 2 1

FOR MARSDEN PRICE

teacher father

CONTENTS

Acknowledgments, ix

Introduction, 3

CHAPTER 1
Whitman in Blackface, 9

CHAPTER 2
Edith Wharton and the Problem of Whitmanian Comradeship, 37

CHAPTER 3
Transatlantic Homoerotic Whitman, 56

CHAPTER 4
Xenophobia, Religious Intolerance, and
Whitman's Storybook Democracy, 70

CHAPTER 5
Passing, Fluidity, and American Identities, 90

CHAPTER 6
Whitman at the Movies, 108

Notes, 139

Index, 177

FIGURES

1. *The Trapper's Bride*, by Alfred Jacob Miller, 1850 *24*

2. *The Trapper's Bride*, by Alfred Jacob Miller, 1845 *25*

3. *Boy With Raised Arm*, by Sidney Goodman *35*

4. *Resources of America*, by Ben Shahn *83*

5. *Father Coughlin*, by Ben Shahn *84*

6. Eadweard Muybridge's serial photographs of a trotting horse *109*

7. Thomas Eakins's *History of a Jump* *110*

8. Scene from *The Carpenter* *113*

9. Whitman figure in *The Carpenter* *114*

10. Lillian Gish rocking the cradle in *Intolerance* *117*

11. Claude Rains and Bette Davis in *Now, Voyager* *121*

12. Roberto Benigni in *Down by Law* *127*

13. Kevin Kline, Meryl Streep, and Peter MacNicol in *Sophie's Choice* *131*

14. Susan Sarandon and Tim Robbins in *Bull Durham* *133*

15. Jason Priestley in *Love and Death on Long Island* *135*

16. Scene from *Love and Death on Long Island* *136*

17. Marilyn Monroe reading *Leaves of Grass* *137*

ACKNOWLEDGMENTS

I began this book at Texas A&M University, expanded its range and altered its orientation at the College of William & Mary, and completed it at the University of Nebraska-Lincoln. I am grateful for support of various kinds from each of these institutions. I owe much to Ed Folsom, Elizabeth Gray, Ezra Greenspan, Sian Hunter, and Marilee Lindemann, each of whom read the entire manuscript and enriched it significantly. Other readers improved the book by commenting on particular sections: Brett Barney, Susan Belasco, Stephanie Browner, Matt Cohen, Jeffrey N. Cox, Linda Frost, Amanda Gailey, Andrew Jewell, Wendy Katz, Diana Linden, Jerome Loving, Arthur Knight, Richard Lowry, Martin Murray, Robert K. Nelson, Mary Ann O'Farrell, Venetria Patton, Vivian Pollak, Larry Reynolds, Michael Robertson, Robert Scholnick, and George Wolf. My wife Renée and daughters Ashley and Gillian helped in ways large and small—and also in ways that defy description. Their presence is everywhere in these pages.

For permission to reprint, in Chapter 1, a single paragraph from my coauthored essay published in *American Literature*, I am grateful both to Robert K. Nelson and to Duke University Press. I am similarly grateful to *Texas Studies in Literature and Language* for allowing me to reproduce, in Chapter 2, a modified version of an essay on Edith Wharton and Whitman. I thank the University of Iowa Press for allowing me to reproduce that part of Chapter 4 dealing with John Dos Passos and Chapter 6 on Whitman at the Movies, both of which appeared earlier in volumes edited by Ed Folsom, *Walt Whitman: The Centennial Essays* and *Whitman East and West: New Contexts for Reading Walt Whitman*, respectively.

To Walt Whitman, America

*I returned to Whitman because he was of America, and I felt
he had something to give me in terms of the American world.*
—Jean Toomer

*The only comfort in a rather Nordic array of dispositions has
been Walt Whitman. . . . He has the careless and forgiving odor
of someone who will let you live.*
—Alvaro Cardona-Hine

I, too, sing America. —Langston Hughes

*With a nearly desperate sense of isolation and a growing
suspicion that I lived in an alien land, I took to the open road.*
—William Least Heat-Moon

I just lifted lines from Leaves of Grass. *. . . It's so American.
And also his vision of a new kind of human being that was going
to be formed in this country—although he never specifically said
Chinese—ethnic Chinese also—I'd like to think he meant all kinds
of people.*
—Maxine Hong Kingston

INTRODUCTION

Walt Whitman is a foundational figure in American culture.[1] The inclusiveness of *Leaves of Grass* resonates especially powerfully in the United States, a country remarkable for its diverse population and for its ongoing struggle to fulfill its meaning and promise. Few writers continue to generate as much interest in the wider culture as the poet of *Leaves of Grass*. In recent years his words have been inscribed in public areas with increasing frequency: on the railing above the main terminal of Reagan National Airport, in the Archives–Navy Memorial Metro Station and in the walkway of Freedom Plaza in Washington, D.C., on the railing at the Fulton Ferry Landing at the foot of the Brooklyn Bridge, at the entryway of the Monona Terrace Convention Center in Madison, Wisconsin (Frank Lloyd Wright insisted that the design should include an inscription from his favorite American poet), on a plaque at the entryway to the Willa Cather Garden at my own university in Lincoln, Nebraska. Whitman was a central voice in Ken Burns's magisterial *Civil War* series for PBS and again for Ric Burns's PBS series on New York. He has been celebrated in musical compositions from classical to pop and invoked in political speeches, television programs, and, with remarkable frequency, films. He has been featured on postage stamps, postcards, and matchbook covers and in cartoons, including a *New Yorker* illustration featuring a copy of *Leaves of Grass* with a zipper down the spine, an allusion to President Clinton's famous gift to Monica Lewinsky. Inexpensive pocket editions of Whitman were distributed to workers and farmers during the Depression, and free copies were given to the American armed forces during World War II. Whitman has been used to sell cigarettes, cigars, coffee (in a variety of ways), whiskey, insurance, and more. Many schools bear the name Walt Whitman, including the first private gay high school in the United States. Hotels, bridges, apartment buildings, summer camps, parks, truck stops, common rooms in guest houses, corporate centers, AIDS clinics, political think tanks, and shopping malls are named after Whitman.

Whitman's importance stretches well beyond U.S. national borders, too, of course. The recently published volume *Walt Whitman and the World*, edited by Gay Wilson Allen and Ed Folsom, indicates that he has had a greater impact on cultures worldwide than any writer since Shakespeare.[2] *Leaves of Grass* has been translated into French, German, Spanish, Italian, Japanese, and Chinese, and selections of his poetry have appeared in every major language. Dozens of books on Whitman's life and poetry have been published on every continent. In his own time, Whitman was pleased when a letter from abroad reached him "sharply," addressed merely "Walt Whitman, America."[3]

In addition to the metonymic feat of making *Leaves of Grass* and his own person merge so that they became almost exchangeable terms, Whitman created similar slippage between himself and his country. Ezra Pound remarked: Whitman "*is* America. His crudity is an exceeding great stench, but it *is* America."[4] Others have also conflated Whitman and America. For example, Malcolm Cowley once remarked that "before Walt Whitman America hardly existed."[5] Claims of this sort are especially interesting when a racial element is added, as when June Jordan argues that "in America the father is white" and, further, that "Walt Whitman is the one white father who shares the systematic disadvantages of his heterogeneous offspring trapped inside a closet that is, in reality, as huge as the continental spread of North and South America."[6] When Jordan, an African American poet, claims her place in a Whitman lineage, she savors the irony of being able simultaneously to honor him and to implicate him in the history of unwelcomed white fathering of black children. By alluding to Whitman's sexuality and the problem of the closet, Jordan touches on two major intertwined emphases of this book: Whitman's sexual legacy and his legacy for an ethnically diverse America.

There are complex issues involved when an artist of color acknowledges a white predecessor. Long before Jordan, James Weldon Johnson, Langston Hughes, and Jean Toomer all recognized the link between language and ideology, how the terminology of race divides people into repellent factions. When they acknowledged their troubled kinship with Whitman they demanded something akin to what the mulatto historically lacked: a nameable white father. Intriguingly, many Harlem Renaissance writers negotiated their positions as writers both black and American through their varying encounters with Whitman. Because Whitman's encompassing impulses start from a particular self, it is useful to recall that Whitman's very name, according to William Swinton's *Rambles among Words*, means "white man."[7] And, in fact, however broad-minded Whitman has sometimes seemed and however liberating he has sometimes been, his primary allegiance was to a particular segment of the population, white working men. Whitman was hardly free of the racism of his culture, yet he has had an extraordinary impact on writers from disadvantaged groups. The general tendency among African American writers is to applaud and at times even revere Whitman. Still, the response has been anything but simple and uniform. For example, Ishmael Reed explores the psychic costs of an affiliation that can lead, he believes, to cultural rather than legal enslavement. For various reasons, then, including the open-endedness of *Leaves of Grass* and the sharply different ways that cultural project could be understood, Whitman left plenty of room for his literary progeny to reimagine America.

There is an irony of course in having Whitman, a childless man dedicated to the love of comrades, as the "father" of children of any sort, white, brown, or other. Whitman's own poetics relied heavily on passing, sometimes in a specifically racial sense, but more often through the creation of a shape-changing, identity-shifting, gender-crossing protean self at the heart of *Leaves of Grass*. Whitman's work invites us to consider both racial and sexual passing. Interestingly, biographers developed a Whitman myth in the early part of the twentieth century about his supposed romance with a woman in New Orleans, and even some of his close friends and disciples believed that he had fathered children. However, he was passing, occasionally pretending to be interested in women while subtly signaling his commitment to calamus love, male same-sex bonds. Sexual passing is at the heart of the poem eventually entitled "Once I Pass'd through a Populous City" in which Whitman changed the pronouns from "he" to "she" to reorient (and to disguise) his depiction of love, attachment, and loss. Whitman's fluidity of identity, his artful negotiation of the terrain at both the margin and the center, have been enabling and empowering for his followers, suggesting various ways to slip the limits of given social roles and to fashion new roles more elastic and responsive to the complexities of experience and desire.

In this study, I address various topics in light of a basic analytical premise: that Whitman is so central to practices and formulations of American culture, past and present, that we may use his life, work, ideas, and influence to examine major patterns in our culture over the last 150 years. Described broadly, some of the topics I pursue include constructions of race and authorial identity, the formation of heterosexuality and homosexuality in literature, intersections between film and literary culture, and connections between Whitman's work and different manifestations of nonconformist politics in the twentieth century. This book could have treated innumerable topics ranging from Whitman's impact on music, architecture, and the fine arts to the way his words and his image have been turned into advertising fodder. Seeking Whitman, one can find him seemingly everywhere. But rather than discussing the entire range of responses to Whitman, I dwell on case studies that illuminate how Whitman mediates understandings of race and sexuality in American culture. For me, these matters are fundamental to Whitman's legacy. I believe my eclectic approach can sketch, though it does not begin to fully portray, the poet's endlessly rich and surprising afterlife.

My opening chapter, "Whitman in Blackface" treats questions of race, region, and what the poet termed "real Americans." I investigate how Whitman crafted a poetic identity on the color line, interstitially, between racial identities. Whitman's early experiments emerged out of a working-class white culture that was fascinated by blackface performance, and he developed key elements of his poetic identity by appropriating aspects of black masculinity. I particularize Whitman's emergence and reception by being attentive to local circumstances, both Whitman's New York origins and the way in which his literary project challenged Bostonian norms for nineteenth-century literary culture. Whitman's poetry first appeared in an age of New England domination of American letters, and many early commentators rejected him on the grounds of his class, region, and sexuality. Whitman celebrated the roiling crowd and was especially fond of the working-class theater and street life in the Bowery. He set *Leaves of Grass* in opposition to literature conceived as conservatively exclusive. The idea that American literature was white, male, and New England–based was asserted in the leading monthlies, in collected editions, in literary histories, and in the voting for a proposed American academy of letters.[8] Eventually the New England construction of literary culture crumbled as modernist writers strove to locate a more usable past. Many modernists sought a literature more responsive to a mixed people and frequently highlighted the importance of Whitman. George Santayana understood these shifting cultural currents as well as anyone, as is clear from "The Genteel Tradition in American Philosophy" and *The Last Puritan* (1935). Chapter 2 analyzes how Edith Wharton benefited from a newly available past. Vastly different from Whitman, Wharton found the poet nonetheless to be a central resource in both her life and art. Wharton's midlife love affair with the journalist William Morton Fullerton was conducted within a Whitmanian aura through the exchange of a copy of *Leaves of Grass* and the periodic invocation of the poet's language of comradeship. Fullerton was a sexually ambiguous figure who contributed in powerful (and sometimes painful) ways to Wharton's thinking about gender roles, a subject of primary importance in her novels.

D. H. Lawrence and E. M. Forster, too, found Whitman's commitment to comradeship to be of fundamental importance, as Chapter 3 indicates. *Studies in Classic American Literature*, Lawrence's account of American culture, culminates with a chapter on Whitman that changes radically through various versions as Lawrence struggles with the implications of male-male love. Both Lawrence and Forster address the love-death nexus, though Lawrence finally shies away from endorsing Whitmanian comradeship while Forster enthusiastically embraces the love between men in *Maurice*. Forster was very much aware, of course, that the "happy ending . . . that fiction allows" was at odds with the actual England he lived in, where *Maurice* had to be left unpublished (lest Forster be charged with supporting criminal activity). Chapter 4 considers the extreme political circumstances of the 1930s when the term comradeship often had a Marxist inflection. Here I study how John Dos Passos and Ben Shahn turn to Whitman as a democratic symbol, as a way to illuminate the dignity of ordinary work and workers, and as an antidote to the rise of international fascism. I close the chapter with Bernard Malamud's mid-century reflections on Whitman and the crises of the 1930s in "The German Refugee." Chapter 5 moves from global politics to identity politics. Here I consider Ishmael Reed, William Least Heat-Moon, and Gloria Naylor on the issue of racial and sexual passing. While Naylor and Least Heat-Moon turn to Whitman as a means of claiming a multiple racial heritage, Reed, as indicated above, sees Whitman much less favorably. In my final chapter, I explore Whitman-based movies, tracing the long engagement of cinema with Whitman from the days of *Intolerance* and the first avant-garde American films, through the middle of the twentieth century, and on to the last twenty years, when Whitman has been crucial for mediating our culture's understanding of same-sex love. These films offer a fresh vantage point for considering how Whitman helped create—and continues to participate in—celebrity culture.

Literary and film narratives that respond to Whitman consistently remake him in the process of trying to achieve America.[9] Whitman attempted to include, encompass, celebrate, and give voice to a variegated populace. These goals, imperfectly realized in his poetry, link his name to inclusive versions of American democracy. George Fredrickson writes of "Whitman's intellectual problem—the still unanswered question of how to give a genuine sense of community to an individualistic, egalitarian democracy."[10] For many thinkers, Whitman's inclusiveness makes him crucial in efforts to build toward a harmonious American society. Nonetheless, Peter Erickson argues that Whitman does not offer a useful model for contemporary multiculturalism largely because his sympathy too often becomes appropriation. There is a way in which Whitman imposes his views on others and presupposes the rightness of his own structures and modes of perception. To some degree, Whitman can be said to be coercive. Yet if he asked readers to accede to his version of America, it was also with the belief that these very readers and writers, paradoxically, must revise him as they strive to realize themselves and remake America.

At another level, Erickson's point about multiculturalism is anachronistic. Whitman was not interested in developing multiple cultures in the United States but instead in helping to realize *one* culture, a complex yet unified and distinctive people. Whitman balanced his celebration of individual development with an insistence that such development could only be fully realized within the aggregate. Whitman attempted to absorb others into his expanded self and into a resulting expanded view of what might constitute his country. For Whitman, American democracy, fully responsive to a varied people, was not an achievement to be celebrated but a hope to be fulfilled: "The word democracy is a great word whose history . . . remains unwritten because that history has yet to be enacted."[11]

CHAPTER 1

WHITMAN IN BLACKFACE

I come back to Walt Whitman.
What in the hell happened to him.
Wasn't he a white man?
—June Jordan[1]

In 1998, Toni Morrison declared that Bill Clinton was our first black president. Or at least, she clarified, he was blacker than any person who would be elected in our lifetimes. Morrison noted that he "displays almost every trope of blackness: single-parent household, born poor, working-class, saxophone-playing, McDonald's-and-junk-food-loving boy from Arkansas."[2] In the ensuing controversy some wondered if Morrison's tropes themselves were not racist. The columnist Clarence Page observed, however, that many people missed Morrison's point: "Clinton knows how it feels to be an outsider and he has used that knowledge to connect emotionally and intellectually with others who felt the same way."[3] This purported ability to connect may account for the steady support Clinton received from the black community despite a mixed record on racial matters. Just as Clinton knew what it was to be an outsider (and benefited from that knowledge), so, too, did Whitman, who articulated an expansive sense of community from a position both "in and out of the game."

A close look at Whitman and race reveals a complicated record. The exceptionally strong egalitarian and inclusive impulse guiding his life's work, *Leaves of Grass*, is periodically disrupted by moments of insensitivity and racism. These shortcomings occur both early and late in his career, and both within *Leaves of Grass* and outside of it. Despite these lapses, we find widespread admiration of Whitman over a long period of time and from a distinguished group of African American writers including, among others, Kelly Miller, James Weldon Johnson, Langston Hughes, Jean Toomer, Richard Wright, June Jordan, Gloria Naylor, Yusef Komunyakaa, and Cornel West. A remark by William James—"a man has as many social selves as there are individuals who recognize him and carry an image of him in their minds"—reminds us of the extent to which "Whitman" exists as an identity created nearly as much by his commentators as by the poet himself.[4] On the issue of race, especially, people have partly found and partly created what they needed in Whitman based on their own dispositions and circumstances. Ronald Takaki, for example, quotes Whitman at the end of *In a Different Mirror*, his multicultural history of the United States, to highlight the attractive possibilities of a harmonious diversity. Notwithstanding Whitman's personal contradictions, entangled in larger cultural contradictions, he is typically remembered for his capacious and loving record of American life in all its teeming, earthy, extraordinary complexity. His work holds out the promise of renovation based on new bonds and crossings, providing a glimpse of something other than the racial separation marking so much of U.S. history (and continuing in present settings from high school cafeterias to urban neighborhoods across the country). Separatism, at times a useful means in the struggle for equality, has appeal as an ultimate goal for some multicultural theorists. But a less atomistic and essentialist goal remains vital for many, a goal based on fluid and cross-culturally enriched identities. Accordingly, many African American intellectuals have found Whitman's inclusive, future-oriented project a useful point of departure.

Whitman's cultural positioning may further explain why many African American writers have responded favorably to him. He was both privileged and not, an Anglo male but also a sexual minority, a person with roots in the working class, and a writer whose book was banned.[5] African Americans have been intrigued by a poet whose reputation was significantly shaped by nineteenth-century debates, when commentary ranged from rapturous appreciation to disgusted rejection. Some nineteenth-century commentators, naive or disingenuous, mistook the persona for the person and emphasized Whitman's claim that he was rude, uneducated, lusty, and vulgar. Frequently, these commentators turned his own rhetoric against him and insisted that he was disqualified as a poet—and all the more as a national spokesman—because he was a sexual, religious, and even subhuman outsider. They described Whitman as bestial, judged him to be insane, suggested that he should commit suicide, urged that he be publicly whipped, called him a "satyr," and tarred him as "Caliban," Prospero's half-human slave, son of the witch Sycorax and a devil and symbol of base and lustful urges.[6] They employed an array of tropes to depict him as an outsider in his own land. They made him, as it were, black.

THE SPACE BETWEEN MASTERS AND SLAVES

Whitman began his career at a time when many white performers were appearing in blackface, some of whom the poet himself witnessed. Nineteenth-century commentators, disturbed by Whitman's violation of codes of gentility, strove to further tar him by associating him with black men and with widely popular New York minstrel shows.[7] Some of their descriptions of Whitman amounted to caricature, but they could claim that they took their cue from the poet himself, who repeatedly explored cross-racial identifications.

Occasionally Whitman asserted these racial crossings directly, as when he declares, in the initial poem of *Leaves of Grass* (1855), "I am the hounded slave," and at other times the crossings were made more indirectly. Whitman's cross-racial identifications are important in two primary ways. First, these racial crossings illustrate how Whitman, as was common in working-class antebellum white male culture, constructed a sense of manhood partly through appropriating black masculinity.[8] Eric Lott has noted that such appropriations of black masculinity typically involved a complex mixture of both admiration and fear, of both yearning toward and warding off, and of both love and loathing.[9] Second, Whitman's racial crossings enable us to situate his work within a rhetorical field significantly shaped by the approach of middle-class white abolitionists to the question of race. Whitman, rarely radical in his antislavery positions, nonetheless shared with these abolitionists a reliance on sympathy in addressing racial slavery.

Whitman was at his most progressive in the years leading up to 1855 and somewhat more conservative thereafter, though unevenly and unpredictably so. He was more daring on racial issues in his manuscripts than in more polished work, as jottings and drafts from approximately 1850–56 reveal. This material was unknown to African Americans in the nineteenth century and remains inadequately studied even today, but I focus on these manuscripts because they help highlight and explain some contradictory elements in Whitman's better known works and because they clarify his overall thought and the forces shaping it.

In composing the first two editions of *Leaves*, Whitman made clear that he regarded racial slavery as a fundamental threat to what he perceived as the country's historical mission to promote freedom and equality. The poet who once penned the motto "No nation once fully enslaved ever fully recovered its liberty" recognized the ideologically contradictory position of the United States as a slave-owning democracy.[10] Despite this perception, his commitment to freedom was stronger than his commitment to equality across ethnic and racial lines. Given his national poetic ambitions, it is not surprising that slavery and freedom reside together in *Leaves of Grass*, uneasily enmeshed, at the heart of things.[11]

In one of his earliest notebooks, "Talbot Wilson"—long thought to date from 1847 but now understood to be from about 1854—Whitman broke into free verse in the manner of *Leaves of Grass*.[12] After asserting that he is the poet of the masters and the poet of the slaves, he projects himself into the highly charged space between masters and slaves, both dangerous and erotic:

> I am the poet of slaves,
>   and of ^{the} masters of slaves
> I am the poet of the body
> And I am
>
> I am the poet of the body
> And I am the poet of the soul
> The ^{I go with} the slaves ^{of the earth} ~~are mine, and~~ equally with
>   the ^{equally with the} masters are ~~equally~~ ~~mine~~
> And I will stand between
>   the masters and the slaves,
> ~~And I e~~ Entering into both ~~and~~
>   so that both shall understand
>   me alike.[13]

Whitman occupies and transforms the cultural space of violation. He underscored the stakes at issue in another notebook from this period: "what real Americans can be made out of slaves? What real Americans can be made out of the masters of slaves?"[14] Whitman's idea of America, a goal rather than an achieved condition, was based on an inclusive and exalted commonality, the "divine average." Masters and slaves were ill-suited to this notion of America not because of whiteness or blackness but because of the polarized qualities—despotism and debasement, authority and dependence—characteristic of slavery itself. In his notebook lines, Whitman seeks to enter slave and master to identify with them, to grasp their meaning and circumstances. Convinced of the inseparability of the body and the body politic, and attempting to offset the effects of rape and the white fathering of property on enslaved women, Whitman strives to remake penetration as a vehicle for purification. His metaphor conveys suggestions of both transgression and transformation, preparing us for the twist at the end: the result of Whitman entering others is not his understanding of them but their understanding of *him*. The insistence that master and slave should adopt *his* view can be regarded as imperious arrogance. But if we merely scold Whitman for presumptuousness we may miss a key point. At a time when abolitionists were deeply committed to intersubjectivity and described it as a white mobility as opposed to black stasis, Whitman grants the power of identification to both master and slave. This is extremely unusual for the antebellum period, when sympathetic mobility was reserved as a particular racial privilege as white abolitionists sought to establish rich human inwardness through flirtations with inward merging. Typically, a corresponding ability was not granted to black subjects. In abolitionist literature it is the white sympathetic onlooker who is inwardly transformed, not—as Whitman has it—both white and black, both slave and master.[15]

Despite the key passage above granting black subjects sympathetic mobility, Whitman's more common approach was to explore white racial crossing. The "Talbot Wilson" notebook, recently recovered by the Library of Congress after being missing for decades, deserves extensive quotation because, in the flickering, not quite visible movement *between* its leaves, we can sense the birth of Whitman's poetic sensibility. At the opening of a sequence of passages that contribute to the first published version of "The Sleepers," Whitman indulges in a male fantasy of size and plenitude.

> I held more than I thought
> I did not think I was big
>   enough for so much exstasy
> Or that a touch could
>   take it all out of me.[16]

This unpromising mixture of wishfulness and bravado is suddenly recognized as something extraordinary when read in conjunction with what follows. That is, this male fantasy is associated culturally and psychologically with the succeeding notebook leaf, treating black rage, revenge, and empowerment. On that succeeding leaf, Whitman launches into a speech in the slave's voice, though readers may hear Whitman, the slave, or both of them. Importantly, in this notebook Whitman links across two leaves a dream of great virility and the release of a black voice:

> I am a curse:
> Sharper than ~~wind~~ serpent's
>   eyes or wind of the ice-fields!
>
> O topple down ~~like~~ Curse!
>   topple more heavy than
>   death!
> I am lurid with rage!
>
> I invoke Revenge to assist
>   me—[17]

The reviewer of the first edition of *Leaves* who associated Whitman with Caliban could not have known about this notebook in which Whitman seems to build on Caliban's famous complaint to Miranda: "You taught me language; and my profit on 't / Is I know how to curse."[18] Caliban, an enslaved victim of imperialism, waged a rebellion in response. Whitman's notebook articulates, in the highly charged context of the 1850s, the desire for black revenge and rebellion. We are not presented with the pathetic and victimized black of much antislavery—yet typically racist—literature. Instead Whitman depicts an enormous force, power, and submerged anger in his black speaker.

In the following notebook passage, Whitman yearns for slaveholders to be punished with sexual and reproductive rot:

> Let fate pursue them
> I do not know any horror
>   that is dreadful enough
>   for them—
> What is the worst whip
>   you have
> May the ~~genitals~~ that
>   begat them rot
> May the womb that begat[19]

Whitman's concern with genitals was anything but arbitrary. In the South and elsewhere in the United States, black men were castrated—sometimes literally, sometimes psychologically—so as to keep them at a distance from white women. Meanwhile some white men raped and impregnated their slave women, thus adding to their holdings in property. Whitman responded by creating a black speaker of potent force. The slaveholders, with whips raised against them by the poet and their sexual license turned into sexual corruption, will be pursued even beyond death. Whitman says he will not listen or offer mercy, the grave will offer no hiding place, and even the "lappets of God shall not protect them."[20] And then we encounter a stunning transformation, as curious as it is complete:

> ~~The sepulchre~~ The sepulchre and the white
> ~~serving the shroud~~
> linen have yielded me up
> Observing the summer grass[21]

This notebook announces profoundly transformative effects yet comes to rest in passivity, a result some may regard as mere acquiescence. Yet out of this strange brew of sexual potency and sexual rot, oppression and punishment, racial crossing and resurrection, a poet emerges, absorbing the lessons of the grass, which he will famously describe as a "uniform hieroglyphic" that grows "among black folks as among white." This was an insight that provided the central image for *Leaves of Grass*, and Whitman's notebooks allow us to see in what political ferment the image was born.[22]

In a manuscript related to this notebook, a tangled draft now held at the University of Virginia, Whitman articulates more fully than in any published version of "The Sleepers" the plight of a particular "slave negro" and his bold response. Whitman's deletion of "slave" in favor of "negro" in this context shifts the emphasis from bondage to race:

> I am ~~black~~ a curse: a ~~black slave~~ negro ~~spoke~~ ~~felt thought~~ thinks me
> You You ~~He~~ cannot speak for ~~your~~him self, ~~slave,~~ negro—I lend ~~you~~ him
>   my own ~~mouth~~ tongue
> ~~A black~~ [illegible] I darted like a snake from [his[?]] ^ [your[?]]
>   mouth.——

~~I~~ My eyes are bloodshot, they look down the river,
A steamboat ~~carries off~~ ^{paddles away} my woman and children.——
[previous two lines canceled with vertical lines]

~~Around my neck I am~~
~~T The~~^{His} Iron necklace and the red sores of ~~my~~ ^{the} shoulders
    I do not ~~feel~~ ^{mind,}
~~The~~ Hopple ~~and ball~~ at ~~my~~ ^{the} ancles, ^ ^{and tight cuffs at the wrists} ~~does~~ ^
    ^{must} not detain me

I ^ ~~will~~ go down the river with ^ ^{the sight of} my bloodshot eyes,
I ~~will~~ go ~~on~~ ^{to} the steamboat that paddles ^ ~~off~~ my ~~wife~~ ^{woman} and _{child}

~~A~~ I do not stop with my wom[an?] and children,
I burst ~~down~~ the saloon doors and crash on [?]
    party of passengers.——
~~But for them, I am too should have been on the steambo~~[at?—— page
    cut off]
~~I should soon~~ [23]

Toni Morrison has argued that, for whites, the experience of selfhood and freedom is grounded in racial difference and inequality, and certainly Whitman's exploration of identity on the color line is partially self-exploration.[24] The bursting of the saloon doors by the "slave negro" is closely related to Whitman's description of himself in "Song of Myself": "Unscrew the locks from the doors! / Unscrew the doors themselves from their jambs!"[25] Whitman acts on his own exhortation and *achieves* himself through this bold black man. It is possible to regard Whitman's lines as solipsistic and to conclude that his self-exploration is self-misrecognition. But the lines are more interesting and more politically charged if we see them as breaching the very borders of identity. Significantly, they raise the prospect of violence and of this "slave negro"'s assertive efforts to establish justice and freedom. Intriguingly, Whitman uses the word "lend," indicating that he does not strive to appropriate the black voice but to enable it, to aid the slave/himself in locating a tongue with the lethal power of a snake. Whitman says that the bestowal of power goes from white to black, even though we witness a mutual exchange and enhancement. For Whitman, "lending" is also borrowing as he appropriates black masculinity to develop his poetic persona. He has freed no slave, taken no part in action on the Underground Railroad.[26] Yet despite the racism in his city and social class, he has made an important intellectual and empathetic breakthrough. He offers one of the first attempts by a white author to narrate through a black voice and provides a compelling illustration of the power of racial crossing in the making of a complex intellectual identity. No doubt it was the egalitarian, boundary-crossing side of Whitman, especially evident in the manuscripts but also apparent in the first two published editions of *Leaves of Grass*, that recommended his work to the radical abolitionist publishers, Thayer and Eldridge of Boston, publishers of the third edition.

In the writings of abolitionists, racial crossing frequently moved along a circuit of pain.[27] Whitman, too, used pain to achieve identification, but as he moved closer to the publication of the untitled 1855 version of "The Sleepers," he deleted the references to "red sores" on the shoulders, the "Hopple" at the ankles, and tight cuffs, perhaps because he recognized that the spectacle of pain too often became pornographic.[28] By the time of the first edition of *Leaves* he had lessened the emphasis on physical pain and chosen to create not a pitiable but a powerful individual, an heir of Lucifer, the arch rebel:

> Now Lucifer was not dead . . . . or if he was I am his sorrowful terrible heir;
> I have been wronged . . . . I am oppressed . . . . I hate him that oppresses me,
> I will either destroy him, or he shall release me.
>
> Damn him! how he does defile me,
> How he informs against my brother and sister and takes pay for their blood,
> How he laughs when I look down the bend after the steamboat that carries away my woman.
>
> Now the vast dusk bulk that is the whale's bulk . . . . it seems mine,
> Warily, sportsman! though I lie so sleepy and sluggish, my tap is death.[29]

As Ed Folsom notes, Whitman admires Lucifer, a figure brave enough to confront even a divine master.[30] At a time when slaves routinely were either degraded or pitied, Whitman emphasizes the divinity of Lucifer in related manuscripts. (In "Pictures," another formative early poem, Whitman had explicitly linked a black Lucifer to revolt.[31]) Christopher Castiglia describes typical black representations as emphasizing "traits of piety, nurturance, and conjugal fidelity threatened by the outrages of slavery."[32] In depicting Black Lucifer, Whitman adheres to the pattern of "conjugal fidelity"—in fact, he boldly insists on black male sexual possessiveness at a time when white masters often threatened the sexual dynamic and integrity within black families. With equal daring, Whitman diverges from the idea of an ordinary piety and from stereotypical white paternalism and black male submission. Whitman has his Black Lucifer likening himself to a (sperm?) whale and making clear that he is a potent force to be reckoned with.

The poet insisted that blacks were destined to reach a high estate: "Where others see a slave a pariah an emptier of privies the Poet beholds what when the days of the soul are accomplished shall be peer of God."[33] Whitman recurrently returns to the idea of a semi-divine origin and semi-divine destiny for blacks. But the middle ground is usually missing when he treats blacks. That is, his tendency is to exalt noble black people in the distant past and distant future and to think of blacks in the present as less than fully equal human beings. Over the long publishing life of *Leaves* (beginning eight years before the Emancipation Proclamation and ending nearly three decades after it), Whitman typically does not depict blacks as ordinary people, common Americans. Clearly, the social landscape that shaped Whitman had marked blacks as distinctive. With "slave negro"—his visibly uncertain term from the "I am a curse" manuscript—Whitman struggled with terminological slippage as he referred to categories that overlapped but did not match. We recall that Whitman doubted that "real Americans" could be made out of slaves, a defensible position for a committed democrat. But this position becomes insupportable when "slave" and "negro" become blurred. Whitman's blind spot was in his inability to envision or his unwillingness to promote the right of blacks to full citizenship, an unwillingness that becomes most clear in the postwar years.[34]

This shortcoming partially undermines one of the otherwise bracing and effective poems of 1855, the untitled work now known as "I Sing the Body Electric." Whitman once planned to put "I Sing the Body Electric" in the final position for the 1855 *Leaves* (he referred to the poem, in notes to himself, as "Blacks").[35] In one section of the poem, Whitman dramatizes his encounter with an enslaved black man on the auction block, in whom he sees "the start of populous states and rich republics." Yet even in recognizing the capacity of blacks for self-government, Whitman significantly mentions "republics" rather than the American Republic, and thus avoids contemplating black involvement in U.S. political decision making. (Interestingly, Whitman used "republics" only twice in the poetry of the 1855 *Leaves,* and the other usage connects the black man with himself in striking fashion since both are said to start republics: in the opening poem, he says "this day I am jetting the stuff of far more arrogant republics.") Although Whitman repeatedly identifies himself with blacks in ways both obvious and subtle, he is more comfortable with blacks participating in remote "rich republics" of the future than in the next election in the United States.[36]

In the context of cross-racial masquerade and ventriloquism, one of the most intriguing sections of the poem treats a stalwart old man.

> The shape of his head, the richness and breadth of his manners, the
> pale yellow and white of his hair and beard, the immeasurable
> meaning of his black eyes,
> These I used to go and visit him to see . . . . He was wise also,
> He was six feet tall . . . . he was over eighty years old . . . . his sons
> were massive clean bearded tanfaced and handsome,
> They and his daughters loved him . . . all who saw him loved him . . .
> they did not love him by allowance . . . they loved him with
> personal love;
> He drank water only . . . . the blood showed like scarlet through the
> clear brown skin of his face.[37]

Perhaps this old man is white because no one tells us so and because, as Toni Morrison argues, the default in American culture is white. Yet he also has "black eyes" and "blood" that showed through the "clear brown skin of his face," phrasing that becomes even more noteworthy in 1860 when Whitman added a hyphen to describe the face as "clear-brown." The tension between clarity and ambiguity is fascinating here, especially since the poem culminates in a question underscoring the ultimate uncertainty of all racial lineages: "Who might you find you have come from yourself if you could trace back through the centuries?"[38]

In this same poem, Whitman's description of slaves at auction, grounded in his experiences in 1848 in New Orleans where slaves were sold within an easy walk of his lodgings, illustrates not only the power and limits of sympathy but also the awakening of his powerful commitment to adhesiveness. Whitman uses the black body to unfetter homoeroticism. His approach differs from that of minstrel shows that periodically invoked homoeroticism only to later circumscribe and contain it.[39] Jay Grossman notes that the slave auction offered a rare instance of the nineteenth-century naked body on display, a staging of the body open to the most intrusive examination.[40] Whitman transformed the slave auction into an occasion to articulate and to love the body, indexing its glories from top to toe. Whitman's imagining of the black body advanced—perhaps even enabled—his overall treatment of sex and the body in *Leaves of Grass*. "I Sing the Body Electric" is critical for Whitman as a poet of intimacy and eroticism. In 1856 he added the remarkable section enumerating parts of the human body that ended the poem in all subsequent versions. In 1860 he provided a gloss on the poem by placing just before it "Enfans d'Adam" number 2 (later titled "From Pent-up Aching Rivers") a poem that clearly comments on the auction and the powerful and unsettling erotics of that spectacle:

> The welcome nearness—the sight of the perfect body,
> The swimmer swimming naked in the bath, or motionless on his back
>   lying and floating,
> The female form approaching—I, pensive, love-flesh tremulous,
>   aching;
> The slave's body for sale—I, sternly, with harsh voice, auctioneering,
> The divine list, for myself or you, for any one, making,
> The face—the limbs—the index from head to foot, and what it
>   arouses,
> The mystic deliria—the madness amorous—the utter abandonment,
> (Hark, close and still, what I now whisper to you,
> I love you—O you entirely possess me.[41]

It is not accidental that Whitman yokes together the "slave's body for sale" and mention of the "divine list" that lovingly itemized body parts from toe-joints to heart-valves, from arm-pits to nipples, from man-root to womb. Despite the poet's striking distinctiveness, he follows a well-known cultural pattern in overcoming white inhibitions and prohibitions about sex and corporeality through recourse to the captive body and the racial other.[42] Race, sexuality, domination, and subordination are entangled here. Whitman's erotics are released not only by black bodies but also by the very hierarchy of slavery. Whitman and white sexuality are liberated even as the slave remains enchained.

Intriguingly, the word "possess" turns the last of these lines in an unexpected way, with Whitman, rather than the slave "possessed"—and in multiple ways.[43] At the end of "From Pent-up Aching Rivers," possession itself is reversed by desire for the body, and the possessor becomes possessed. The reversal is important because in the slippage from master to slave, slave to master, hierarchy is undone, and eventually the terms themselves erode. Whitman's use of "possession," connected here to ownership and bondage, is part of his metaphoric use of slavery. Enslavement for Whitman in 1855 was a complex metaphor central to his initial articulation of *Leaves.* He once remarked: "Every man who claims or takes the power to own another man as his property, stabs me in ~~that~~ the heart of my own rights." To own people was to violate what Whitman saw as the "primal right— the first-born, deepest, broadest right—the right of every human being to his personal self."[44] But, in a different context, Whitman also said: "What is it to own any thing?—It is to incorporate it into yourself, as the primal god swallowed the five immortal offspring of Rhea, and accumulated to his life and knowledge and strength all that would have grown in them.—"[45] His way of knowing risked the very mastery he both abhorred as a social reality yet needed as a poetic force. Thus, though he found the roles of both masters and slaves repugnant, he reacted in typically complicated and fascinating ways, finding mastery and utter dependence powerful tropes. His famous open letter to Emerson of 1856 is a dramatic case in point, which I have elsewhere discussed in terms of a master-slave relationship.[46] Whitman could imagine himself becoming a slave in the sense of giving himself over to a project, to his muse, to inspiration, to the war effort. Regarding his hospital service, for example, he told Horace Traubel: "What did I get? Well—I got the boys, for one thing. . . . I gave myself for them: myself: I got the boys: then I got Leaves of Grass." His work with soldiers became his "religion," his "lodestar." It was his "master," and, as he said, it "seized upon me, made me its servant, slave."[47]

ENTHRALLED AND ENTANGLED: THE TRAPPER'S BRIDE, THE RUNAWAY SLAVE, AND THE TWENTY-NINTH BATHER

The centrality of slavery to Whitman's thinking can be illuminated if we take a close look at three consecutive passages in the initial poem of the 1855 *Leaves* (the untitled poem now known as "Song of Myself"). Interestingly, when Whitman produces his first developed characters in his book —respectively, the trapper and his bride, the fugitive slave, and the twenty-ninth bather—he links them through a consideration of bondage. He examines the way bondage connects with sexuality, romance, economics, domestic intimacy, and marriage. As both an actuality and a trope, bondage offered Whitman a means of emphasizing commonalities that cut across gender, race, and circumstance.

The first of these tightly clustered scenes was prompted by *The Trapper's Bride*, the work of the Baltimore artist Alfred Jacob Miller.[48] Existing in multiple versions in both oil and watercolor, *The Trapper's Bride* records an event Miller witnessed during a trip West from near present-day Kansas City, Missouri, to Fort Laramie, Wyoming, in 1837. Miller had been commissioned by an adventurous Scotsman, Captain William Drummond Stewart, to accompany him and to "sketch the remarkable scenery and incidents of the journey."[49] In effect, Miller was to provide souvenir sketches of the American West. After their trip, Miller accompanied Stewart back to Scotland for eighteen months where he reworked some of his prairie sketches into full-scale oils for Stewart's ancestral home, Murthly Castle. Peter Hassrick comments on the aura of Miller's works: "His characters, whether trappers or Indians, seemed suspended in idyllic haze."[50] This result was achieved partly through the intervention of Stewart, who made Miller alter any Indian without "sufficient dignity in expression and carriage."[51]

Although Miller was willing to bestow admirable physical qualities on Indians, his overall opinion remained uncompromisingly harsh: he held that an Indian "uses every stratagem, fair and foul, to preserve . . . [his] worthless life."[52] Ultimately, Miller's painterly eye and hand were better than his extensive commentary on his own work. Dawn Glanz argues that *The Trapper's Bride* depicts "an Indian ceremony, taking place on Indian soil . . . beyond the jurisdiction of the white man's laws, customs, and traditions."[53] But of course the view of the ceremony, and the resulting painting and commentary, were not beyond Miller's personal jurisdiction and, like all of his work, should be considered in light of his equal mix of admiration and loathing of Indians. Because of a lack of both knowledge and sympathy, Miller failed to accept on its own terms the common tribal practice of gift exchange at the time of marriage, and thus he found marriage conducted *au façon du pays* to be debased. He misunderstood the custom of the country, which typically involved the man paying bridewealth to the woman's family,[54] and when he witnessed the event recorded in *The Trapper's Bride*, he concluded that he was encountering de facto prostitution or slavery. He spoke of the "price of acquisition . . . $600 paid for in the legal tender of this region: viz: Guns, $100 each, Blankets $40 each, Red Flannel $20 pr. yard, Alcohol $64 pr. Gal., Tobacco, Beads &c. at corresponding rates."[55] One assumes that Miller would not have found anything amiss in a European woman providing a dowry to the groom's family. His inability to see beyond his own cultural norms was common to many nineteenth-century Euro-Americans who mistakenly assumed that the marriage customs of tribal peoples were tantamount to practices of slavery.[56]

Glanz and Joan Troccoli have argued that *The Trapper's Bride* is an emblem of "the Jeffersonian ideal of a peaceful amalgamation of the races" and the "hope of reconciliation between civilization and the wilderness."[57] Superficial aspects of the trapper's Anglo appearance have led these and other critics to assume that Miller's painting portrays the marriage between a white man and an Indian maiden.[58] But the trapper is by no means unambiguously white. Trappers were in fact bicultural or liminal figures and were often regarded in the nineteenth century as "White Indians."[59] Equally to the point, Miller himself had difficulty categorizing the particular trapper he depicted in *The Trapper's Bride*: "A Free Trapper (white or half-breed) . . . is a most desirable match"[60] (see fig. 1).

The figure of the bride is also complex, though in a different way, because she (paradoxically) appears to be chaste and carnal at once. Small, innocent, almost childlike, she is dressed in white and sharply distinguished from the half-nude Indian woman in red who appears in Miller's 1845 and 1846 renditions of the scene (see fig. 2). Yet if Miller distinguishes the bride from this obvious sexual temptress, he makes the bride, too, sexually suggestive in less obvious ways. For example, the artist depicts her in such a way that her pelvis juts forward, and her white dress hugs and highlights the contours of her body. Miller probably intended her bare feet to be erotic

FIGURE 1. *Alfred Jacob Miller,* The Trapper's Bride, *1850, oil on canvas. Courtesy Joslyn Art Museum, Omaha, Nebraska.*

also. His patron, Stewart, is known to have been attracted to the bare feet of young native women.[61]

Whitman also underscores the erotic appeal of the Indian bride, though he instead emphasizes her "voluptuous" nature and the length of her hair, which reaches her feet. (In none of Miller's versions—or at least in none

FIGURE 2. *Alfred Jacob Miller,* The Trapper's Bride, *1845, oil on canvas.*
Courtesy Eiteljorg Museum of American Indian and Western Art, Indianapolis;
© *Eiteljorg Museum of American Indian and Western Art.*

of the five different versions I have seen—does the bride possess the statuesque build associated with voluptuousness, nor does she have the extraordinary profusion of hair that Whitman gives her.) Edgeley W. Todd, one of the first to comment on how *The Trapper's Bride* figures in "Song of Myself," was misleading, then, when he argued that Whitman provides "simply a verbal translation of what he saw in the painting," and that "not a single detail in the poem is without its counterpart there."[62] Subsequent critics have also failed to examine how Whitman purposefully veers away from Miller. Perhaps the most significant difference between painter and poet is that Miller masks conflict while Whitman explores it. That is, in Miller's depictions the trapper's rifle might as well be a staff given the meek, pacific, and longing expressions of the trapper and his friend. Yusef Komunyakaa, in a poem about the 1846 version of Miller's work, aptly describes the two men as sitting "like Jesus / & a shepherd in rawhide."[63] In contrast, in Whitman's lines, the rifle plays a much more threatening role. Unlike Miller, Whitman records a troubling scene, one that conveys a sense of the uneasy, conflicted, and destructive aspects of the contact of cultures:

> I saw the marriage of the trapper in the open air in the far-west . . . .
>   the bride was a red girl,
> Her father and his friends sat near by crosslegged and dumbly
>   smoking . . . . they had moccasins to their feet and large thick
>   blankets hanging from their shoulders;
> On a bank lounged the trapper . . . . he was dressed mostly in skins
>   . . . . his luxuriant beard and curls protected his neck,
> One hand rested on his rifle . . . . the other hand held firmly the wrist
>   of the red girl,
> She had long eyelashes . . . . her head was bare. . . . her coarse straight
>   locks descended upon her voluptuous limbs and reached to her
>   feet.[64]

Here the trapper holds his bride as if she were recently captured rather than recently wedded. The idea that the trapper "held firmly the wrist of the red girl" is Whitman's own invention—Miller's renderings of the scene do not show this type of grasp. The poet's phrasing describes a coercive relationship, which conveys a truth about the imperial nature of western expansion and the role of trappers as one of the first in a series of forces that ultimately "demoralized, depopulated, and eventually dispossessed Indian people in the trans-Mississippi West."[65] In Whitman's lines, the trapper "lounged," an informal posture at odds with the rapt attention of the trapper in all of Miller's versions of *The Trapper's Bride*. There is a striking incongruity between "lounged" and "held firmly" because the relaxation implied by the one is at odds with the exertion required by the other. Whitman's trapper strikes a pose of confidence in an encounter fraught with anxiety. Even the description of the trapper's curls hints at danger: his neck needs to be "protected."[66]

Whitman juxtaposes the account of the trapper and his bride with his treatment of the runaway slave. The scenes are related both through theme and imagery, including a "rifle" that is an important element in both scenes. Both passages also emphasize bare feet: we recall that the bride's hair reached to her feet, and Whitman describes himself as tending the black man's feet.

> The runaway slave came to my house and stopped outside,
> I heard his motions crackling the twigs of the woodpile,
> Through the swung half-door of the kitchen I saw him limpsey and
>   weak,
> And went where he sat on a log, and led him in and assured him,
> And brought water and filled a tub for his sweated body and bruised
>   feet,
> And gave him a room that entered from my own, and gave him some
>   coarse clean clothes,
> And remember perfectly well his revolving eyes and his awkwardness,
> And remember putting plasters on the galls of his neck and ankles;
> He staid with me a week before he was recuperated and passed north,
> I had him sit next me at table . . . . my firelock leaned in the corner.[67]

Earlier in the poem, we have been prepared to think of feet in connection with acts of intimacy by the famous union of body and soul in which the totality of sexual engagement is underscored by the line: "And reached till you felt my beard, and reached till you held my feet." The runaway slave, with his awkwardness and revolving eyes, may seem an unlikely focus of erotic interest, though the reference to the opening to the speaker's own room is worth noting. In addition, the most tender touch—actual as opposed to fantasized—described in Whitman's sequence of bondage scenes is between the speaker and the runaway. Soon after these scenes, a black drayman enters the poem, and he is sharply contrasted with the runaway. With his "polish'd and perfect limbs," the black drayman clearly is a person with great appeal for the speaker: he fits into a pattern of streetcar and train conductors whom Whitman found especially fascinating. The poet makes a before-and-after statement by replacing the runaway slave with the black drayman, or, if you will, metamorphosing the one into the other through the power of freedom and Whitman's baptismal bath.[68] No longer driven by hounds as was the runaway, the drayman is himself a driver. One index to the transformation is in the contrast between the "revolving eyes" of the runaway and the "calm and commanding glance" of the drayman.

The third of these scenes of bondage involves Whitman's famous twenty-ninth bather, a wealthy woman confined behind the windows of her house, yearning for the freedom enjoyed by the naked bodies she sees cavorting in the water. Significantly, she sees "white bellies" bulging to the sun, luxuriating in a race- and gender-based relative freedom. The twenty-ninth bather experiences what women's rights advocates sometimes called "the slavery of sex" and is imprisoned and confined by the codes of her time.[69] As Vivian Pollak notes, she "owns" the fine house but does not own herself.[70] Like the trapper, she is situated on a "bank." The woman also shares with the trapper a number of paradoxically empowering traits. The elevated position of both reinforces their more privileged social standing. Both the trapper and the twenty-ninth bather are bolstered by finances. Both are situated on a "bank," a word that, when enunciated, calls to mind the alternative meaning of financial institution. Both senses of the word are relevant here given the wealth of both the trapper and the twenty-ninth bather relative to their partners. The twenty-ninth bather passage is notable for its breaking of bounds, its violation of decorum, its acknowledgement of female sexuality, and its acceptance of voyeurism and nonprocreative sexuality. But there are notable effects of hierarchy at work, too, not only based on wealth but also on knowledge, because she can gaze at the men bathing and know them, while they remain unaware of her. Liberation and equality are available only in her remarkable fantasy. Indeed, in all three scenes, Whitman pursues erotic fantasy as an antidote to slavery. More practically, Whitman's lines on the runaway slave also prefigure his later role as the devoted comforter of wounded Civil War soldiers to whom he provided sustaining aid, hope, and love, serving black and white alike.

As we will see in the next chapter, focusing on Edith Wharton, Whitman's promised liberation could also be limiting for women. We might think of Wharton as a sister of sorts to the twenty-ninth bather, the wealthy woman who yearns to escape the confining mores of her time and place, who seeks a greater sexual freedom and expressiveness, and who believes she finds it in a group of men drawn to comradeship. Interestingly, the twenty-ninth bather passage ignores the very problem Wharton will explore: what happens to the woman who wants to follow Whitman's recommended trajectory away from the stifling prison of class privilege and into the physical release of passion, touch, and camaraderie when she comes to realize that what she has entered is not a scene of heterosexual passion, but a scene of male-male liberating touch? These young men do not even know the lady is there among them, and, even if they did, would they care? If she were really there, would they all turn toward her, or would they take a look, then turn back toward each other? Whitman's poem doesn't probe these questions, but they are precisely what Wharton *does* probe.

TRACKING WHITMAN IN BOSTON AND THE BOWERY

Early reviewers not only described Whitman as like "Caliban" but as the "Bowery Bhoy in Literature." In the antebellum period the Bowery had been a locale for minstrelsy, among other entertainments. To hang the label of the "Bowery" on Whitman was to do more than suggest a lack of racial purity on his part. The epithet suggested a broad-reaching contamination: commentators who mentioned the Bowery did so to condemn Whitman through association with immigrant groups, moral degeneracy, and working-class culture. In the postbellum period, when the Bowery became more seedy, commentators continued to insist on Whitman's association with this prominent street. For example, in 1882, the *New York Examiner* described Whitman as "the 'Bowery Bhoy' in literature, a rowdy with . . . the itch for writing. . . . He could not have been bred anywhere but in a certain part of New York city a generation ago—in any other place or at another time he could no more have been developed than Plymouth Rocks can be hatched out of cobble-stones."[71] It is intriguing that a New York paper would criticize Whitman in terms that underscored Plymouth Rock, a national symbol but also very much a symbol of regional rival New England. When this commentator and others cited Whitman's ties to New York's Bowery, they linked him to a particular geographical space that served as a trope for a moral condition. Whitman, however, was not inclined to dis-own the Bowery: he noted that the scale of the Bowery is "convention-ally lower" than in Broadway, "but it is more pungent. Things are in their working-day clothes, more democratic, with a broader, jauntier swing, and in a more direct contact with vulgar life."[72] Dotted with theaters, the Bow-ery was known for its sexualized street life throughout the nineteenth cen-tury. Race and ethnicity are regularly interwoven with sexuality in con-structions of Whitman, with circular reasoning holding that the racial and ethnic other was oversexed and because Whitman was oversexed, he him-self was the other. Whitman wished to be the poet of both Broadway and the Bowery, but it was his celebration of the Bowery that offended that powerful group of people who wanted a literature constructed according to the gentlemanly dictates of the Boston Brahmins. Those who labeled him a Bowery boy attempted to relegate him to a particular regional and class niche.[73]

The final part of this chapter addresses the question of Whitman and blackface from a broader perspective by considering the Boston-New York contrast and the shifting way in which competing versions of literary cul-ture operated in conjunction with issues of race and class. Whitman at-tempted to make himself "the age transfigured," to "flood himself with the immediate age as with vast oceanic tides."[74] Taking on various hues and identities (and frequently risking the danger of taking over these identi-ties), Whitman worked in a way somewhat akin to a blackface performer as he disrupted genteel expectations and crossed gender and racial lines. In other important ways, however, he was revising the form of blackface performance itself since his ultimate goal was to unsettle and defamiliarize existing identities and to make visible and audible all aspects of a multi-faceted and multiracial society. For him, fluidity and receptiveness were requirements of national realization.

Ironically, though Whitman himself had been eager to set the terms and conditions of American identity ("What real Americans . . . ?"), he had his own national credentials questioned by those dedicated to a New England–and Anglo-Saxon–centered view of American culture. One literary history, coauthored by Barrett Wendell and Chester Noyes Greenough, observed that "[Whitman's] democracy . . . is the least native which has ever found voice in our country."[75] George Woodberry claimed: "A poet in whom a whole nation declines to find its likeness cannot be regarded as representative."[76] Barrett Wendell complained in his *Literary History of America* that Whitman's violation of traditional standards and values resulted from his being "of the artisan class in a region close to the most considerable and corrupt centre of population on his native continent," no doubt meaning New York.[77] Wendell, whose wife, Edith Greenough Wendell, served as president of the Colonial Dames' Plymouth Executive Committee,[78] did not hesitate to declare that Whitman was "less American than any other of our conspicuous writers."[79]

In response to great waves of immigration that occurred between 1880 and 1920, the so-called Brahmins had become ever more insistent about a particular perspective on American culture, asserting that the real, pure, or true Americans were Anglo-Saxons. The great migrations coincided with the founding of such groups as the Society of Mayflower Descendants and the Sons and Daughters of the American Revolution. The migrations also coincided with the efforts of publishers who commissioned numerous professors (almost all from New England) to write literary histories for high school and college use with the hope of unifying the heterogeneous American people under the "aegis of New England" by fashioning a national history anchored in that region. Nina Baym has noted that "conservative New England leaders knew all too well that the nation was an artifice and that no single national character undergirded it. And they insisted passionately . . . [on] instilling in all citizens those traits that they thought necessary for the future: self-reliance, self-control, and acceptance of hierarchy."[80] These New England histories of American literature claimed that the inclusive Whitman was un-American because of his supposed lack of moral earnestness and because he had failed to gain any popular following whatsoever. The poet was steadfastly opposed by those who, far from being interested in exploring blackface, strove to whitewash American culture.

If we look in more detail at how one prominent New Englander, Thomas Wentworth Higginson, responded to Whitman, we can study an especially vivid and illuminating case of increasing Boston conservatism. In the antebellum period, Thomas Wentworth Higginson and other Bostonians had been more radical than Whitman in their support of abolition, being willing to resort to violence to aid blacks, as in the case involving the fugitive slave Anthony Burns. But by the 1880s Higginson's growing conservatism was in fact part of a significant New England pattern of retreat.[81] Higginson was now ready to defend the disenfranchisement of blacks if it would help bring about sectional reconciliation. He was also adamant about attacking Whitman in a series of essays from 1881–98. In the closing decades of the century, the roles of Whitman and Higginson reversed, at least in so far as image and cultural meaning were concerned. Whitman, less radical in the 1850s in the face of the slavery crisis than many Boston intellectuals, had become by the 1880s increasingly associated with the teeming masses, the immigrants, the downtrodden of all types. Meanwhile some of the same Boston intellectuals who had led the charge for the emancipation of blacks had come to be associated with propriety, exclusiveness, and backsliding on racial issues.

There was some hypocrisy mixed in with prudery that manifested itself in Higginson's uneasiness over Whitman's sexual bravado. Whitman's sexual explicitness made him "primitive" (like the Indians and the blacks) and often stood as the great unspoken reason the Boston literary establishment could not abide him. Many of their arguments against him were simply disguised ways of saying "he talks dirty." The Boston banning of *Leaves of Grass* in 1881—blamed on Higginson by at least one person close to Whitman[82]—did not focus on poems treating homoeroticism. Throughout Higginson's writings on Whitman, however, his disapproval of the poet took this particular turn and emphasized male-male love. He consistently criticized what he called "the mere craving of sex for sex," or the "sheer animal longing of sex for sex," or "the blunt, undisguised attraction of sex to sex."[83] His veiled defamations of Whitman's sexuality are all the more interesting given that Higginson himself was a man of somewhat fluid gender identifications. His famous "Letter to a Young Contributor" (the *Atlantic Monthly* essay to which Emily Dickinson responded) had alluded to Cecil Dreeme, a cross-dressing character in Theodore Winthrop's *Cecil Dreeme* (1861) whose transvestism provokes a homosexual response. Dreeme was a character based on William Hurlbut, a close friend of Higginson's youth, about whom he once remarked: "I never loved but one male friend with passion—and for him my love had no bounds—all that my natural fastidiousness and cautious reserve kept from others I poured on him; to say that I would have died for him was nothing."[84] Moreover, his own *Army Life in a Black Regiment* (1870) exhibits an erotic fascination with black skin and bodies: "I always like to observe [black soldiers] when bathing,—such splendid muscular development, set off by that smooth coating of adipose tissue which makes them, like the South-Sea Islanders, appear even more muscular than they are. Their skins are also of finer grain than those of whites, the surgeons say, and certainly are smoother and far more free from hair."[85] Higginson's attacks on the homoerotic aspects of Whitman's verse and life may have stemmed directly from potentialities and inclinations he uneasily felt in himself.

Whitman's key role in the development of modernism, in the overthrow of the Brahmin past, and in debates over the nature of what is truly "American," are all well dramatized in *The Last Puritan* (1936; composed 1890–1935), a novel by the one-time Harvard professor George Santayana, who never became an American citizen and who always retained the sharp edge of an outsider in his criticism of American culture. Santayana attacked the Puritan past and undercut several Brahmin writers while championing Whitman because the Puritans had been used to support a particular view of the present, because the past had been mustered to the defense of a privileged order.[86] Whitman's great appeal for Santayana and for a handful of other Harvard intellectuals of the 1890s was in his promise to free people from what Santayana called "moral cramp." The main character of *The Last Puritan*, Oliver Alden, is told by his mother—who identifies herself with the Daughters of the American Revolution—that "nobody reads Walt Whitman except foreigners."[87] She has so sheltered her son Oliver that he thought the poet "was English." With staccato insistence, Jim, his English friend, corrects this view: Whitman is the "great, the best, the only American poet . . . the only one truly American." Given that Oliver's father, Peter Alden, wants his son to "understand America" and wants to free Oliver from the distorting effects of his mother's outlook, there can be no mistaking the centrality the novel grants Whitman.[88] It is only away from Boston, at sea on a ship significantly called the *Black Swan*, that Oliver can enjoy a harmonious blend of the sensual and the spiritual.

Nonetheless, Oliver is trapped by his ancestry, doomed by his spiritual and emotional inheritance. His story dramatically exemplifies the "mortal consequences that the dead hand of the . . . past inflicts upon its heirs."[89] *The Last Puritan* challenges conventional accounts of the rise of New England culture most powerfully, then, by its very plot trajectory, which traces a declining arc. Santayana's novel insistently invites us to consider large movements of cultural change. "In a new nation," J. V. Matthews has observed, "an aesthetically and emotionally satisfying myth of origins is not only a necessary ingredient of an evolving national identity but a prerequisite for a sense of direction and future development."[90] For various reasons, the New England myth of origins did not survive intact, as we know from the extensive displacement of once "classic" writers. In fact, New England culture was almost as well adapted to accepting (and even promoting) discontinuity as it was to insuring perpetuation of its own power. Santayana dramatizes the forces that helped, through Whitman, reconstitute American culture and in so doing clarifies the importance of freeing literature from the over-refinement of an elite class.

ALI, WHITMAN, AND "ME WE"

In *The Sense of Beauty*, a book based on lectures Santayana gave at Harvard from 1892 to 1895, he discussed the aesthetic pleasures of democracy:

> [O]ccasionally the beauties of democracy are presented to us undisguised. The writings of Walt Whitman are a notable example. Never, perhaps, has the charm of uniformity in multiplicity been felt so completely and so exclusively. Everywhere it greets us with a passionate preference; not flowers but leaves of grass, not music but drum taps, not composition but aggregation, not the hero but the average man, not the crisis but the vulgarest moment; and by this resolute marshalling of nullities, by this effort to show us everything as a momentary pulsation of a liquid and structureless whole, he profoundly stirs the imagination. We may wish to dislike this power, but, I think, we must inwardly admire it. For whatever practical dangers we may see in this terrible levelling, our aesthetic faculty can condemn no actual effect; its privilege is to be pleased by opposites, and to be capable of finding chaos sublime without ceasing to make nature beautiful.

Aggregation rather than composition, and the pleasures of multiplicity and a liquid structureless whole: this might define the democratic voice, a voice that often expressed itself through the reiterative parallelism of nineteenth-century oratory and the ongoing traditions of the black church. Richard Wright was not necessarily invoking Whitman when he employed a lengthy lyrical parallelism near the opening of *Black Boy*, though he elsewhere explicitly refers to the poet. And it was more likely the rhythms of, say, Langston Hughes rather than Whitman that lay behind Muhammad Ali's incantatory answer to a reporter's question prior to his historic fight

FIGURE 3. *Nationally renowned figure painter Sidney Goodman created the mural* Boy With Raised Arm. *Photograph by Jack Ramsdale. Image courtesy Philadelphia Mural Arts Program.*

with George Foreman in Zaire for the heavyweight championship of the world. I have lineated Ali's response to highlight his use of parallelism as he explained his motives for boxing:

> I'm going to fight for the prestige, not for me, but to uplift my little
>   brothers who are sleeping on concrete floors today in America,
> Black people who are living on welfare,
> Black people who can't eat,
> Black people who don't know no knowledge of themselves,
> Black people who don't have no future,
> I'm going to win my title and walk down the alleys,
> Sit on the garbage can with the wineheads,
> I want to walk down the street with the addicts, talk to the
>   prostitutes,

I can show them films,

I can take this documentary,

I can take movies and help uplift my people in Louisville, Kentucky, Indianapolis, Indiana, Cincinnati, Ohio.

I can go through Tennessee, and Florida, Mississippi and show the little black Africans of them countries who didn't know this was their country.[91]

There is something uncanny about Ali's echoing of Whitman's sympathy for prostitutes and the downtrodden, and about Ali and Whitman's shared fondness for catalogues of place names. In the final two lines, Ali contrasts —purposefully, I suspect—free border states and slave states, the latter being paradoxical places black people could be in and from but not of, both in the nineteenth century and in recent times.

Following a lecture Ali gave at Harvard University, when he was asked for a poem, he paused for a moment and said "Me we," thereby composing perhaps the shortest poem in the English language.[92] As George Plimpton has noted, "It stands for something more than the poem itself." In a re-markable way, Ali's two-word poem captures fundamental Whitman goals: to talk about the self to discuss all of us, to use the self to create community. In fact, if one were limited to two words in summarizing *Leaves of Grass*, one could not do better. Yet we should not overstate the similarity between Ali and Whitman. Ali's prose-poem in Zaire makes a more modest and particular claim than Whitman as to whom he speaks for and as. Whitman's assertion that he can comprehensively and unproblematically be the nation's body has left him open to criticism (can a white male body represent all bodies? can any body, of any hue, represent all bodies?), even as cohesion retains an ongoing appeal.[93] African American commentators continue to find Whitman to be a provocative and useful resource in the ongoing search for something more complicated and satisfying than separation, a unified rather than a universalist culture.

CHAPTER 2

EDITH WHARTON AND THE PROBLEM
OF WHITMANIAN COMRADESHIP

As Chapter 1 noted, "Walt Whitman" became, for many, a name signaling the outsider. Whitman himself cultivated this association by explicitly identifying his poetic voice with the American underclass, enslaved African Americans. African Americans have, in turn, responded to Whitman's poetry and its democratic reach to historically oppressed members of society. But this identification of Whitman with the underprivileged is not consistent among readers of his poetry. Some members of old blue-blood families also saw reason to identify with Whitman and his work. Rather than seeing him as a liberator of the politically oppressed, a reader such as Edith Wharton saw Whitman as a liberator of the psychically oppressed, a force who helped overthrow the burden of the genteel tradition. Her constructions of Whitman changed as her thinking and experience developed. In general, he was an enabling force in Wharton's explorations of fundamental issues concerning friendship and love, explorations that led—in both life and art—to discoveries that were often exhilarating and occasionally profoundly troubling.

Wharton held Whitman to be a significant philosopher[1] and preeminent lyric poet. Her high estimate of his work manifested itself repeatedly: in 1898 *Leaves of Grass* appeared on her list of favorite books, a list dominated by French fiction and devoid of American novelists; and, in this same year, when she visited with George Cabot "Bay" Lodge, they enjoyed a mutual "reverential love for the poetry" of Whitman.[2] In 1904 Wharton shared her enthusiasm with Henry James, who agreed that Whitman was the greatest of American poets—a shared judgment all the more striking for being made at a time when the reputation of *Leaves* remained decidedly mixed.[3] In 1906, Wharton wrote to Bliss Perry, praising his recently published *Walt Whitman*, although she felt he misplaced his emphases and undervalued the poet's conscious artistry and control of rhythms.[4] The inadequacy of Perry's treatment of love, friendship, and sexuality (though not overtly mentioned by Wharton) probably tempted her to enter the new field of Whitman studies. By 1908 she was making notes for her own extended critical treatment of Whitman, a project that never came to fruition.[5] That she even considered the undertaking is curious because she had already found her métier. This was not just any novelist contemplating a significant tangential move that would divert her from fiction to criticism: this was the author of *The House of Mirth* (1905), which had recently enjoyed "the most rapid sale of any book ever published by Scribner."[6]

Certainly we have to look beyond Perry to explain why Wharton would consider funneling her energies into criticism. Her intensified interest in Whitman emerged out of the same longings—for greater freedom and for sexual, emotional, and spiritual fulfillment—that marked her midlife affair (lasting from 1908 until probably 1911) with William Morton Fullerton. Whitman, as a poet whose work infused sexual relationships with both a spiritual glow and with the best elements of friendship, was enticing for Wharton, who passed, almost overnight, from what Cynthia Griffin Wolff calls a "nunlike purity" to what the novelist herself described as a "triumphant discovery" of passional life.[7] For Wharton, love and literature were often elaborately intertwined, and taking notes on Whitman and pursuing the Fullerton affair were part of the same pattern of needs and aspirations.

Even as her affair with Fullerton was commencing, Wharton recognized both its dangers and her own role in choosing an experience capable of being transformed into "beauty." In an undated letter, probably from 1908, she wrote her lover:

> I'm so afraid that the treasures I long to unpack for you, that have come to me in magic ships from enchanted islands, are only, to you, the old familiar red calico & beads of the clever trader, who has had dealings in every latitude, & knows just what to carry in the hold to please the simple native—I'm so afraid of this, that often & often I stuff my shining treasures back into their box, lest I should see you smiling at them!
>
> Well! And if you do? It's *your* loss, after all! And if you can't come into the room without my feeling all over me a ripple of flame, & if, wherever you touch me, a heart beats under your touch, & if, when you hold me, & I don't speak, it's because all the words in me seem to have become throbbing pulses, & all my thoughts are a great golden blur—why

should I be afraid of your smiling at me, when I can turn the beads & calico back into such beauty—?[8]

Passion, exploitation, love, and articulation; self-abasement versus mutuality; balance versus asymmetry—these are only some of the themes and oppositions swirling in the great golden blur. Both yearning and withholding, Wharton shifts focus with a dizzying rapidity. She feels the certainty of passion in throbbing pulses, yet she also registers a sense of confusion about the relationship and about the kind of discourse that might best describe it: magic and treasures? calico? an exchange with a canny trader? an exploitative relationship in which she assumes a vulnerable position similar to that she imagines for the racial other, the "simple native"? Her striking and diverse metaphors adhere to no single discursive field, but they nonetheless adumbrate the fiction-enriching power of the relationship: the novelist already believes that she will ultimately turn beads and even silences into beauty.

That Wharton never developed her notes on Whitman into a full-fledged critical study reflects not waning interest in the poet but the disarray of love. Responding rapturously to Fullerton, as had many men and women before her, she was initially unaware of just how complex his romantic history was; and once she learned it, she was not particularly deterred. (Fullerton's romantic life included both men and women, and partners significantly older and significantly younger than himself.) Busy with many projects, she found herself unable to read, much less write. On 25 April 1908 she wrote of Fullerton in "The Life Apart," her love diary: "For the first time in my life *I can't read.* . . . I hold the book in my hand, & . . . see your name all over the page!" There were even moments when her deepest identity seemed threatened: "This pinch of ashes that slips through my fingers? Oh my free, proud, secure soul, where are you?"[9]

Wharton's inability to complete her Whitman study is part of a more general difficulty she had in completing extended prose works during the Fullerton affair.[10] However, she found that her impulse to write poetry, dormant for years, had returned. Moreover, poetry she had written earlier now seemed to her eerily fitting and predictive of her current moods.[11] Her poetry—both that written before and that written during the affair—frequently explores the troubling dynamics of submission and domination. Other poems, however, especially "Terminus," savor a more sharing and loving sexuality, a sexuality celebrated for its joyousness. The opening line of "Terminus" sets the mood of a work Whitmanesque in form and texture: "Wonderful was the long secret night you gave me, my Lover."[12]

Wharton dropped her critical study of Whitman but never abandoned the concerns that first prompted it. In fact, one can overhear her dialogue with Whitman in many of her later works. A series of efforts—"Literature" (drafted c. 1914), *The Custom of the Country* (1913), *Hudson River Bracketed* (1929), *The Gods Arrive* (1932), and *A Backward Glance* (1934)—treat the discovery of vocation and the nature of the literary artist. They discuss, more precisely, Wharton's own expanded understanding of her vocation. She strove to redefine her fictional scope—to treat matters more "in the round," in a way that encompassed the joys and anguish of human sexuality—and she did it by thinking through Whitman.

For Wharton, the example of Whitman was more appealing than that of Hawthorne, the seemingly unavoidable father figure for male novelists in the nineteenth century.[13] Unlike the many writers who invoked Hawthorne as a thematic source and as an institutionally sanctioned model for authorship, Wharton looked to a poet who lacked strong institutional sanction and whose status was much more in doubt, particularly in the early years of her interest in him. Wharton perceived Whitman's ability to occupy both the margin and the center (or, more accurately, to occupy the center *from* the margin): that is, he combined literary prestige with oppositional status by becoming himself a center of power even as he insisted on his distance from all privileged positions.

Paradoxically, to understand these two New Yorkers we should recall how Bostonians once dominated American high culture. For most of Whitman's career, and the beginning of Wharton's career, the great American authors were the revered New Englanders: Holmes, Hawthorne, Lowell, Whittier, and Longfellow. One need only read Wharton's *Old New York* (1924) to recall the extent to which figures such as Poe (even though he was long since dead) and Whitman threatened polite society in America's Gilded Age. In Wharton's formative years, the American canon featured New England men, localized around Cambridge, Concord, and Boston, and it was a canon conspicuous for its Puritanical reticence and evasiveness concerning sexuality. (Years later she described how Whitman fared in the cultural ambience of her girlhood in the 1870s: *"Leaves of Grass*, then just beginning to circulate among the most advanced intellectuals, was kept under lock and key, and brought out, like tobacco, only in the absence of 'the ladies,' to whom the name of Walt Whitman was unmentionable, if not utterly unknown."[14]) Though Wharton was of course neither a Bostonian nor a Harvard graduate, many of her closest associates had been fundamentally influenced by this intellectual climate, and she herself was marked by it through what she absorbed and what she struggled against. Her husband, Edward ("Teddy") Wharton, was of old Boston stock. Her close friend Sara Norton was the daughter of Charles Eliot Norton, Distinguished Professor of Fine Arts at Harvard. Her friend and critic Walter Berry, the one "true love" of her life according to Wolff, was a product of Harvard. Her lover Morton Fullerton was, along with George Santayana and others, one of the founders of the *Harvard Monthly*. Her intellectual companion "Bay" Lodge was yet another Harvard graduate and the scion of a distinguished Brahmin family. And her close acquaintance, Howard Sturgis, the "richly sugared cake" of Queen's Acre, was a member of an English branch of an old Bostonian family.

Wharton's career as a whole contributed to a heightened awareness of gender issues as she explored human relationships from the vantage point of a privileged economic position. In life and fiction she moved back and forth between the rigid mores of New England, the only slightly more tolerant ways of New York, and the relatively relaxed and open life of Paris; she negotiated her literary career through the decades that witnessed the passing of an older American literary canon and the struggle by several (sometimes conflicting) groups to capture the meaning of "Whitman," to define him in ways amenable to their own various needs.[15]

Wharton allied herself with men such as Sturgis, Lodge, Fullerton, Berry, Santayana, and Henry James whose ambiguous sexuality was especially suggestive for her art, for their lives threw into question established gender roles.[16] A shift in gender roles was occurring as the century turned, and the homosocial desire of these intellectuals, manifested partly in their desire to "embrace" Whitman, points to multiple needs, not the least of which was to free American culture from a high culture that seemed fatigued, sterile, and fawningly Anglophilic. Wharton's connection with this network of men went hand in hand with her interest in Whitman, a poet widely admired by these individuals, the acknowledged source of much avant-garde thinking about sexual mores, and a rallying point for reformers of literature. There was at this time a growing sense of homosexual consciousness to which Whitman contributed significantly. These men appealed to Wharton because they seemed to offer freedom from conventional limitations and perspectives.

Wharton and Fullerton apparently met in 1907, when Wharton was forty-five and in the twenty-third year of her marriage to Teddy Wharton, a union that was far from successful. (Along with physical incompatibility, the Whartons' marriage was undermined by Teddy's virtually total lack of interest in her intellectual work, except insofar as it produced income.) Fullerton, three years younger than Wharton, possessed a "combination of dreamy idealism, literary sophistication, and sexual vitality [that] proved widely appealing" to people of both sexes.[17] He had a penchant for unleashing the sexual energy (and/or fantasies) of individuals notable for their sexual reserve, including Santayana, James, and Wharton.[18]

Wharton's more than 300 letters to Fullerton and her love diary are especially important for understanding their relationship. Here Wharton's love is both represented and constituted. Writing of love—and loving through writing—entangled the making of love and of literature. When she asked Fullerton to return her letters (feigning a casual attitude) she remarked: "In one sense . . . I am indifferent to the fate of this literature."[19] This passing remark reveals that Wharton recognized that, for her, billets-doux and belles lettres were intimately linked.

Even before meeting Fullerton, Wharton had imagined the special power of letters. In *The Touchstone* (1900) she discussed how letters can bring a lover closer than can actual presence.[20] The novelist's notion that separation could actually increase intimacy makes understandable why this correspondence, especially in its early stages, yielded such satisfaction. Letters transported the lovers into the world of imagination and freed them from the frustrations and limitations of ordinary life. Through writing to Fullerton, Wharton liberated an inner being, granting freedom to an idealized "other self" within the epistolary realm. Wharton prepared the way for her own rejection of conventional restraints by immersing herself in liberatory thinkers such as Whitman and Nietzsche. As Gloria Erlich notes, these thinkers enabled Wharton "to build a bridge between religious and sexual antinomianism."[21] Thus in her love diary she remarks: "I feel as though all the mysticism in me—the transcendentalism that in other women turns to religion—were poured into my feeling for you, giving me a sense of *imma-*

nence, of inseparableness from you" (20 April 1908). And she describes herself in these pages as beyond good and evil ("Jenseits von Gut und Böse") as she moves toward a religion of passion.[22] That Whitman was one of her high priests is clear from her dismay (she "reeled under the shock") upon learning that her editor, William Brownell, was "not a Walt-ite." Her jaunty tone does not hide her annoyance with Brownell for conveying a "sardonic laugh between the lines" in responding to her essay linking the French poet Anna de Noailles and Whitman. She commented: "If one isn't *for* Walt, one is so indignantly and contemptuously against him! But being a Whitmanite, like being an agnostic, cultivates forbearance and humility, since the anti-Whitmanite and the Christian are licensed to say what they please about one's belief, while it's understood that one may not talk back."[23] Wharton claims to accept silencing even as she makes her views known forcefully to Brownell and insists on her unshaken allegiance to Whitman.

From the start the Wharton-Fullerton affair was mediated by the texts of other literary figures. Early in the relationship (February 1908), she observed: "I have found in Emerson . . . just the phrase for you—& *me*. 'The moment my eyes fell on him I was content.'"[24] Yet Emerson quickly recedes in significance as Whitman comes to the fore. Fullerton did not create Wharton's interest in Whitman, but he certainly intensified it, and a shared passion for Whitman energized their relationship.[25] She wrote to Fullerton in 1910, listing her current reading: Nietzsche, Emerson, Reynolds's *Discourses on Art*, Dostoyevsky, and Melville. She follows her crisp catalog with an extended and enthusiastic discussion of Leon Bazalgette's translation of *Leaves of Grass* sent to her by Walter Berry. It is "a tour de force!!" she exclaims. "'When lilacs last' is unbelievably well done. The book must surely have a great influence on the young Frenchmen of letters. . . . I am going to get his Life of Whitman at once, for a man who can so translate him is sure to have interesting things to say of him."[26]

Wharton seems to have seen in Fullerton—or projected onto him—some of the traits she admired in Whitman. She says of the poet in her notes: "His epithets, his images, go straight to the intrinsic quality of the thing described, to 'the inherences of things.'"[27] She noted analogous traits in her lover with pleasure: she told Fullerton that she admired "what you say on that humble poor paper, on which the fashionable & conventional are never expressed. You say in your note of last night: 'we are behind the scenes together—*on the hither side*.'"[28] And just as she praised Whitman's "sense of the absolute behind the relative," so, too, did she applaud Fullerton's ability to "discriminate between the essential & the superfluous."[29]

Both Wharton and Fullerton claimed to seek "comradeship" or, as they sometimes said, "camaraderie." Before she ever met Fullerton, Wharton indicated why she valued comradeship. In *The Touchstone* she says of the relationship between Margaret Aubyn and Glennard: "Her intellectual independence gave a touch of comradeship to their intimacy."[30] For Wharton, independence and intimacy were both valued and interrelated. She stressed her "need of an equable friendship," noting that "what I like best in your letter . . . is the word 'camaraderie.' I was never sure that you cared for it, or felt it . . . that you thought I *gave* it."[31] Not long after, she asks: "Do you want to know some of the things I like you for? . . . Well—one is that kind of time-keeping, comparing mind you have—that led you, for instance, in your last letter, to speak of 'the camaraderie we invented, *or, it being predestined, we discovered*.'"[32] This passage—somewhat puzzling in its claim that they invented camaraderie—may indicate they regarded themselves as originators in adapting the Whitmanian model to a heterosexual relationship. Certainly in other passages speaking of comradeship, Wharton thinks of Whitman as a guide, as for instance, when she alludes to a well-known section near the end of "Song of Myself": "I could be the helpful comrade who walked beside you for a stretch & helped you carry your load. . . . But the last words of all, Dear, is that whatever you wish, I shall understand; I shall even understand your *not* understanding."[33] The woman-as-comrade, Wharton suggests, seeks to be a strong partner ready to share life "for a stretch" (rather than a romanticized eternity) and robust enough to ease the other's burden.

That Wharton's letters to Fullerton are everywhere marked by references to "comrades" and "camaraderie" displays her longing for Whitmanian reciprocity and symmetry,[34] her effort to reconceptualize traditional hierarchical roles. The Wharton-to-Fullerton correspondence repeatedly calls for an equal friendship. Like Whitman, Wharton thought of *comrade* as a flexible term applicable either to a committed friendship or to a loving, sexual relationship based on mutuality.

Neither partner moved effectively toward comradeship. To approach such an ideal with Fullerton was possible only in the letters, not in life: the actual man, notwithstanding his intelligence, attractiveness, and charm, seems to have been mercurial, duplicitous, and infrequently in possession of the "radiant reasonableness" Wharton once attributed to him.[35] Concurrently with his liaison with Wharton, Fullerton was engaged in amorous adventures with his first cousin, Katherine Fullerton,[36] and was being blackmailed by a mysterious long-time lover known now only by the last name of Mirecourt in a scheme involving three of Fullerton's past lovers— Mirecourt herself; Margaret Brooke, the Ranee of Sarawak (a woman fifteen years his senior);[37] and the sculptor Ronald Gower.[38]

But Wharton, too, acted in ways at odds with her rhetoric of equality. She frequently played the self-sacrificing and self-effacing mother, a role Fullerton encouraged.[39] Before this relationship, Wharton had established a persona that was strong, assured, and independent.[40] Yet in the love diary the persona Wharton had earlier constructed began to be displaced by the alternative roles she was now trying out. She began to enact the part of a self dangerously drawn toward the difficulties of the romantic heroine.[41] She was too prone to "worship" him;[42] too given to the slavish reverence of sexual enthrallment; and too ready—proud woman though she usually was—to be dominated. Louise Kaplan argues persuasively that Wharton was paying off psychological demons: "Under the cover of suffering, crimes flourish. . . . If the slave pays by surrendering her soul to her master, then she can continue with her forbidden occupations until the next bill comes. One forbidden occupation is her sexuality; the other is her intellectual ambition."[43] Thus Wharton exclaims: "I want to lose everything to you!"[44]

An irony of the Wharton-Fullerton relationship is that, while the two invoke the rhetoric of comradeship, Wharton was constantly reminded of asymmetry: she had full awareness of "how unequal the exchange is between us."[45] When the relationship began to deteriorate, Wharton attempted to adjust its character. She wrote to Fullerton, probably in the late summer of 1909:

> It is impossible, in the nature of things, that our lives should run parallel much longer. I have faced the fact, & accepted it, & I am not afraid, except when I think of the pain & pity you may feel for *me*.
>
> *That* I long to spare you; & so I want to tell you now, Dear, that I know . . . how little I have to give that a man like you can care for, & how ready I am, when the transition comes, to be again the good comrade you once found me.
>
> My only dread is lest my love should blind me, & my heart whisper

"Tomorrow" when my reason says "Today." . . . To escape that possibility, can't we make a pact that you shall give the signal, & one day simply call me "mon ami" instead of "mon amie"? If I felt sure of your doing that, I should be content![46]

Wharton seems to call for a clear distinction between friend and lover, but she uses the term "comrade," which clarifies little about the degree of intimacy implied. Given that Wharton had been reading *Leaves* with Fullerton, a man she knew was drawn to both sexes, what does she signal in offering to be his comrade, his *ami*?[47] The confused coding results in part from language itself, from her employing (inevitably) words "already imprinted with the meanings, intentions, and accents of previous users."[48] The polyvocal character of Wharton's utterance—especially notable in the use of the Whitmanian term "comrade"—creates complexity. And if, as I believe, the incorporation of the values of friendship into marriage (and quasi-marital unions) was of great importance to Wharton, this development nonetheless came at a certain cost: when love began to resemble friendship, the borders between friendship and love became blurred.[49]

Whitman's poetry promoted this blurring. In the letter quoted above Wharton distinguishes between "amie" and "ami," and, as a close reader of Whitman, she may have noticed the poet's use of the word "amie" in the 1855 "Song of Myself" ("Extoler of amies and those that sleep in each other's arms"; "Picking out here one that shall be my amie, / Choosing to go with him on brotherly terms").[50] Since Wharton's French was impeccable, it is likely that she would have noted the oddity of Whitman's usage: he employs the feminine form of the ending (amie) in applying it to male friends. The poet's gender crossing was clearly purposeful: in the essay "America's Mightiest Inheritance" (1856) Whitman defines and distinguishes between the words "Ami (ah'-me, masculine)" and "Amie (ah-me, feminine)—Dear friend."[51] James Perrin Warren observes that the word "amie" is an especially important element in Whitman's vocabulary; the term is "sexually ambivalent, and . . . is an early version of the 'Calamus' theme of the 'need of comrades.'" Whitman turns to French to describe a relationship for which English lacks vocabulary. The poet's word "amie" is meant to "project a new social relation between men, and . . . to help bring about the new social relation."[52]

In her most hopeful moods, Wharton turned to Whitman to pursue a similar goal—an altered sense of human connectedness—that would bring to relations between men and women a new equality and depth of feeling. In her darker moments, on the other hand, she experienced the pain of women's exclusion from the new social relation.

Wharton herself recorded Fullerton's prescient (if self-serving) remark: "you told me once I should write better for this experience of loving."[53] To be sure, the turmoil and the satisfactions of love were important for the novelist's career: "Wharton began to write about . . . sexual passion; the passions for acquisition, for experience, for love."[54] She achieves a fresh tone, as if she were undertaking a new life. In fact, as "The Life Apart" notes, the affair had made her feel like a "new creature opening dazzled eyes on a new world."[55] Even when the luster of the affair had worn off, a new world remained to be explored as a possibility in fiction. The shift in Wharton's fiction is widely recognized, but we lack an account of how Whitmanian comradeship—a source of the love rhetoric during the affair—was handled after its close. Comradeship continued to develop as a term of central importance for her, one she would explore in *The Custom of the Country*, *The Age of Innocence* (1920),[56] *A Son at the Front* (1923), and *A Backward Glance*.

Wharton responded to *Leaves* on a very personal level. She points to the central importance of the "Whitman" she created and used to fashion a new self: the very title of her autobiography, *A Backward Glance*, is drawn from Whitman's capstone essay "A Backward Glance O'er Travell'd Roads." The multiple crossings involved in identifying herself and her work with Whitman made it easier to escape a sense of anxious indebtedness. The poet could serve Wharton as an autobiographical mask *because* he was so different from her (in terms of class, gender, and preferred genre) yet crucially like her in being marginalized in a patriarchal, homophobic society. Of course in obvious ways Wharton was vastly different from Whitman, yet this does not negate underlying affinities. Moreover, Candace Waid rightly notes that Wharton was more concerned to distinguish herself from women authors than from men, and that, like many women artists of her generation, Wharton thought of her creative self as masculine.[57] In *Hudson River Bracketed*, Wharton has a literary critic disparage the use of "raw autobiography" in writing fiction, noting that "the 'me-book' . . . however brilliant, was at best sporadic, with little reproductive power."[58] For both Wharton and Whitman, the coming to terms with their sexual "difference" from canonized writers was a slow process; both waited until their mid-thirties to publish their first books. But once they emerged, both writers produced striking insights informed by their powerful identification with silenced groups.

Wharton's autobiographical "Literature" is an important unpublished account of the development of the artist. This is one of Wharton's various experiments with self-presentation, a fictionalized autobiography tracing the imaginative development of a male child, Dick Thaxter. Wharton uses this occasion to represent many of her own childhood memories, including the crucial discovery of rhythmical language. This fragmentary novel rearticulates the admiration for Whitman's rhythmical sense she stressed both in her letter to Perry and in the notes she took on the poet. (She told Perry regarding his book on Whitman: "I liked your Walt Whitman.—I only wish you had gone into more detail about his rhythms. It seems to me in *that* side that he was the great and conscious artist, & the great originator, & most likely, therefore, to live & be fruitful."[59]) Wharton stresses the power of rhythm in Dick's development. When he hears the biblical passage "O my son Absalom, my son, my son Absalom, would God I had died for thee, O Absalom, my son, my son!" the "wonder of the linked syllables seemed to catch his little heart in a grasp of fire." An even more decisive moment occurs, however, when Dick, browsing in his father's library, stumbles upon "poetry of a new kind":

> Out of the cradle endlessly rocking,
> Out of the mocking-bird's throat, the musical shuttle,
> Out of the Ninth Month midnight,
> Over the sterile sands . . .

"Never had words shaken out such wild lights, beat on him in waves so multitudinous. It was the swing of the sea itself, the sea of the poem tirelessly tossing, and he the child, awed, melted, trembling, crying out."[60] Here the chain of substitution and transformation is made explicit with Wharton writing herself into the role of male child, and the male child melting into Whitman's identity. Eventually, Dick's mother sees the light on in his room and tries to stop the boy from reading. But, fittingly, the moon is full, and with the silver flood on his page, and with straining eyes, he reads on. (The ingredients of this scene—the silver moon, the flooding page, the straining eyes—are strongly reminiscent of "Out of the Cradle,"

Whitman's own rendering of the discovery of literary vocation.) Whereas Whitman translated the hints from bird song to poetry, Dick Thaxter translated *Leaves of Grass* into a successful career as a dramatist. With a few deft strokes, in other words, Wharton highlights the matter of cross-genre influence.

The account of Dick "*reading aloud a story of his own* from one of the other people's books [Wharton's emphasis]" further stresses the autobiographical nature of the work, for this recalls Wharton's own famous behavior of "making up," her practice, as a very young child, of creating stories while pacing a room with a book (often upside down) before her. The only noteworthy difference between her account of "making up" in *A Backward Glance* and the account in "Literature" is in the assertion she makes about the status of the child's text.[61] In "Literature" we are told: "the story, as [Dick] walked, grew out of the book, seemed to curl up from it in a sort of silvery mist; he had to turn the pages as he would have done if he had really been reading what was printed on them. And his own story, somehow *was* printed on them while he read: it overlay the other like a palimpsest."[62]

The significance of this passage is clarified if we recall Freud's "A Note on the 'Mystic Writing-Pad'" and Jacques Derrida's consideration of the implications of "arche-writing." Freud's essay describes a toy sold for children, a writing pad on which messages written with a stylus could be made to disappear by lifting a double-layered covering that rested on the wax base. However, a faint imprint from the stylus remained embedded in the base, even after the impermanent writing on the cover had vanished. For Freud, the wax base could be likened to the unconscious, while the outer layer of celluloid and waxed paper represents the conscious mind.[63] Derrida extends these ideas, asserting that the writing that becomes visible on the pad through the use of the stylus was already there: the use of the stylus only makes visible part of the wax block that preexisted the act of writing. Thus, the unconscious mind can be said to be constituted by writing. As Derrida remarks, in a passage relevant to Dick Thaxter/Edith Wharton's experience, "Writing supplements perception before perception even appears to itself. 'Memory' or writing is the opening of that process of appearance itself. The 'perceived' may be read only in the past, beneath perception and after it."[64] Wharton communicates through her fictionalized account the shared nature of language and written creation, the dawning insight of the child that there are traditions out of which one emerges and to which one adds. Wharton displays a deep concern with the question of what makes an artist and recognizes the permeable boundaries of both art and the self.[65]

The Custom of the Country, drafted in part during the affair with Fullerton, explores a host of matters crucial to Wharton—the nature of art and the self, the implications of adultery, and the question of divorce. In this novel Ralph Marvell struggles to complete his literary work (like Wharton) in the company of a spouse unsympathetic to literary efforts. Ralph is engaged in two projects, a dramatic poem on "The Banished God" and a critical work (again like Wharton) on "The Rhythmical Structures of Walt Whitman."[66] Wharton and her character Ralph, though fascinated by Whitman's rhythms, are more deeply interested in exploring the possibilities of "comradeship." Not long after marriage, Ralph has the "not wholly agreeable surprise" of watching his wife, Undine, attract the attention of a cavalry officer and shortly thereafter of seeing her whirl through an evening of dances with a marquis. But at this early stage, he can still fool himself into thinking that "she showed qualities of comradeship that seemed the promise of a deeper understanding."[67] Ralph is destined never to find this understanding with his wife. Instead, in a scene that memorializes conflicting visions of marriage and relationships, he kisses Clare Van Degen under a portrait that shows Van Degen casting "the satisfied eye of proprietorship" on his wife. The violation involved in Ralph's kissing her "vehemently" beneath this portrait adds to the passion of the moment, and "Clare Van Degen, in the light of this mood, became again the comrade of [Ralph's] boyhood."[68]

Along with much else, *The Custom of the Country* analyzes the destruction of an American writer; it traces the decline and eventual death of a writer who turns from imagining Whitman and banished gods to treating men as insects—that is, from heroic ideals to deterministic naturalism. In doing so, it presents a biting account of the difficulty facing American artists. As Candace Waid argues, Undine's "attraction to and embodiment of a language and aesthetic based on ornamentation, decorative color, and deceptive surface . . . represents the aesthetic that Wharton identified with the feminine." Ralph Marvell succumbs to artifice, which he confuses with authentic forces of nature; he finds himself destroyed by the meretricious beauty characterizing both Undine and the language of lyric poetry and nature writing.[69]

Various signals invite readers to see elements of Wharton in Ralph (the artist figure fascinated by Whitman and haunted by unfinished projects). Similarly, Wharton stages another gender transformation, by attributing to Undine key characteristics of Fullerton. Both Undine and Fullerton were strangely amoral and extraordinary in their vitality, shape-changing abilities, and nimble amorous versatility. What Wharton ultimately recognized is that Fullerton's great appeal was offset by failings—like Undine's—that were closely linked to the debasing of language. Wharton's letters to Fullerton call for him to adopt a "franker idiom" and to eschew the false trappings of journalistic style.[70]

Wharton's planned work on Whitman had pointed to a corrective course. She held that Whitman's adjectives and descriptive passages abandoned false ornamental language, that the "sense of the absolute behind the relative" provides Whitman's adjectives with "their startling, penetrating quality, their ultimateness."[71] (As noted above, before her disillusionment she thought Fullerton personally possessed a similar ability to cut to essential matters, even though she never had illusions about him as a writer.) A key problem in *The Custom of the Country* is that Marvell and Undine both indulge themselves in adjectives. In contrast, Wharton, as a memorable passage in *A Backward Glance* makes clear, consciously shed as many adjectives as she could. The Marvell-Undine relationship is doomed because Ralph is unable to detect the false and ornamental in life even as he tries to purge it from art.

Following her affair with Fullerton, Wharton sometimes questioned Whitman as a model for comradeship. Fullerton, we recall, had complicated—perhaps even destroyed—the romance with homosexual and incestuous desire; *A Son at the Front*, set in Paris, can be read as Wharton's sustained meditation on these complications and on the network of male friends who seemed to promise comradeship but instead remained either detached (like Walter Berry) or not truly committed to equality (Fullerton). What John Campton wants with his Harvard-educated son George is "comradeship."[72] Campton turns to no other women after divorce and is apparently repelled by heterosexual life.[73] His erotic response to his boy is depicted most tellingly in a scene in which he views his boy asleep as the "sheet, clinging to his body, modelled his slim flank and legs."[74] On the eve of his son's departure for the front, Campton's yearning for his boy is intensified by the thought of potential loss and death.

The Whitman influence in *A Son at the Front* is seen as early as the epigraph drawn from *Specimen Days*: "Something veil'd and abstracted is often a part of the manners of these beings." The veil here refers to Campton's partially blocked vision, his failure to comprehend the nature of his love for his son. Wharton was preoccupied with incest, as the "Beatrice Palmato" fragment and many other works testify. Whitman's concern with incest has not received much attention from critics, though his intense relationship with his mother and close ties to his brothers Jeff and Eddie leave this area open for further inquiry.[75] *A Son at the Front* suggests that Wharton understood *Specimen Days* to be Whitman's exploration of very complicated erotic territory—his mingling of the paternal and the sexual in the loving care he bestowed on soldier boys. Most critics have taken Whitman's infusion of family metaphors into his descriptions of nursing, his constant references to the soldiers as his "sons" or "brothers," as an attempt to obscure the sexual element underpinning these encounters, but it is possible that Whitman's discussion of soldiers in terms of family metaphors served instead to intensify eroticism.[76]

As Judith Sensibar notes, Wharton's invocation of Whitman stresses the "contrast between Campton's blindness to and Whitman's understanding and acceptance of similar fantasies."[77] Wharton returns to the epigraph when she has the portrait painter employ Whitman's words when he labors to justify his inability to put his son "in focus" and thus understand him. Unlike Whitman's hospital labors—marked by commitment, sacrifice, healing love, and an ultimate transformation into art—Campton is so self-obsessed as to make the wounded men he visits uncomfortable rather than soothed. It seems probable that George functions in his father's carnal reveries to displace "a more possible and thus more dangerous attraction for Anderson Brant."[78] At the end of the novel, Wharton portrays Campton as a type of reincarnated Whitman visiting the wounded soldiers and attempting to transform life into art. Yet Campton is something of a parody of Whitman because, unlike the author of *Leaves*, he is unable (or unwilling) to plumb his own depths and so cannot make successful artistic use of his homoerotic or bisexual fantasy life.[79]

Wharton returns to the fascination of Whitman's nursing capacities—and spiritual mentoring—in *The Spark* (1924), offering in this story a radically different perspective from that seen in *A Son*. (Wharton's interest in

Whitman's hospital work probably results from a biographical parallel: like Whitman, Wharton served the wounded and displaced, particularly Belgian refugees, in World War I. For her work she was made Chevalier of the Legion of Honor, the highest order the president of France could bestow.) The spiritual efficacy of Whitman's hospital work with Hayley Delane is recounted in a story whose purpose is to examine the extensive effects of a chance encounter with a generous spirit.[80] The narrator of this tale, intrigued by Delane, gradually puts together facts about his life. It becomes clear that Delane had run away from school to join the army and had been wounded at Bull Run. During several months in hospitals he met that "queer fellow in Washington."[81] Whitman's importance is not limited to what he did for Delane: the narrator has benefited from Hayley Delane just as Delane has benefited from Whitman.[82] As a schoolboy the narrator looks upon Delane as "a finished monument" and values him little. Yet with the passage of time, and after his graduation from Harvard, he grows more sensitive to Delane. The narrator becomes one of the more thoughtful and considerate members of society as influence filters down from Whitman to Delane to the "I" of the story. Wharton's benign model of influence notwithstanding, the overall story blinks at none of the falsity and hypocrisy of Old New York nor does it divert attention away from the anti-intellectual elements of this culture. Whitman may be celebrated as a life-giving spiritual source, but Wharton holds no illusions about the good that might do him as a literary man. Delane is anything but pleased to learn that "Old Walt" wrote poems: "'I rather wish,'" he remarks, "'you hadn't told me that he wrote all that rubbish.'"[83]

Beginning in 1914 Wharton attempted to write a *Künstlerroman* that would not demand the suicide of the potential writer, as did *Ethan Frome*, *The House of Mirth*, and *The Custom of the Country*. *Hudson River Bracketed* and *The Gods Arrive* raise the suicide theme only to reject it. Instead they provide a story about a writer who gives himself to poetry and lives.[84] Yet it is Halo Tarrant rather than Vance Weston (the ostensible artist and hero) who is the real creative genius in Wharton's final completed novels.[85] These two connected novels offer together a nine-hundred page meditation on the question of comradeship. From the very start of the Halo Tarrant-Vance Weston relationship, when she slips a "comrade-arm"[86] through his, the novelist weighs the (sometimes) conflicting claims of companionable and sexual relations. Before they become sexually involved, Halo serves as Vance's muse in *Hudson River Bracketed*, helping him produce his first noteworthy book.

In *The Gods Arrive*, Wharton shifts her perspective on Vance Weston, and he becomes a much less sympathetic character. Fullerton again may have been crucial because, after a silence of almost two decades, he had written her a letter praising *Hudson River Bracketed* while letting her know that he had not read any of her other recent works. She wrote back an elegantly ironic letter,[87] and then let her new novel carry her weightier response. In *The Gods Arrive* once Halo and Vance become lovers, Halo has to talk herself into accepting a sense of loss: "She told herself that in becoming his mistress she had chosen another field of influence, that to be loved by him, to feel his passionate need of her, was a rapture above the joys of comradeship; but in her heart she had dreamed of uniting the two."[88] As Vance becomes increasingly unreliable and unfaithful (like Fullerton), she blames herself and strives to fight off jealousy: "How unworthy, she thought, for the lover and comrade of an artist to yield to such fears—and a comrade was what she most wanted to be."[89] Whatever she does may well be doomed because of Vance's emotional and creative immaturity and his attitude toward women. In fact, Vance abandons Halo for a time in favor of the bogus intellectual Alders, and Vance registers surprise that Alders and Halo become jealous of one another. Vance cannot see women as equal partners with men and so lacks faith in the possibility of blending (hetero)sexual love and intellectual communion: "Intellectual comradeship between lovers was unattainable; that was not the service women could render to men."[90] Vance's attitudes and limitations—so like those of her former lover—suggest that Wharton continued to work through the Fullerton affair even in this late novel.

The notion of comradeship is also central to *A Backward Glance*, published two years after *The Gods Arrive*. Wharton applies this term to Egerton Winthrop, "Bay" Lodge, Geoffrey Scott, and Henry James (who provided "mental comradeship" and who was the "jolliest of comrades, the laughing, chaffing, jubilant yet malicious James").[91] In addition, she says of Walter Berry: "It is such comradeships, made of seeing and dreaming, and thinking and laughing together, that make one feel that for those who have shared them there can be no parting."[92] Whatever her frustrations with comradeship, it was finally a term and a concept too crucial for her to abandon.

A marriage might be temporary, but comradeship, she asserts with a final romantic flourish, is eternal.

Both vilified and vindicated by his culture, Whitman's career offered an intriguing example to Wharton, an artist deeply conflicted, especially early in her career, about her own artistry. Whitman's own uncertain status, coupled with his compelling power and relevance to her concerns, fortified and emboldened her. Yet the Wharton-Whitman link was not simply positive. During her love affair, Wharton's "Whitman" and Fullerton's "Whitman" were at odds, and she ultimately came to realize that the homosexual Whitman, an empowering and energizing conception for many people, was likely to deprive her of lasting physical communion with any individual from the one group of men that consistently took her seriously as an intellectual.[93] The difficulties of dealing with a liminal figure such as Fullerton and his bisexual drives—problematic for both women who love men and for men who love men—led Wharton to an idiosyncratic yet powerful conclusion as her liberating Whitman gradually metamorphosed into an exclusionary Whitman.[94]

CHAPTER 3

TRANSATLANTIC HOMOEROTIC WHITMAN

Attempting to contribute to a distinctive national literature, Walt Whitman cautioned himself in an early private notebook to "take no illustrations whatever from the ancients or classics, nor from the mythology, nor Egypt, Greece, or Rome—nor from the royal and aristocratic institutions and forms of Europe.—Make no mention or allusion to them whatever, except as they relate to the New, present things—to our country—to American character or interests.—Of specific mention of them, even for these purposes, as little as possible."[1] Whitman's creation of himself as "one of the roughs"—primitive, uncouth, rude, and savage—constituted a complex defense against the polish, sophistication, and sheer achievements of Europe, achievements that stood on the foundations of the ancient world.[2] Fully expecting to reach a mass audience in the United States, Whitman was surprised to find his poetry more enthusiastically received abroad than at home. This chapter, building on the work of Eve Kosofsky Sedgwick, Richard Dellamora, Ed Folsom, and others, examines how British readers, in particular, appropriated Whitman for their own purposes.[3] The American poet became especially important for a group of writers who, despite some inconsistencies, were struggling to establish a positive homosexual identity within a British culture that naturalized hatred and fear of same-sex love, categorizing such love as both morbid and criminal.[4] My discussion first examines the intertwining of love and death in Whitman's homoerotic poetry and then considers what happened when Whitman's ideas were read across the Atlantic by John Addington Symonds, Edward Carpenter, D. H. Lawrence, and E. M. Forster. I close by considering a recent novel (and now film), *Love and Death on Long Island*, which returns us to both Forster and Whitman and dramatizes and reverses the cultural movement across the Atlantic.

Intriguingly, in Whitman's sentence urging himself to take no illustrations from Egypt, Greece, or Rome, the word "Greece" is circled. "Greece" was—among other things—a signifier of male-male love in the nineteenth century, and although early in his career Whitman made few overt connections between his work and the classical past, British readers regularly linked him to the Greeks. Oscar Wilde remarked that "There is something so Greek and sane about his poetry, it is so universal, so comprehensive."[5] John Addington Symonds, a prominent biographer, poet, and literary critic, went further, claiming that "Walt Whitman is more truly Greek than any other man of modern times."[6] The socialist, poet, and student of sexuality Edward Carpenter admired Whitman's "face of majestic simple proportion, like a Greek temple as some one has said; the nose Greek in outline."[7] And D. H. Lawrence exclaimed: "What a great poet Whitman is: great like a great Greek."[8] Besides serving as shorthand for male-male intimacy, references to Greece (because of its honored role in the development of democracy) could also contribute to the critique of aristocratic privilege. Whitman's language of comradeship was employed by his British followers to advance an egalitarian alternative to a society fraught with inequities.

Whitman's most sustained exploration of the interconnections between comradeship, democracy, and same-sex love is found in his "Calamus" poems. This group of poems had an earlier incarnation under a different title, "Live Oak, with Moss." The "Live Oak" sequence (drafted probably 1857–59 and never published by Whitman in its original form, a form only recently gaining the attention it deserves) dealt in part with loss and separation, but contains no mention of death.[9] This absence of death and the life-affirming joy and ecstasy of "Live Oak" are crucial in Whitman's first full articulation of manly attachment. At some time during the composition of the third edition of *Leaves of Grass* (1860), Whitman decided to break up—perhaps to disguise—"Live Oak," a coherent group of a dozen poems telling a story of the beginning, development, and loss of love. He reshuffled the poems, modifying some; and he began to interject repeated and powerful meditations on death. Significantly, it was this later account of same-sex love that was passed on to his British followers, the more conflicted account of male eroticism found in "Calamus" that became key when newly emergent homosexual identities were coming into recognizable form in Britain.

It is worth asking why Whitman shifted focus dramatically and emphasized death. Possibly he experienced the death of a loved one (as Malcolm Cowley once speculated) or, as is more likely, he underwent a repression of desire or a loss of love so intensely felt that love, death, and repression became nearly equivalent. Finally, however, I resist the temptation to turn to biography for an explanation of Whitman's change, because relevant facts are scarce and because such a move might risk being, in any event, a too literal-minded reading of Whitman's rhetorical shifts. Perhaps a better way to explain his change is to say that "Live Oak" constitutes a private poetry, a series he never published as such. In preparing his homoerotic poems for publication, Whitman was drawn almost inevitably into the language of death because of the available discourses on homoerotic love. Both the elegiac tradition, which allowed for a socially sanctioned articulation of male-male passion, *and* the counter discourse, religious and legal prohibitions against sodomy, presented same-sex affection as death-oriented.

The pivotal poem as Whitman transformed the unpublished twelve-poem "Live Oak" sequence of 1857–59 into the forty-five-poem "Calamus" sequence of 1860 is a poem appearing in neither group. "A Child's Reminiscence" (better known by its final title "Out of the Cradle Endlessly Rocking") was published in the *Saturday Press* on 24 December 1859. "A Child's Reminiscence" appeared after the composition of the death-free early "Live Oak" poems and before the publication of the death-haunted "Calamus" series.[10] This poem concerns the male poet's bond with the male bird and his song of loss. It is also the poem in which Whitman sings of the birth of his vocation. Although he had already published two editions of *Leaves*, Whitman writes as though he is discovering poetry anew for a pair of distinct reasons: first, he takes a fresh direction in writing poetry that is overtly allusive and deferential to the literary past, and, second, he conceives of himself as the "outsetting bard of love." Whitman later cut the words "of love," but this initial articulation indicates his awareness that in the very late 1850s his career was developing in a new way. He was exploring unfamiliar territory in his sustained treatment of personal love—particularly same-sex love—in poetry.[11] This treatment of love finally focuses on the mysterious "word out of the sea," repeated five times consecutively: "death."

The title "Calamus" better suits the expanded elegiac sequence of 1860 than it does the less somber manuscript sequence. The name "Calamus" ultimately derives from a Greek tale by Nonnus concerning Carpos and Calamus. These two beautiful youths loved one another and led an idyllic life until Carpos died suddenly. Calamus lamented him and, after elegizing Carpos, threw himself into a river and turned into the reed named for him (*Acorus calamus*). This reed, familiarly known as sweet flag, is notable for its phallic appearance. The word "calamus" has also been applied to a reed pen, and to the writings produced with such a pen, and to a wind instrument made of reed. Beyond signifying a phallic grass, then, "calamus" also reinforces Whitman's recurrent concerns with music and writing, particularly in an elegiac context. For Whitman to call his central poems on male-male intimacy "Calamus" was to emphasize anguish, loss, and death, elements important in the elegiac tradition of homoerotic texts and poignant material out of which to fashion an affirmation of manly attachment.[12]

Whitman's fascination with death has attracted useful commentary, though critics have not noted that death was a later imposition on a sequence originally far more positive in its mood and overall attitude toward same-sex affection. At times in the "Calamus" poems Whitman claims to embrace love and death equally, as in the poem ultimately called "Scented Herbage of My Breast":

Death or life I am then indifferent—my soul declines to prefer,
I am not sure but the high soul of lovers welcomes death most;
Indeed, O Death, I think now these leaves mean precisely the same as
  you mean.

The speaker disrupts usual distinctions between love and death because of his sense of extreme opposition to society. Whitman imagines, in the future, an ennobling death that will liberate him from the walking death of sexual repression.[13] Seeking language sufficiently intense to register the power of his love, Whitman argues that, in Michael Moon's words, "Death is . . . the most appropriate figure for . . . the experience of falling in love and being rejected by the beloved." Death is also a figure for "forming an inseparable attachment to another man."[14] Whitman sought to reconceive death so that he could remake life, as is clear in another poem, "Calamus" number 27:

O love!
O dying!—always dying!
O the burials of me, past and present!
O me, while I stride ahead, material, visible, imperious as ever!
O me, what I was for years, now dead, (I lament not—I am content;)
O to disengage myself from those corpses of me, which I turn and
  look at, where I cast them![15]

Although Whitman labels as "dead" the past self that he "was for years," he is not rid of this identity, since in self-divided fashion he looks at that part of himself that he would—but cannot fully—disengage from. When he republished this poem in later editions, Whitman erased the original meaning of this text by omitting its opening line ('O love!') and undoing what Moon calls his "intentionally 'morbid' linking of 'love' with perpetual death."[16]

In 1978 Joseph Cady argued—against an American critical consensus—that the "Drum-Taps" poems contained powerful homoerotic elements.[17] Intriguingly, British homosexual critics anticipated Cady's insight by more than a century. In particular they focused on "Vigil Strange I Kept on the Field one Night" (one of the few homoerotic poems presented to British readers through William Michael Rossetti's carefully selected English edition of Whitman's poetry).[18] In 1871, Roden Noel, for example, noted that "There is a rare freshness of personal feeling about that ['Vigil']: the charm of it seems to me unutterable. He watches by a dying comrade whom he loved—a boy—on the field of battle, returns to find him dead, buries him in a blanket in a rude dug grave there." In the same year Symonds published his poem "Love and Death: A Symphony," which salutes Whitman's Civil War poetry while invoking the Theban lovers "by death made holy." Carpenter's interest in the homoerotic element in the "Drum-Taps" poems is apparent in the use he makes of these poems when he writes the section "The Dead Comrade" in his long Whitmanian poem *Towards Democracy*, first published in 1883.[19]

Symonds's phrase "by death made holy" points to a significant divide within Whitman's British homosexual followers. Two main groups existed, one (represented by Symonds) that trusted male-male love when it was spiritualized and the other (represented by Carpenter) ready to realize male affection in the flesh and to promote political change as part of a larger social program addressing cultural inequities. Collectively, these writers formulated a complicated response to male-male desire that construed such desire as a means toward a new paradigm of social relations and a challenge to identity altogether.

Carpenter serves as an especially important middle figure linking Whitman to Forster and Lawrence. Tracing how Forster and Lawrence—each influenced by Carpenter—react differently to Whitman and death is revealing. John Simons argues that Carpenter "set about the construction of a masculinity which tried to reunite the individual man with a world of feeling and emotion, and to disestablish the power which accrued to him solely by virtue of his gender. This revision of inherited ideas about masculinity is what truly defines Carpenter as a radical."[20] Carpenter held that established models of masculinity were critical to the perpetuation of injurious social structures. Whitman was pivotal in Carpenter's life because he embodied a homosexual masculinity that enabled the Englishman to see beyond the models available within Carpenter's class and country. For Carpenter, homosexuality became not only a form of sexual transgression, but also part of a more "extensive pattern of transgressivity which challenged norms of social and class position and aesthetic value."[21]

Lawrence engaged with Carpenter's *The Intermediate Sex* at precisely the time he was drafting various versions of his famous essay on Whitman, which concludes *Studies in Classic American Literature*. Carpenter's *The Intermediate Sex* contends that sex has advanced beyond biological purposes and that the growing frequency of "uranism"—a term for homosexuality he borrowed from Karl Ulrichs—represents the evolution of a distinctive third sex destined to usher in improved social relations.[22] Lawrence was at first enthusiastic about the possibilities of male-male love, only to retreat, in a panic. He remarked, characteristically, that "the quick of the universe is the *pulsating, carnal self*, mysterious and palpable. . . . Because Whitman put this into his poetry, we fear him and respect him so profoundly."[23] Lawrence's mention of both fear and respect captures the divided feelings that mark his many comments on Whitman. If, as Wynn Thomas observes, Lawrence's attitude toward the poet was "prickly and . . . chronically ambivalent," one can nonetheless trace developments within that ongoing ambivalence.[24] Lawrence's perspectives changed notably from 1913 to 1923, his key decade of strenuous engagement with both Whitman and Carpenter, as he refined his own understanding of affection, sympathy, comradeship, and homosexuality. These were productive but in many ways bitter years for Lawrence: during World War I he and his wife Frieda were suspected of being spies for Germany, and, in what seems to have been mainly political harassment, *The Rainbow* (1915) was censored for "indecency." Lawrence finished *Women in Love* in 1916 but had to wait five years to get it published. And he tried (unsuccessfully) to leave England for the United States, believing that the New World might in fact bring renewal. Bruised yet hopeful, Lawrence began to develop the essays that became *Studies in Classic American Literature* (1923), a book that culminates with a chapter on Whitman.

In 1913 Lawrence first acknowledged his conflicting impulses with regard to homosexuality. For example, in a letter to Henry Savage, Lawrence wrote, "I should like to know why nearly every man that approaches greatness tends to homosexuality, whether he admits it or not: so that he loves the *body* of a man better than the body of a woman—as I believe the Greeks did, sculptors and all, by far. . . . He can always get satisfaction from a man, but it is the hardest thing in life to get one's soul and body satisfied from a woman, so that one is free for oneself. And one is kept by all tradition and instinct from loving men, or a man."[25] Lawrence's desire for bonding that would leave the self intact anticipates his later concern with the dangers of "merging." At times Lawrence believed that sexual relations with women "threatened his physical and spiritual integrity," and thus male love seemed a "'real solution' to the struggle for dominance and conflict of wills" he thought were characteristic of heterosexual love. Comradeship appealed to him as more profound and fully as sacred as marriage.[26] In another letter to Savage also from 1913, Lawrence engaged in an extended analysis of Whitman, lamenting that the poet—both very fine and very false—gave himself, body and spirit, to the abstract. Lawrence faulted him for being not the "joyous American" but a generalizer trying to "fit a cosmos inside his own skin" and pouring his seed not into stalwart American brides but into space.[27]

While writing his major novels and much of his poetry, Lawrence continued to explore issues that pervade and sometimes entangle his commentary on Whitman. Like Whitman, Lawrence routinely rewrote his works, at times altering quite sharply their import.[28] That Lawrence could not settle on a consistent set of ideas about Whitman is clear from the curious and abrupt changes as he alters the essay over the course of numerous drafts of his "Whitman."[29] For the purposes of this chapter, I will distinguish between three major forms of the Whitman essay: the earliest surviving manuscript draft from September 1919, the version published in *The Nation and the Athenæum* (23 July 1921), and the final published version that appeared in *Studies in Classic American Literature* (1923).

Lawrence believed that his publisher Benjamin Huebsch might find it "politic not to publish" the 1919 manuscript version of "Whitman,"[30] presumably because of the essay's remarkably frank account of male-male love. Lawrence's treatment of Whitman here served as a critical juncture in his consideration of homosexuality. He objects to Whitman's loss of the integral self through sympathy, his process of *merging*, which threatens to lead to "soul-death." In this version of the essay Lawrence treats male-male sexual practices quite directly (for example, discussion of vaginal sex is contrasted with that of anal sex). Lawrence believes that Whitman offers the final deathly culmination of the American practice of subordinating the "blood" to the mind, the sensual self to consciousness. According to Lawrence, Whitman gives himself away merely as a means of knowing his own sensuality and thus fails to grasp the separateness of the other. In 1919 Lawrence thinks of Whitman as both the "greatest of Americans" and as the "arch-humbug," simultaneously a "great prophet" and a "great swindle."[31]

By the time of the essay in *The Nation and the Athenæum*, Lawrence has begun to shy away from considering male-male sexual practices. Now homosexuality functions more as a metaphor. He begins to turn Whitman's idea of comradeship into a model of soldierly attachment, a relationship that Lawrence will later turn into a leader-follower relationship, a surprising development given Whitman's emphasis on equality. While being somewhat evasive on the question of homosexuality, the *Nation and the Athenæum* essay is the most positive version in terms of Lawrence's overall attitude toward Whitman. It is certainly a clearer and more coherent essay than the jaunty final version. Many of the most striking and most puzzling features of Lawrence's final articulation in *Studies* can be glossed by considering it in conjunction with the *Nation and the Athenæum* version. The different tone of the two essays is set by their openings. The *Nation and the Athenæum* article begins with an assertion: "Whitman is the greatest of the Americans," while *Studies* opens with a question: "Post-mortem effects?" And whereas the *Nation and the Athenæum* version closes with a type of hushed reverence for the sheer loveliness of Whitman's lines, "the perfect utterance of a concentrated, spontaneous soul," and Lawrence's prayerful "*Ave America!*," the version in *Studies* emphasizes, in contrast, how love and merging brought the poet to the edge of death:

For the great mergers, woman at last becomes inadequate. For those who love to extremes. Woman is inadequate for the last merging. So the next step, is the merging of man-for-man love. And this is on the brink of death. It slides over into death.

David and Jonathan. And the death of Jonathan.

It always slides into death.

The love of comrades.

Merging.

So that if the new Democracy is to be based on the love of Comrades, it will be based on death too. It will slip so soon into death.

The last merging. The last Democracy. The last love. The love of comrades.

Fatality. And fatality.

Lawrence continues:

Whitman would not have been the great poet he is if he had not taken the last steps and looked over into death. Death, the last merging, that was the goal of his manhood.

To the mergers, there remains the brief love of comrades, and then Death.

He quotes from Whitman's "Out of the Cradle," including the line "Death, death, death, death, [death]" and concludes:

Whitman is a very great poet, of the end of life. A very great post mortem poet, of the transitions of the soul as it loses its integrity. . . .

Only we know this much. Death is not the *goal*. And Love, and merging, are now only part of the death-process. Comradeship—part of the death process. Democracy—part of the death-process. The new Democracy—the brink of death. One Identity—death itself.[32]

The dramatic difference between Lawrence's last two versions of the Whitman essay—published only two years apart—can be explained, I think, because they treat matters of real importance and emotional weight about which he was deeply conflicted and because this was precisely the time when Lawrence was struggling to come to terms with Carpenter and with his own early socialism (which he would later abandon in favor of a more authoritarian politics). The central difference between the two essays is in Lawrence's treatment of comradeship and same-sex desire. The *Nation and the Athenæum* article claims that the "Calamus" poems show Whitman at his finest, a poet who recognized that if we do not stand "on the brink of death" we shall have "no beauty, no dignity, no essential freedom."[33] Lawrence further asserts that Whitman the poet prepares the way for a new great era of mankind. According to Lawrence this new era will be founded on, first, the "great sexless normal relation between individuals," second, the "powerful sex relation between man and woman, culminating in the eternal orbit of marriage," and, third, the "sheer friendship, the love between comrades, the manly love which alone can create a new era of life." He holds that the "life-circuit" now rests solely on the "sex-unison of marriage," a circuit that should never be broken but must be surpassed. "The new, extreme, the sacred relationship of comrades awaits us," and nothing less than the "future of mankind" depends on these relations.[34]

By 1919, however, Lawrence, still admiring of Whitman, was already beginning to retreat from Carpenter's position toward that of the platonizing, spiritualizing homosexual apologists. He said in a letter to Goodwin Baynes: "You are a great admirer of Whitman. . . . So am I. But I find in his '*Calamus*' and Comrades one of the clues to a real solution—the new adjustment. I believe in what he calls 'manly love,' the real implicit reliance of one man on another: as sacred a unison as marriage: only it must be deeper, more ultimate than emotion and personality, cool separateness and yet the ultimate reliance."[35] Two years later, Lawrence clearly doubts Whitman's claim that manly love will yield the inspiration for the future. "Will it though? Will it?," he asks of the poet. "Are you sure?" Lawrence answers: the "merging of man-for-man love" hovers on the brink of death and "slides into death." Indeed, Whitman's poems are to Lawrence "really huge fat tomb-plants, great rank grave-yard growths."[36] At the time of the *Nation and the Athenæum* essay, Lawrence saw Whitman as the hope of America, in fact of all people. But by 1923 he was no longer persuaded that comradeship was the future of the world. As a poet, Lawrence had learned much from Whitman: "the quick of all the universe, of all creation, is the incarnate, carnal self. Poetry gave us the clue: free verse: Whitman. Now we know."[37] Over the course of a decade, Lawrence went from both loving and fearing Whitman to both admiring and condemning him. Whitman was so deeply Lawrencian that Lawrence very much needed to declare his independence.

E. M. Forster's engagement with Whitman, Carpenter, and same-sex love leads him to very different conclusions than Lawrence about what homosexual love might mean for male identity, authorship, and society.

Forster credited the writing of his posthumously published novel *Maurice* to his visit to Milthorpe, where Edward Carpenter lived with his long-term working-class lover George Merrill. Forster refers to Carpenter as a "Whitmannic" poet and "a believer in the Love of Comrades."[38] Robert K. Martin demonstrates that *Maurice* contrasts two kinds of homosexuality, one dominated by Plato and John Addington Symonds and the other by Edward Carpenter and his translation of the ideas of Walt Whitman. Symonds shapes the first half of *Maurice*, in which homosexuality is defined as a higher form of love, and its supposed spiritual superiority is preserved by its exclusion of physical consummation. In the second half, homosexuality includes physical love.[39]

Near the end of the novel, when the relationship between Maurice and Alec Scudder briefly declines, they meet outside the British Museum, and the death of hope is everywhere in the air: "the great building suggested a tomb, miraculously illuminated by spirits of the dead." When it appears that Maurice will be blackmailed by Alec, Maurice says: "I'd have broken you. It might have cost me hundreds, but I've got them, and the police always back my sort against yours. You don't know. We'd have got you into quod, for blackmail, after which—I'd have blown out my brains." To which Alec responds: "Killed yourself? Death?" And Maurice explains, "I should have known by that time that I loved you. Too late . . . everything's always too late." Finally, however, when Alec purposefully misses the boat that would have taken him to the Argentine, "Maurice went ashore, drunk with excitement and happiness. He watched the steamer move, and suddenly she reminded him of the Viking's funeral that had thrilled him as a boy. The parallel was false, yet she was heroic, she was carrying away death." In passages such as these, *Maurice* clearly considers the love-death nexus, only to turn away from it. As Forster remarked: "A happy ending was imperative. I shouldn't have bothered to write otherwise. I was determined that in fiction anyway two men should fall in love and remain in it for the ever and ever that fiction allows, and in this sense Maurice and Alec still roam the greenwood."[40] Unfortunately, it was just that happy ending that rendered *Maurice* unpublishable. Until 1967 homosexuality was illegal in England, and the novel—first drafted in 1913 and not published until 1971—could have been taken as supporting crime and thus left Forster subject to prosecution.[41]

Maurice concludes that he and Alec "must live outside class, without relations or money; they must work and stick to each other till death," a conclusion that owes much to Carpenter's own life choices.[42] Forster also echoes Whitman's "Song of the Open Road":

Camerado, I give you my hand!
I give you my love more precious than money,
I give you myself before preaching or law;
Will you give me yourself? will you come travel with me?
Shall we stick by each other as long as we live?[43]

Carpenter, a man of the upper middle classes who directly challenged the "dominant image of homosexuality presented by the homosexual apologists," gave Forster an invaluable example of love between two men that thrived by moving outside mainstream society.[44]

Forster's comment about what he can achieve "in fiction anyway" helps us see that one reason for the death obsession in the homosexual writers of his period is the lack of adequate social scripts for their love: at some level they felt themselves invisible, unrecognized, and, as it were, dead. Our own time is different in part because writers like Forster himself are now a resource, and because Kinsey, the Stonewall riots, and gay pride marches reside in recent memory. It is no longer necessary to think of gay life suffering the death of social non-existence. I acknowledge this major historical difference because I close by moving forward in time to treat Gilbert Adair's *Love and Death on Long Island* (1990) and the recent film by the same title directed by Richard Kwietniowski (1997). In the final chapter of this book, I examine the use made of Whitman by moviemakers. Here, I want to anticipate that exploration by looking at a film that serves to pull together the concerns examined in this chapter: it is a movie that looks back to Forster and Whitman while also looking forward to key changes in cultural attitudes about sexuality. Finally, it is a movie that brings this discussion back to the United States.

Love and Death on Long Island concerns the life of a reclusive English writer, Giles De'Ath (the name is spelled almost like *death*), who has lived shielded from modernity in his study and who accidentally locks himself out of the house during a rainstorm. He finds shelter at a nearby movie theater, selecting a film based on E. M. Forster's *The Eternal Moment*. After taking a wrong turn in the theater, Giles (played by John Hurt) finds himself viewing not the Forster film but *Hotpants College II*, featuring randy undergraduates bent on voyeurism. These male gazers are contrasted with Giles who, dismayed, begins to leave until he is mesmerized by a face, that of a young actor named Ronnie Bostock (Jason Priestley).

Before seeing this film, Giles had lived in his own type of time warp. His new love for Ronnie propels him out of a Victorian way of life—all quill pens, formal manners, and fastidious orderliness. Giles now stumbles into a world of faxes and VCRs so that he can pursue knowledge of a teen idol movie star. Buying teen movie magazines (and hiding them as if they were pornography), he clips pictures and articles that he carefully itemizes for a notebook labeled "Bostockiana." In the film, these scenes are simultaneously funny and touching because of the dignity John Hurt brings to the part of Giles. In both novel and film Giles's sexual life remains hazy: as one critic notes, "he has been married, now lives as a widower, and there is no indication that he has (or for that matter had) any sex life at all."[45] We might wonder about the title: why is death mentioned given the changed historical circumstances and given that no one dies? Beyond the pun on names—love equals Ronnie and death equals De'Ath—there is an interesting clue in a lecture Giles gives entitled "The Death of the Future." As he lectures, Giles spins off into a seemingly irrelevant disquisition on smiles (all the time fantasizing about Ronnie's repertoire of facial expressions). In this commingling of thoughts on death and meditations on beauty and eroticism, Adair and film director Richard Kwietniowski are invoking an idea implicit in much we have seen before: when sufficiently passionate and intense, love melts into death. This idea, found everywhere from Shakespeare's *Romeo and Juliet* to Whitman to Wagnerian opera, sees the highest love involving a mystical movement of the soul into a realm of total union with the beloved possible *only* in death because love on this side of the grave is earthbound, frustrated, and always imperfectly realized. At the end Ronnie rejects Giles's love, and Giles sends a love letter destined to haunt Ronnie's days because he has refused the possibility of an extraordinary, unmatchable, once-in-a-lifetime love.

Interestingly, the film, unlike the novel, has recourse to Whitman. The film *Love and Death on Long Island* quotes *Leaves of Grass* when Giles arrives on Long Island from London, and Ronnie quotes *Leaves* again at the end, suggesting that he has benefited from his encounter with De'Ath, though their relationship never reaches a fully realized romance. These invocations of Whitman—nowhere to be found in the novel—are fitting in a complex way. Certainly Kwietniowski highlights themes present in Adair's original novel. Whitman's major relationships were with significantly younger men, precisely the type of bond explored in *Love and Death*. The class politics of Whitman's sexuality were important to his reception in Britain, and this film emphasizes the class contrast between an elegant, upper-class Englishman and an American B-movie star who, though rich, lacks taste, learning, and sophistication. Yet in more fundamental ways, the Whitman material superimposed on the plot does not fit with the Whitman absorbed by British writers such as Forster, the Whitman of "Calamus." In fact, curiously, Whitman is used as part of the film's swerve *away* from the death/love connection. (Whitman's "Now, Voyager" serves as a touchstone, indicating that Ronnie is now ready to brave the unexpected in future journeys.) The film, unlike the novel, leaves us optimistic about Ronnie, suggesting that he has benefited from his encounter with Giles, and Giles appears ready to return refreshed to his life as a writer. Adair's novel claimed higher stakes for the love: the narrator, projecting into the future, foresees that Giles's life has been "transformed and perhaps even cut off in its prime" and that Ronnie, because he would not destroy Giles's haunting love letter, will ultimately be destroyed by it.[46]

The novel *Love and Death on Long Island* presents homoeroticsm in ways consistent with the elegiac tradition and what we might call the public Whitman of "Calamus." The film version of *Love and Death*, in its affirmations and hopefulness, echoes (perhaps unwittingly) a different Whitman, the private poet of "Live Oak." In the 1990s, Adair, Kwietniowski, and gay culture generally had reasons both artistic and medical to be attentive to discourses of death. To my mind, the novel and film are each successful in different ways. The novel makes enormous claims for the power of a lost love; the film speaks to the optimism and resiliency and capacity for joy within a post-Stonewall gay culture living under siege.

CHAPTER 4

XENOPHOBIA, RELIGIOUS INTOLERANCE,

AND WHITMAN'S STORYBOOK DEMOCRACY

In August 1938 the *Boston Globe* reported that a trunk of personal papers belonging to Walt Whitman had been discovered and excitedly urged its readers to master Whitman's *Leaves of Grass* and *Complete Prose* because his "fecundity, breadth of soul, passion for beauty and strength and democracy have made him a symbol of American idealism at its noblest." These claims provoked one outraged reader to lament that Whitman's work was not banned and to assert that he "is a notorious Communist." Two months later, Ben Shahn elicited similarly heated responses when he planned to quote from a Whitman poem in a federally funded mural, *Resources of America*, in the Bronx General Post Office. Shahn's use of an excerpt from "Thou Mother with Thy Equal Brood" in a preliminary sketch was decried as "irreligious," "pagan," expressive of "Asiatic" philosophy, and as "background for two false and fatal pseudo-messianic movements," Bolshevism and Nazism. These topical controversies prompt questions about the range and power of Whitman as an icon within twentieth-century political crises and help illuminate the treatment of Whitman in John Dos Passos's *U.S.A.* and Bernard Malamud's "The German Refugee." Taken together, both fiction and topical controversies clarify how Whitman's legacy is entangled with contentious issues involving immigration, religious and ethnic diversity, and the nature of Americanism.[1]

The outraged *Globe* reader, A. Maurice Farrell of Cambridge, argued that "Walt Whitman is a notorious Communist, and his writings have been for years denounced by respectable and eminent authorities, from both pulpit and press, as vile and unspeakable maunderings. His so-called 'poems' were suppressed for years in this very city by the public authorities. It is unfortunate that a lazy and careless public have permitted this well-merited ban to be lifted of recent years."[2] Though simplistic, Farrell's labelling of Whitman as a communist was understandable. Whitman had served as an icon for American Leftists for decades: Horace Traubel, Emma Goldman, Newton Arvin, Mike Gold, Langston Hughes—these were only some of the intellectuals intent on constructing him as a semi-miraculous father figure who, in Gold's words, "rose from the grave to march with us."[3] (In the United States and abroad, it seemed not to matter that Whitman had rarely given more than qualified support to political radicalism; he was nonetheless hailed as a prophet of socialism and communism.) Another reader, F. F. Hill of Roslindale, fired back his own response to the *Globe*, taking issue with Farrell and arguing that Whitman had achieved a status akin to Plymouth Rock: "Some misguided soul chose to apply a coat of red paint to Plymouth Rock and the only result was contempt for the ill-balanced mind which deliberately chose to desecrate so sacred a shrine. Through your columns a similar mind has seized the opportunity to pour red paint over the one truly great figure in American literature. Not that it can in any way affect the immortal name and reputation of the good gray poet. . . ."[4]

Hill defends Whitman behind the sanctity of Plymouth Rock, a symbol he regards as foundational and indisputably "American" (geologists have since concluded that Plymouth Rock itself is probably of African origin).[5] Hill also ignores the irony that the rock has its meaning because of the pilgrims, who were initially as much strangers in the land as any latter-day immigrants. In a curious defense of Whitman, Hill harnesses the power of a New England–based American origins myth, despite the poet's own deeply conflicted relationship with New England and his notable pride in being a New Yorker. Moreover, Hill ignores Whitman's audacious constructions of himself as a beginner and as a mythic point of origin, as "the born child of the New World."[6]

Hill's New England–oriented view of American culture, whether he realized it or not, was a cultivated way of seeing. As discussed in Chapter 1, the latter part of the nineteenth century saw the explicit effort of the New England elite to codify "American" as "Anglo-Saxon." These efforts often took the form of literary histories designed for the classroom. In trying to mold a "history" of American literature into white, middle-class, Protestant values, many critics objected to Whitman, grumbling that he was "less American" than other writers and decidedly unrepresentative of American culture.

It is no wonder, then, that Whitman appealed to disaffected students such as John Dos Passos, who was educated at Choate Preparatory School and Harvard from 1907 to 1916. Whitman offered hope of freeing literature from the overrefinement of an elite class and suggested—because he had been depicted as if he were an unassimilated, slightly suspicious immigrant—that the literary realm might soon include more than blue-blooded patricians. Dos Passos was situated so as to understand all sides of the debate concerning Whitman's "Americanness." His "Against American Literature" (1916) praises Whitman's rejection of gentility and associates him with a vital, earthy, and "foreign" ethnicity: "Walt Whitman failed to reach the people he intended to, and aroused only a confused perturbation and the sort of moral flutter experienced by a primly dressed old bachelor when a ruddy smiling Italian, smelling of garlic and sweat, plumps down beside him in the street car."[7] What perspective does Dos Passos take here?—the old bachelor or the smiling Italian? Dos Passos was refined, wealthy, privileged, *and* he was a second-generation Portuguese American. Dos Passos's grandfather was a Portuguese-speaking shoemaker; Dos Passos's father—a quintessential American success story—rose to be a famous corporate lawyer, a personal friend of President McKinley, a staunch defender of imperialism, and the author of, among other books, *The Anglo-Saxon Century and the Unification of the English Speaking People.* The oddity and irony of his father's book is perhaps exceeded only by a casual remark made by Dos Passos's mother (and recorded in the third autobiographical Camera Eye section of *U.S.A.*): "one night Mother was so frightened on account of all the rifleshots but it was allright turned out to be nothing but a little shooting they'd been only shooting a greaser that was all."[8]

Dos Passos had an unusual childhood. Because he was the illegitimate son of John Randolph Dos Passos and Lucy Madison, John Madison (as the boy was known until the age of fourteen), spent much of his time abroad. There his parents could travel openly together. It is possible to see Dos Passos's rebelliousness as expressing hostility toward his father.[9] "I wished I was home but I hadn't any home," he says in *The 42nd Parallel.*[10] Homelessness was at the root of his emotional life and shaped the pattern of his quest for self-identity. As Blanche Gelfant notes, "The passionate attention he gives to the contemporary social scene reveals his search for some group to which he can belong."[11]

For Dos Passos, committing himself to America was a matter of choice, as the title of his late novel *Chosen Country* suggests. At Harvard, his foreign accent, swarthy look, and continental mannerisms set him apart from other students—a separation marked even in his nickname "Frenchy." His early stories show uncertainty in cultural focus: his settings are almost always foreign, though his favorite protagonist was a naive, well-educated Brahmin.[12] Yet ultimately, as he responded to strikes by workers and the onset of World War I, he came to hate Harvard and Brahmin ideals:

> And what are we fit for when they turn us out of Harvard? We're too intelligent to be successful businessmen and we haven't the sand or the energy to be anything else—
>
> Until Widener is blown up and A. Lawrence Lowell assassinated and the Business School destroyed and its site sowed with salt—no good will come out of Cambridge.

On another occasion, thinking back to the circumstances of World War I, he asked why Harvard graduates were such a "milky lot." And why "couldn't one of us have refused to register and gone to jail and made a general ass of himself?" Nobody had guts, he concluded, except the East Side Jews and a "few of the isolated 'foreigners' whose opinions so shock the *New York Times*." These people, so real and alive, show the emptiness of "all the nice young men" turned out by these "stupid colleges of ours," these "instillers of stodginess—every form of bastard culture, middle-class snobbism."[13]

As a youth, Dos Passos had interacted infrequently with "muckers." Yet these few interactions were telling: they introduced him to his opposite or double and offered the possibilities of another social role. As Dos Passos remarked: "I've always wanted to divest myself of my class and the monied background";[14] his interest in Whitman also served this goal. The "mucker" and the vagabond offered Dos Passos a "romanticized and readymade identity" that seemed whole and vital; and he dreamed that by adopting external features of a lower class (tattered clothes, plainspokenness, vagabondage) he could assume a new role.[15] No wonder Whitman is invoked, echoed, alluded to, quoted at length, or directly discussed in virtually every one of

Dos Passos's significant works, including *Streets of Night, Manhattan Transfer*, the three volumes of *U.S.A., Midcentury*, and *Century's Ebb*.

In *U.S.A.* Dos Passos identifies himself directly with Whitman. In this trilogy his hostility toward his father and his turn toward Whitman appear at the outset. The opening of *U.S.A.* might in fact be read as a calculated revision of his father's *The Anglo-Saxon Century*. The father, in his opening pages, praises Anglo-Saxon dominance and the glories of British activities in the Boer War and of American efforts in the Philippines; the son opens his trilogy by considering these exact same matters. Yet the opening newsreel of *U.S.A.* marks its difference by insisting on the costs to the soul that such imperial power brings. Dos Passos presents scraps of newspaper stories that speak of the United States replacing England as the leading industrial and imperialist nation. In *U.S.A.* "celebration" of the American century is inseparable from reckoning with the deaths in the Philippines. In coming to power, the United States begins to die.

The Camera Eye section of *U.S.A.* that immediately follows deals with a revolutionary moment. Written from a subjective point of view, rendering a memory of Dos Passos's childhood, this section provides more evidence of his debt to Whitman's democratic vision of humanity in the leaf of grass.[16] The boy's first recorded experience is of fleeing with his mother down a street in Belgium from a crowd that mistakenly believes they are British. Dos Passos feels keenly the effects of British imperialism in the Boer War, the effects of unjust persecution; as he flees, he focuses on the fact that "you have to tread on too many grassblades the poor hurt green tongues shrink under your feet."[17] Whitman's "metaphor of the grass," Lois Hughson notes, "expresses his ability to see his self as proxy for all selves which are, at the level of experience he is invoking, identical to his, and so virtually to abolish otherness."[18] The vision of Dos Passos, on the other hand, does not abolish all otherness. To his way of thinking, power inevitably brings gradation, the dominance of one requiring the submission of another.

Throughout the trilogy Dos Passos establishes a division between political power and the true soul of America, which is seen to reside precisely in those who are powerless. In 1932 Dos Passos wrote, "We have had a proletarian literature for years, and are about the only country that has. It hasn't been a revolutionary literature, exactly, though it seems to me that Walt Whitman's a hell of a lot more revolutionary than any Russian poet I've ever heard of."[19] Yet when Dos Passos links himself with Whitman in Camera Eye 46 of *U.S.A.* he is overcome by misgivings:

> you suddenly falter ashamed flush red break out in sweat   why not
> tell these men stamping in the wind that we stand on a quicksand?
> that doubt is the whetstone of understanding is too hard hurts instead
> of urging   picket John D. Rockefeller the bastard if the cops knock
> your blocks off it's all for the advancement of the human race   while
> I go home after a drink and a hot meal and read (with some difficulty in
> the Loeb Library trot) the epigrams of Martial and ponder the course of
> history and what leverage might pry the owners loose from power and
> bring back (I too Walt Whitman) our storybook democracy.[20]

He feels shame at the futility of what he is asking men lacking his advantages to do. He is haunted in this passage—too extensive to quote in full—by his money and by his continuing interest in money. Yet finally, despite his self-contempt and despite the impracticality implied in the epithet "storybook democracy," he rededicates himself to a Whitmanian democracy in which the true Americans are the poor, the dispossessed, the vagabonds.[21] The true Americans are also the Isadora Duncans and the Frank Lloyd Wrights of the world. Both are explicitly linked to Whitman, as, for example, when Dos Passos says of the dancer: "She was an American like Walt Whitman; the murdering rulers of the world were not her people; . . . artists were not on the side of the machineguns; she was an American in a Greek tunic; she was for the people."[22]

Behind the rage and the apparent proletarian sympathies of *U.S.A.* is a conservative desire to restore what many contemporary radicals wanted to move beyond.[23] Dos Passos's analysis is ultimately more mythic than historical, resting on a view of an idyllic golden age reminiscent of Whitman's yearnings for primal purity in "Passage to India." The novelist looks back to the time of the founders, to a time before America's dominant role in world affairs, and his goal, like Whitman's, is to return to original innocence and insight, to a "storybook democracy" of justice and equality, freedom and opportunity. Such a belief in a golden age, whatever shortcomings it has as history, contributed to Dos Passos's "fervid characterization of the world of power" and promoted a "fidelity to the voice of the submerged groups which is one of the triumphs of *U.S.A.*"[24]

After the executions of Sacco and Vanzetti—so important to the writer's career and so pivotal in the trilogy—Dos Passos made clear that he was deeply affected by Vanzetti's eloquence and intelligence as well as his being an Italian American immigrant punished for his beliefs. As Dos Passos saw it, Sacco and Vanzetti were executed for being "anarchist wops." Dos Passos, too, was an anarchist wop.[25] Sacco and Vanzetti were versions of himself—simultaneously stigmatized outsiders and believers in the American dream of a better life.[26] At the crisis point of the Sacco and Vanzetti ordeal he cries out in anguish over their fate but also in admiration for what they had achieved:

> America our nation has been beaten by strangers who have turned our language inside out who have taken the clean words our fathers spoke and made them slimy and foul
>
> their hired men sit on the judge's bench they sit back with their feet on the tables under the dome of the State House they are ignorant of our beliefs they have the dollars the guns the armed forces the powerplants
>
> they have built the electricchair and hired the executioner to throw the switch
>
> all right we are two nations
>
> . . . .
>
> but do they know that the old words of the immigrants are being renewed in blood and agony tonight do they know that the old American speech of the haters of oppression is new tonight in the mouth of an old woman from Pittsburgh of a husky boilermaker from Frisco who hopped freights clear from the Coast to come here in the mouth of a Back Bay socialworker in the mouth of an Italian printer of a hobo from Arkansas   the language of the beaten nation is not forgotten in our ears tonight
>
> the men in the deathhouse made the old words new before they died[27]

The strangers, here, are not the immigrants but those who have corrupted American language, principles, ideals. Through the three volumes of *U.S.A.*, Dos Passos undergoes a range of experience (recorded in the Camera Eye sections), maturing in insight until he achieves recognition that his role— a role he shares with both Whitman and Sacco and Vanzetti—is to be a reviver of democracy.

SHAHN AT THE CROSSROADS

The great illustrator of the Sacco and Vanzetti case was Ben Shahn, who, like Dos Passos, was an admirer of Whitman. Shahn developed as a social realist painter by contributing to Diego Rivera's *Man at the Crossroads* (1933), a controversial mural for the Rockefeller Center that was ultimately destroyed, apparently because Rockefeller disapproved of Rivera's decision to include a depiction of Lenin. Shahn achieved notoriety when he completed, during seven months in 1931 and 1932, twenty-three gouache paintings entitled *The Passion of Sacco and Vanzetti*. Prominently connected with left-wing movements through his involvement in the antifascist American Artists' Congress, the John Reed Club, and the Popular Front, Shahn's politics sparked suspicion in some quarters.[28] In 1937, when he worked on a mural for the Jersey Homesteads, a Jewish workers' co-op, he was observed by an agent from the FBI. Following some surveillance, the agent concluded that there was nothing "communistic" about Shahn's intentions. Still, lingering suspicion about Shahn's political convictions helps explain one aspect of the controversy that developed shortly after he and his wife Bernarda were selected to produce murals for the Bronx General Post Office as one of the Treasury Department's New Deal arts projects.[29] Shahn's work, *Resources of America*, features Whitman in its central panel and emphasizes that human beings are resources as valuable as soil and water. In its completed form, and as it remains today, the central mural, one of thirteen, shows Whitman addressing a group of workers lined up in very orderly fashion, with Whitman's huge hand pointing to his words scrawled on a chalkboard, in a somewhat unlikely teacherly pose. It is not the most aesthetically successful of the murals in the Bronx post office. Whitman's huge hand seems strangely out of proportion, though it does serve to suggest, perhaps, that the artist's hand supports and ennobles the many other hands Shahn depicts in the other murals. For Shahn, Whitman's poetry was its own form of labor. The poet, a weaver of words, is a textual worker akin to the cotton picker and the textile worker. Shahn strove to instill a sense of commonality and potential solidarity between workers in New York and those elsewhere in the country. As he explained in somewhat fractured fashion, "having experienced America myself, I decided to those people who are as provincial as only city people can be, to show them the best and scope of America."[30]

What was so controversial about the Whitman mural? Shahn initially posted a sketch or "cartoon" for public viewing, indicating that he meant to use these Whitman lines in the central panel:

Brain of the New World, what a task is thine,
To formulate the Modern—out of the peerless grandeur of the
   modern,
Out of thyself, comprising science, to recast poems, churches, art,
(Recast, may-be discard them, end them—may-be their work is done,
   who knows?)
By vision, hand conception, on the background of the mighty past, the
   dead,
To limn with absolute faith the mighty living present.[31]

Shahn's initial selection of the Whitman passage resulted from a convergence of personal circumstances and political beliefs and pointed to his own desire for a space beyond religious difference and bigotry. Moreover, the idea of recasting the past and remaking the self, familiar American themes, had particular resonance for Shahn himself. In 1935 he abandoned his Jewish first wife, Tillie Goldstein Shahn, and began seeing a Christian woman, Bernarda Bryson, who would become his second wife. When Shahn left Tillie and their children, he became alienated from many friends and from his Jewish family (he remained interested in Jewish traditions without being strictly observant). In his politics, Shahn had also concluded, because of his work with labor organizations and his admiration of Charney Vladeck (the socialist founder of the American Labor Party), that Jews should emphasize class rather than ethnic or religious affiliation.[32] At this time, as Diana L. Linden argues, Shahn was in the process of "redefining Jewishness in terms of class, labor, and secular life."[33]

However much Shahn yearned to inhabit a space beyond narrow definitions of religion and ethnicity, local and world events continued to deepen old divisions and prejudices. In the fall of 1938 Shahn and Bernarda moved from Greenwich Village to Yorkville, New York's "Little Germany," where they would be closer to their work on the Bronx mural. In Yorkville many residents spoke in German and some greeted one another, "Heil Hitler."[34] The extraordinary amount of anti-Semitic propaganda both on the world stage and in his own immediate surroundings contributed to Shahn's concerns.

The Whitman passage he originally selected is poignant in a prewar context laced with anti-Semitism. Reflecting on recent events, James Weschler wrote in the *Nation* on 22 July 1939 that New York City itself had become a "laboratory for carefully developed fascist experimentation."[35] Fordham University contributed to this impression when it invited Hilaire Belloc, the renowned poet, essayist, and commentator on Catholic doctrine, to join the faculty as a visiting professor in 1937–38, even though Belloc had made himself notorious because of the pro-Franco and anti-Semitic positions taken in *The Jews* (1937). In addition, Father Charles E. Coughlin, the radio priest, whose broadcasts at their peak reached some forty million people, had turned unmistakably to overt anti-Semitism only a month before the Bronx mural controversy, in November 1938. One of Coughlin's many unfounded claims was that Jewish bankers from the United States had bankrolled the Russian Revolution. (In another incident, Coughlin plagiarized from one of the speeches of Hitler's propaganda minister, Dr. Paul Joseph Goebbels, and actually outdid Goebbels by heightening the anti-Semitism of the propaganda.) Coughlin consistently insisted to his followers that the United States, though a Christian country, was controlled by communists and non-Christians.[36] Based near Detroit, Coughlin was a national figure with a powerful following in two cities that had always embodied Whitman's fondest hopes for democracy, Brooklyn and New York. The first chapter of the Christian Front, a right-wing group prone to violence, was founded in Brooklyn and received Coughlin's unofficial support.[37] Sheldon Marcus explains that "many Christian Fronters espoused Nazi ideals and utilized Nazi methods. . . . Elliott Shapiro, then associated with the Anti-Defamation League, recalls: 'The ADL received many complaints from Jewish people in Brooklyn who were being beaten by gangs of individuals who screamed that they were "Father Coughlin's brownshirts."'" Meetings between the Anti-Defamation League and church officials of the Brooklyn archdiocese proved to be unsatisfactory because, as Shapiro notes, church officials expressed an inability to "'control the everyday acts of Brooklyn parishioners'" and "'denied any knowledge that it was Catholics who were beating up the Jews.'"[38] Frank Hogan, president of the American Bar Association, pointed out the irony of Catholic intolerance toward Jews, without mentioning Father Coughlin by name:

One hate breeds another. . . . Wherever Jews are persecuted, there too, other creeds and races will sooner or later be persecuted. . . . We Catholics cannot permit men of ill will to preach in America bigotry and anti-Semitism without raising our voices in protest. . . . Some Americans have swallowed hook, line, and sinker the falsehood that the Jews are in league with the Bolshevik tyrants of Russia. I raise my voice against the spread of this lie. . . . Democracy, Christianity, and Judaism are all bound together by the silken strands of justice. . . . If there is an attack upon any of these then both the others will suffer.[39]

Given that the inclusivity Whitman had come to represent was at odds with the "100 percent Americanism" that reactionary groups advocated,[40] Shahn, a Lithuanian Jewish immigrant, was seen as doubly un-American in his proposed use of the poet. The tentativeness of the offending lines from "Thou Mother with Thy Equal Brood" afforded Shahn no protection. Protests rang out from scattered individuals and many Catholic leaders and organizations. Congressman Donald O'Toole, a member of the Post Office and Post Roads Committee, sent a telegram to Postmaster General James A. Farley insisting that the quotation "is repulsive to a majority of our people and promotes irreligion." He further indicated that "in these godless days some mention might be made of the recognition of the existence of God by the American people."[41] Critics of the proposed mural claimed that Whitman was out of step with American popular sentiments, an idea Shahn disputed.[42] They also asserted that he was "Asiatic" in his philosophy, meaning *not* that he was versed in Eastern religions but that his thought was of a piece with communism, a blight that, according to many in the slippery world of the 1930s, could and should be blamed on the Jews.[43]

The most severe criticism of the mural came on 11 December 1938 from the Reverend Ignatius W. Cox of Fordham University. He addressed approximately 3,000 parishioners on the subject of "Is There Government Propaganda for Irreligion?":

Not to speak of the vagueness of all this, the note of religious skepticism is quite clearly conveyed, and some sort of an absolute faith in the living present is indicated. The wording is an insult to all religious-minded men and to Christianity. It does indulge in propaganda for irreligion. As such the mural should never be executed. But the wording does show us the need modern man feels for redemption and actually implies the background for two false and fatal pseudo-messianic movements which are competing with Christianity for the allegiance of men's mind. They are Bolshevism of the Russian Asiatic type and Nazism of the European type. . . . Both are condemned by the church and neither can be overcome except by the church.[44]

In Cox's address, delivered at the Church of Our Lady of the Angels in Whitman's hometown of Brooklyn, the poet is linked with opposed extremes on the political spectrum, communism and nazism.[45]

Bowing to pressure, the Treasury Department directed Shahn to change the inscription. He protested that a particular interest group had claimed power to dictate art policy: "I question whether it is the right thing for a limited group of people to try to impose their particular Index on the general public. With Democracy rather on its mettle these days anyway it gives one something of a shock to hear 'Verboten!' directed against a traditionally celebrated American poet."[46] Shahn's use of the word "Index," carefully chosen, refers to the Catholic Index of prohibited books, and his use of "Verboten!" indicates that he sees a sympathy with fascism in some U.S. Catholic spokespersons in the late 1930s, a justifiable conclusion. (Shahn had linked the word "Verboten!" to Nazi persecution of the Jews in the Jersey Homesteads mural he completed just before working on the Bronx mural.)[47] After a delay of three months and after giving four other Whitman quotations serious consideration, Shahn altered the inscription to lines that first appeared in the 1860 poem "Chants Democratic" number 21. Interestingly, Whitman excluded from the 1881–82 *Leaves* the very lines that Shahn ultimately used for his mural:

> For we support all, fuse all
> After the rest is done and gone we remain,
> There is no final reliance but upon us
> Democracy rests finally upon us,
>   (I, my brethren begin it)
> And our visions sweep through eternity[48]

We may wonder why Shahn did not fight even more powerfully for artistic freedom, especially since he had been a bold defender of Diego Rivera earlier in the decade during the debate over the ill-fated Rockefeller Center mural. The Rivera debacle, however, had left him concerned about the fate of his own mural.[49] Moreover, although he was willing to undergo personal sacrifice for the sake of principle, it was another matter when he was doing something that might compromise the entire arts program of the federal government, already under attack by conservatives. Finally, too, Shahn's options were limited because, even though his quotation had been approved by the jurors, he had agreed in writing to make changes in the design if Christian J. Peoples, director of procurement, requested them, and Peoples found the Whitman passage to be "contrary to the spirit of our own Constitution."[50]

Willing to stand up for himself as a Jew, Shahn was also trying to pick his fights judiciously.[51] Treasury Department officials were worried that he would find a way to allude to the original quotation. Shahn avoided all reference to the previous quotation while finding a passage with more political edge that indicates that democracy relies on and finds its meaning in workers (see fig. 4). Shahn concluded that he could use his second choice of Whitman lines without compromising his work. He had found another Whitman excerpt that reinforced the theme of his murals and addressed the controversy at hand by contradicting the claims of Father Ignatius W. Cox. He also made a subtle point about censorship by quoting lines Whitman had self-censored from *Leaves of Grass* on his own artistic grounds rather than because of external pressure. Later, Shahn took out his animosity by painting several caricatures of Father Coughlin in the late 1930s and early 1940s (see, for example, fig. 5) and by spoofing Father Cox and the irreligion scare in his easel painting "Myself Among the Churchgoers."[52]

The controversy over the Whitman lines shaped Shahn's emphases in proposals for later murals in St. Louis and in Queens, New York, in both of which he stressed freedom and civil liberties.[53] The Treasury Department's Section of Painting and Sculpture solicited proposals for nine mural studies to decorate the St. Louis Post Office in the spring of 1939, as Shahn was finishing the Bronx mural. Shahn's proposed designs for St. Louis—including a scene depicting the major religions in the United States—were not selected by the jury, who disapproved of what they called his "political distractions." The successful proposal, by Edward Millman and Mitchell Siporin, depicts only Christianity through the portrayal of early settlers joined in communal prayer. However, officials did invite Shahn to submit designs based on his St. Louis proposal the next year for a project in New

FIGURE 4. *Ben Shahn,* Resources of America, *1938.*
Photograph by David Linden.

York City. This was the *Four Freedoms* project that appeared in the Wood-
haven Branch Post Office in Queens. Compressing his St. Louis studies,
Shahn developed on a single canvas a treatment of constitutional rights
in the United States, with a subtheme of immigration, again making freedom of religion a central concern. Shahn emphasized the importance of the
Bill of Rights in his work by lettering in the First Amendment: "Congress
shall make no law respecting an establishment of religion or prohibiting
the free exercise thereof; or abridging the freedom of speech or of the press
or the right of the people peaceably to assemble and to petition the government for a redress of grievances." Officials from the Treasury Department
haggled with Shahn over the perspective and scale of his work, and they
objected to the "printed label," which they regarded as unnecessary. Shahn
responded with a vigorous defense of his choice:

FIGURE 5. *Ben Shahn,* Father Coughlin, *1939, ink and wash on paper. Courtesy Philip J. and Suzanne Schiller. Photograph by Michael Tropea.*

The thing that I have tried to put into this mural, I feel very strongly. I feel that it has profound significance for every American, more significance every day because of increasing threats to our rights and liberties. I feel that if I, as an artist, can bring home to the people who see this work any added realization of how these basic rights project into their lives and activities, then I've done as good a piece of work as I want to, and don't much mind breaking the rules for pure art.[54]

Having had his own freedom of speech abridged over the Whitman inscription because of a combination of political fear and anti-Semitism, Shahn insisted on the centrality of the First Amendment.

MALAMUD, "THE GERMAN REFUGEE," AND THE SPIRIT OF GOD

Bernard Malamud's "The German Refugee," published in 1963, provides us with a remarkable postwar lens through which to further consider the issues that swirled around the Bronx mural, especially the connections between Whitman and Americanism, religious intolerance, and xenophobia. Either by chance or by design, Malamud's story speaks directly to the issues raised by the Bronx mural controversy.[55] Malamud responds to the attractiveness of Whitman's dream of brotherhood *and* questions whether it can have any meaning whatsoever in an age haunted by the Holocaust. Focusing on two individuals, Martin Goldberg and Oskar Gassner, Malamud's story is set in New York City in the sweltering summer of 1939 (immediately following Shahn's work on the Bronx mural and his studies for the St. Louis Post Office). Rather than focusing on the domestic anti-Semitism that complicated Shahn's work, Malamud stresses international events that are the distant but conditioning events of his fiction: Kristallnacht, Hitler's claim to Danzig, and the crossing of the German army into Poland and the onset of World War II. In a story about a German refugee, it is intriguing that Malamud is silent about the Roosevelt administration's general refusal to lift immigration quotas and welcome refugees.

It is helpful to consider the precise temporal setting of Malamud's story. Refugees made headlines in the summer of 1939, especially because of the case of 907 German refugees on the S.S. *St. Louis*, a ship that was not allowed to dock in the United States. The story of their fate illustrates the dire implications of Roosevelt's policies. Between 1938 and 1941, the Nazi government continued to allow Jews to leave Germany, but they often had no place to go. Although these German refugees had met U.S. immigration requirements and possessed quota numbers that should have provided them safe entry, their entrance dates varied from three months to three years after their arrival in Cuba on what they hoped was the way to the United States. The refugees thought the U.S. would waive the delay. However, neither Cuba nor the United States offered safe haven, and the refugees were left uncertain of their fates while diplomats and politicians debated for weeks. Finally all efforts proved unsuccessful, and the ship turned back to Europe, where most of the passengers ultimately perished at the hands of the Nazis. This much-publicized case has special relevance to Malamud's story because of the fear that the refugees would turn to mass suicide. Ironically, Oskar in "The German Refugee" commits suicide after arriving in the United States and after achieving a certain degree of acculturation. The Nazis made the most of the U.S. refusal to aid the S.S. *St. Louis* refugees: "We are saying openly that we do not want the Jews while the democracies keep on claiming that they are willing to receive them—and then leave the guests out in the cold! Aren't we savages better men after all?"[56]

In Malamud's "The German Refugee," Martin, the narrator, is a young American student who teaches English to immigrants, and Oskar is a former Berlin critic and journalist who has been employed to lecture at the Institute for Public Studies. Oskar's initial lecture is meant to be a prelude to a series of lectures and, ultimately, a class on the literature of the Weimar Republic. Oskar struggles with learning English and is shackled by writer's block. It is only when the narrator jots down some ideas about Oskar's topic—Whitman's impact on German poetry—that Oskar, provoked into disagreement, can write. The narrator had assumed that German writers responded to the love of death in Whitman, but Oskar corrects him, noting that a love of death runs through German literature. Instead, German writers found in Whitman *brudermensch*, a sense of brotherhood. But *brudermensch*, he notes, does not live long on German soil. We ultimately come to realize that Oskar himself has failed to live up to the ideal of fellow feeling. After experiencing an unhappy and childless marriage, he has abandoned his wife, whom he suspects of being anti-Semitic. Oskar's lecture is a success, but two days later the narrator finds him in his apartment dead from taking gas. We learn that Oskar has received a letter indicating that his gentile wife has, after his departure, converted to Judaism, only to be taken to a Polish border town and killed.

"The German Refugee" is about immigration, religion, love, and tolerance. The story subtly explores the consequences of a Jew's being intolerant and even complicit in Nazi-type thinking. Oskar has had little faith in his wife because she is a gentile. And Martin, too, thinks it is enough to identify a group: "I asked no questions: Gentile is gentile, Germany is Germany."[57] The progress of the story involves Oskar's painful realization of the inaccuracy and destructiveness of his conclusions and the guilt he must bear because of its effects on his wife and on his own life. "The German Refugee" is an extraordinary story in part because the disastrous effects of categoric intolerance are embodied in an individual who is a victim both of himself and of the Nazis. The story requires us to see complicity in evil where one might not have expected to find it. Thus, Oskar, a victim of the Nazis, is also a victimizer of his wife. It is possible that Malamud expects the reader to follow this interpretive logic out at the cultural level, too, so that we see the ironies and complexities of the United States, on the brink of World War II, as both a place of refuge and an inhospitable shore, as a haven from lethal forms of anti-Semitism and as a place itself flirting with fascism.

A superficial reading of "The German Refugee" might conclude that Malamud invokes Whitman in order to suggest that his claims in "Song of Myself" are now discredited. Oskar goes ahead with his lecture despite the invasion of Poland and the fall of Warsaw. He quotes "Song of Myself," which in this context may appear to be an anachronistic assertion of nineteenth-century values in the face of a modern reality that is the absolute denial of the assertion. We are told he reads the poem as if Whitman were a German immigrant.

And I know the Spirit of God is the brother of my own,
And that all the men ever born are also my brothers, and the women
    my sisters and lovers,
And that the kelson of creation is love.[58]

We read Whitman's lines about the spirit of God, the brotherhood of man, and the centrality of love more skeptically in Malamud's story than we do in their more familiar context within "Song of Myself." "The German Refugee" treats the start of the war (from a postwar perspective) and offers an analysis akin to that of Elie Wiesel, who observed: "at Auschwitz, not only man died, but also the idea of man."[59] Malamud employs a strategy common to writers of Holocaust literature: to "counterpose . . . . forms that are essentially civilized and humane" against "terrifying accounts of dehumanization."[60] He does this by offering us various texts and voices within the story. We hear from Whitman through direct quotation, we hear indirectly from Oskar's mother-in-law, and of course we hear throughout the story from the narrator. It would be an oversimplification to see the story as an opposition between *Leaves of Grass* (as a hopelessly optimistic romantic text) and the modern hard-edged document of the mother-in-law reporting her daughter's death. Here is how the narrator renders the mother-in-law's letter:

> She writes in a tight script it takes me hours to decipher, that her daughter, after Oskar abandons her, against her own mother's fervent pleas and anguish, is converted to Judaism by a vengeful rabbi. One night the Brown shirts appear, and though the mother wildly waves her bronze crucifix in their faces, they drag Frau Gassner, together with the other Jews, out of the apartment house, and transport them in lorries to a small border town in conquered Poland. There, it is rumored, she is shot in the head and topples into an open ditch with the naked Jewish men, their wives and children, some Polish soldiers, and a handful of gypsies.[61]

At the end of the story we are left to reckon with the results of the failure of love, both in the awful death of Frau Gassner and, more broadly, in the Holocaust itself.[62] The narrator, the character who changes most in the story, mediates between Whitman's text and that of the mother-in-law, creating a third text through the development of his own matured voice.

As Lawrence Lasher notes, Martin changes from being the "limited, first-person narrator, locked into a completed past, into the omniscient narrator who 'sees' through to the truth and speaks in an on-going present tense."[63] The change in tense is intrusive and startling, but effective. Whitman does something similar in the very section of "Song of Myself" that Oskar quotes. That is, he describes a past event—"How you settled your head . . . And parted . . . And reach'd . . . Swiftly arose . . . ." And then he switches to the present: "And I know . . . And I know."[64] In both cases a striking treatment of tense, together with the vivid rendering of the event captures the overwhelming experience of a life-changing event.

Malamud's story pushes us to consider the impotence of literary culture to control mankind's most brutal instincts. Yet I would not agree with those who see Malamud in this story rejecting Whitman completely. Frau Gassner has been, as she says in a letter to Oskar, for twenty-seven years "your own true wife"; she has acted as if a kelson of the creation is love, in the hopes of making it so. The reality of her love—like the love the narrator, in a different way, shows Oskar—is not negated by Oskar's suicide or by the barbarity overtaking the world.

If we think of *Leaves of Grass* as a living document accruing meanings that evolve with time and changing readers, the book was altered but not negated by the Holocaust. Malamud's gloss on these lines from "Song of Myself," as intriguing as any to be found in the critical literature, leaves us with a more sober and chastened Whitman, a sense that his affirmations can, at best, be approved only as ideals, not as descriptions of reality.

With remarkable regularity, Whitman has been pulled into debates over immigration, communism, and national identity and purpose. His comments on various groups of people are not altogether favorable nor altogether consistent, but the inclusivity, and tolerance, and nonhierarchical thrust of *Leaves of Grass* is unmistakable. Within and beyond print, battles over Whitman's twentieth-century meanings were interarticulated with battles over the meanings of America. The mural controversy makes abundantly clear that these debates were not restricted to literature or the elite but crossed art forms and class lines and engaged all groups from ordinary citizens to political leaders.

CHAPTER 5

PASSING, FLUIDITY, AND
AMERICAN IDENTITIES

The reaction to Whitman and his project by writers from marginalized groups can be illuminated by considering the heavily freighted term "passing." The responses of William Least Heat-Moon, Ishmael Reed, and Gloria Naylor are part of a much larger cultural pattern of minority writers talking back to Whitman, writers who extend, refine, rewrite, battle, endorse, and sometimes reject the work of a poet who strove so insistently to define American identity and to imagine an inclusive society. All kinds of "passing"—both real and literary—involve a performative transformation. To pass is to enact a narrative or an identity dependent on fabrication. At a biographical level, Whitman passed from dandy and man-about-town to one of the roughs in proletarian chic, taking on for his poetic alter ego "Walt" a good number of idealized characteristics inconsistent with what is known about ordinary Walter. We should also consider what it means for literary passing to be so central in a text such as "Song of Myself": for example, what does it mean when Whitman pretends to be the "friendly and flowing savage," when he impersonates the Underground Railroad man assisting a runaway slave, and when he presumes to speak as if he were a figure akin to Edith Wharton, imprisoned "aft the blinds of the window" in the famous section concerning the twenty-eight bathers? And, conversely, what does it mean when minority writers invoke Whitman (whose name, as indicated in the Introduction, means "white man" according to one etymological source)?[1] What is at stake when a white writer or a person of color reaches across a racial or ethnic divide? When contemporary white thinkers yearn for a cultural space that is not racially and ethnically inflected—a natural race-free space, they might say—we suspect that they really yearn for a white space. When minority writers invoke a writer such as Whitman, are they seeking a raceless space of "humanity" that we suspect is apocryphal? If it is apocryphal, are they then engaging in literary passing, moving intellectually into white space in a way just as complicated and nuanced and fraught with difficulties and ambiguities as any of the familiar boundary-crossing, border-blurring cases of traditional passing? When is such crossing legitimate and when illegitimate? For example, was it legitimate, not so long ago, for Anatole Broyard to tell his sister Lorraine that "he had resolved to pass so that he could be a writer, rather than a Negro writer"?[2] (This decision required that his darker-skinned sister no longer visit him.) Are the issues different, in any significant way, when a minority writer moves into "white" space as opposed to when a white writer crosses into color? Generalizations are often difficult to make because the particular meanings of different "passings" are as various as the writers involved.

"Mulatto" last appeared as a category on the U.S. census in 1920. In succeeding years we have been slow to employ nonpejorative terms for biracial or multiracial identity. Only in the 2000 census did a "multiple race" category emerge, allowing an individual to check "one or more races to indicate what this person considers himself/herself to be."[3] Significantly, "multiple race" is a term rarely encountered in common usage. Thus, the 2000 census notwithstanding, our cultural habit of oversimplifying racial matters remains in place. Typically in the United States one is characterized as, say, "white" or "black" but not "white-and-black." These simplifications have carried over into literary studies so that, frequently, individual writers and literary movements such as the Harlem Renaissance are viewed from a single-race perspective.[4] As George Hutchinson notes, "the idea of biracial persons achieving healthy identities by embracing their multiple ancestry has been virtually unthinkable to both writers and critics."[5] (Possibly the prominence of Tiger Woods, who has referred to himself as Cablinasian— Caucasian, Black, Indian, and Asian—is starting to bring about a rethinking of these issues.) Jean Toomer once remarked about people puzzled by mixed-race identity: "They never realized that racial strains do not exist separately in a man but blend to form a new product. . . . They never understood that the real factors operating in the United States . . . are creating a new people in this world, a people to whom all Americans, without exception, belong. . . . At one time . . . they were under the compulsion to be this or that. They could have been self-determined to be this *and* that."[6] Toomer believed that a "new American" race was being formed and resisted others' attempts to categorize him in a simple sense as a black man. But, sadly, Toomer's own history shows that negotiating American racial politics is never easy and rarely clear. As David Bradley has noted, because Toomer refused to deny the largest part of his ancestry, he has been called an "apostate," and some argue that "if *Cane* is not a 'black' text, . . . then it is escapist and 'inauthentic.'"[7]

Although one finds a range of responses to Whitman, minority writers have been remarkably generous in their overall attitudes toward the poet. This may result from Whitman's curious sense of needing readers and writers of the future to complete his work, just as his vision of democracy was of an unfulfilled, always yet-to-be-realized goal. Moreover, his broad endorsement of the socially powerless underpins his claim to inclusiveness. Among minority writers, Ishmael Reed takes an unusually dim view of Whitman, and when he attacks the continuing enslaving processes of the western cultural tradition, Whitman becomes a key target. Reed serves as a useful contrast to William Least Heat-Moon and Gloria Naylor who, in more common fashion, present Whitman as a democratic hero and a model for new forms of self-creation. All three writers are worth close attention because they illustrate and examine the complexities involved in questions of lineage, inheritance, and identity.

FROM WHITMAN TO BLACK ELK: NEGOTIATING IDENTITIES IN *BLUE HIGHWAYS*

Blue Highways details William Least Heat-Moon's circumnavigation of the United States by way of the less-traveled highways, those often marked in blue on maps. An exploration of both self and country, *Blue Highways* sold over one million copies, was named a notable book of 1983 by the *New York Times* and one of the top five best nonfiction books of the year by *Time* magazine, and received a Books-Across-the-Sea Award and a Christopher Award. It "moved from the hard- to the soft-cover best-seller list without skipping a beat."[8] For all its success, *Blue Highways* raises complicated issues surrounding passing in a new way. Recently, worldwide, a number of people have been accused of misappropriating the cultural identity of indigenous people (certain Australian painters, for example, have been accused of falsely claiming to be aborigines, and some New Zealand writers, most notably Keri Hulme, author of *The Bone People*, have been accused of having a less than entirely authentic connection to Maori culture).[9] In our more immediate context, Rayna Green, in an article entitled "The Tribe

Called Wannabee: Playing Indian in America and Europe," excoriates those she describes as "notable impostors." These individuals either "write in an Indian persona, on Indian subjects, or . . . they make their reputation by writing about putative Indian gurus who show them the true Indian way of life, healing them from the ills of civilization. In the first mode, writers (such as 'William Least Heat Moon' of *Blue Highways*) whose early work is not popular, drop their Anglo persona and take up an Indian one, finding a loyal and devoted following in the impersonation phase." Others who have joined Green in attacking Heat-Moon include Gerald Vizenor and Jim Crace, who remarks that *Blue Highways* is a "bogus concoction."[10] The charges are serious and, whatever people conclude about Heat-Moon, it is clear that, in various contexts, a number of whites are impersonating Indians, and these acts by nonnative writers point to what Wendy Rose calls a "process of 'cultural imperialism' directly related to other claims on Native American land and lives."[11] Some Native American thinkers are convinced that the purpose is to displace Indians even with regard to their own customs and religion and to usurp the power to determine who is and who is not an authentic Indian. Given Native American sensitivities on this issue and that Heat-Moon claims Osage ancestry, I contacted the Osage nation on this question. Sean Standing Bear and David J. Ward both responded. Ward wrote to me as follows:

> The only litmus test at present to verify a person as a Native American Indian, and which is used by the Federal Government, is Tribal Membership. To be considered a Native American Indian one must be enrolled in a Federally Recognized Tribe or Indian Nation. There are great numbers of people who are descendants of Native American Indians but can not document their lineage. For these people Tribal affiliation is extremely difficult and in most cases impossible. For the Osage, Tribal affiliation is simple. To be eligible for membership in the Osage Nation one must be descended from one of the 2229 people listed on the Osage Allotment of 1906. I am a member of the Osage Nation descended from Bridget A. Barber and Clara M. Barber Allotment numbers 906 and 907 respectively.[12]

It is true enough that "tribal affiliation is simple"—this is a question of citizenship, and the tribe itself, like any sovereign nation, can decide who is in and who is not. But both Indians and non-Indians have been—and remain—interested in more than enrollment: sometimes the concern is with "blood quantums" and sometimes with cultural identification. And usually there is slippage as one moves across categories. I am not inclined to tell the Osage who counts as an Osage. But as a critic interested in William Least Heat-Moon and especially his use of Whitman, I am intrigued by the complexity of these questions of identity and ready to accept liminality. It seems to me less useful and less possible to reach definitive conclusions about individuals than it is to interrogate the grounds of debate and the debate itself. If passing violates or overcomes racial and cultural boundaries, then the exposure of it, which can be thought of as "outing," enforces these divisions even as it implicitly acknowledges their tenuous nature. Michael Elliott notes that if "racial and cultural definitions [were] rigid, fixed, and always recognizable, neither passing nor outing would be possible."[13] Jerry Reynolds's 1993 series, "Indian Writers: Real or Imagined," explores the claims of writers who identify themselves as Native American but are not enrolled in any tribal organization.[14] There are problems, however, with the central criterion used by both Reynolds and my Osage correspondent David Ward: tribal enrollment. Some tribes have never come to terms with the U.S. government and so have not been recognized as tribes. Meanwhile other tribes frequently find themselves entangled in curious paradoxes because of the painful history of U.S.-Indian affairs. Ward Churchill argues that "to take too much account of enrollment is irredeemably racist in its view. . . . The federal government was not involved in deciding who belonged to Indian communities when the treaties were signed. . . . At that time . . . Indians knew their own free of federal restraint." Moreover, the Indian Arts and Crafts Act, which provides penalties for artists who sell their art as Indian-made without being able to prove their Indian identity, has highlighted just how many Indians are not enrolled in recognized tribes. One of the best known of these artists, Jimmie Durham, has declared with biting irony: "I am not Cherokee. I am not an American Indian. This is in concurrence with recent U.S. legislation, because I am not enrolled on any reservation or in any American Indian community."[15]

The situation of "wannabe Indians," then, offers an intriguing twist, a new turn in the history of passing in the United States, in that passing has typically involved less powerful groups attempting to be taken for—and sometimes to permanently blend into—more powerful groups. Wannabe Indians alter the usual directional flow of passing. The sometimes genuinely puzzled and sometimes outraged reaction to them reflects an effort on the part of marginalized cultures to preserve their integrity by shunning those who do not deserve to be regarded as community members. Reactions to passing depend on context: that is, we are more likely to approve of passing by a runaway slave, say a Harriet Jacobs, than we are an individual donning the trappings of an Indian to capitalize on the current hunger for Indian spiritualism or Indian gambling revenues. We are also more inclined, I think, to allow Whitman to play the woman, to play the abolitionist aiding a fugitive slave, and to play the friendly and flowing "savage" because of genre: that is, Whitman engages in fictions that acknowledge their fictitiousness—as he also did in his explicit statement to Anne Gilchrist, warning her not to "construct . . . an unauthorized & imaginary ideal Figure, & call it W.W." because the "actual W.W. is a very plain personage."[16]

Many social practices suggest that one could be only white, or black, or Native American, or Asian American, etc. And we often encounter sharp lines in legal reasoning. A person is simply a member of a tribe or not; a group constitutes (legally speaking) a tribe or not. If we were to defend William Least Heat-Moon, it would be along the lines of fluidity of identity, and it would be because of a sense that cultural identifications ought to be seen not as one thing or another but as locations on a continuum. Part 3 of Jerry Reynolds's series on wannabe Indians, "Indian Writers: The Good, the Bad, and the Could Be," even while engaged in outing, points to the inevitable uncertainties in his task. And of course ironies abound—Rayna Green, who has also made a practice of outing wannabe Indians, comes in for scrutiny by Reynolds because Green herself is not enrolled in any tribe. Reynolds also analyzes, with profound skepticism, the Indian claims of Richard Strickland, a Cherokee and Osage Indian (not enrolled in either tribe) who served as the director of the Center for the Study of American Indian Law and Policy at the University of Oklahoma. He further studies a number of other prominent writers, though he omits, for whatever reason, William Least Heat-Moon from consideration.

Heat-Moon explains that his concept of *Blue Highways* was to make a "book not so much about me, but, to use the expression, about Everyman—or maybe in this case I should say Anyman, any person who finds that it's time to start anew and who begins by putting himself into motion."[17] Yet if this book is about renovation of the self, it would have been helpful, as John

Updike pointed out in a review, for Heat-Moon to be more forthcoming about "where he is from, where he has been, or what he has done."[18] In fact, Heat-Moon does comment briefly on the issue of "blood": "Nevertheless, a mixed-blood—let his heart be where it may—is a contaminated man who will be trusted by neither red nor white. The attitude goes back to a long history of 'perfidious' half-breeds, men who, by their nature, had to choose against one of their bloodlines. As for me, I will choose for heart, for spirit, but never will I choose for blood."[19] If Heat-Moon fails to provide adequate discussion of his real or assumed background, so too the attacks on him as "bogus" are equally thin in terms of evidence and explanation. Few give any reason for judging him to be non-Indian. And if lack of tribal enrollment is the unspoken key, then few speak frankly about the problematic nature of this criterion.

It is appropriate, then, that Heat-Moon's engagement with Whitman becomes a struggle with the nature of the self and ego. "Hadn't I even made a traveling companion of the great poet of ego, the one who sings of himself, who promises to 'effuse egotism and show it underlying all,' who finds the earth his own likeness?"[20] Heat-Moon's struggle is conducted as he negotiates the terrain between *Leaves of Grass*—from which he can learn how to remake the self, how to perform the self through writing—and *Black Elk Speaks*, which he assumes offers access to unquestionable Native authenticity. Finally *Blue Highways* fails to be persuasive in achieving some important goals, in part because Heat-Moon's recorded encounters with Native Americans fall flat. Heat-Moon's project is also compromised by a basic design flaw: his choice of *Black Elk* as a model of stable Indian identity. In contrast with Whitman, whose protean qualities and elusive, multifaceted sense of self are celebrated, Heat-Moon implies that we will find a stable, authentic self in Black Elk. He does little to acknowledge the complexity of how Black Elk is constructed as a character whose story is told to John G. Neihardt through Black Elk's son Ben Black Elk, recorded in stenographic notes by Neihardt's daughter Enid, and then finally shaped and recreated by Neihardt. Heat-Moon is silent about the identity slippages in *Black Elk Speaks* as Neihardt's voice passes for Black Elk's.

Despite the trickiness of these questions of authenticity, *Blue Highways* is structured to record a passage from William Trogdon to William Least Heat-Moon as he progresses through Whitman to Black Elk. He pursues this course by way of the road: "With a nearly desperate sense of isolation and a growing suspicion that I lived in an alien land, I took to the open road."[21] He is in search of possibilities, new materials for constructing the self. He strives to follow the Whitmanian open road but in accordance with Indian beliefs: "I went clockwise. That's the Indian way."[22] He has asserted that the "spiritual movement in the book" is "based on the Hopi Maze of Migration, the Maze of Emergence," and he named his truck "Ghost Dancing," invoking the "ceremonies of the 1890s in which the Plains Indians, wearing cloth shirts they believed rendered them indestructible, danced for the return of warriors, bison, and the fervor of the old life that would sweep away the new."[23] At the outset of the book he has lost his teaching job, faces the prospect of divorce, and is keenly aware of his isolation.

On a visit to Fort Raleigh, Heat-Moon cites Whitman in a discussion of Anglo-Indian relations. The second European expedition of 1585, led by Sir Walter Raleigh's cousin, Sir Richard Grenville, regarded "Indians as savages and ignored their kindnesses. . . . They began stealing from the natives. During the skirmishes that ensued for the next months, Grenville's men were not satisfied with shooting the red people — they beheaded in the old European manner. Commander Ralph Lane even launched one attack with the watchword, 'Christ Our Victory!'"[24] Following these remarks, Heat-Moon quotes Whitman: "*While how little the New after all, how the Old, Old World!*" This apparently casts Whitman as a sympathizer with the Indians or at least a pained observer of the course of genocide. Other Indian writers, as Ed Folsom has shown, have been less sure what Whitman's attitudes would have been.[25] Thus, if Heat-Moon is passing into Native American consciousness, he takes an unusual position on an issue a number of other Indian writers feel passionately about. As Jonathan Yardley has remarked, "Heat Moon is an indefatigable romantic; although he makes occasional gestures in the course of his narrative to the brutalities inflicted on Indians by whites, and though he muses from time to time about what it means to be of mixed blood . . . Blue Highways makes clear that more than anything else he is passionately . . . in love with small-town America."[26] Repeatedly Heat-Moon hits a Whitmanian note of nostalgia for what Allen Ginsberg called Whitman's "lost America of love."[27] The low point of his journey comes at Central Michigan University, where he tries to sleep in a dorm room one summer night and is insulted as "Tonto" by a traveling businessman.

For some, Heat-Moon is too white to count as Indian, and for others he is too Indian to be white. When Anatole Broyard, the daily book reviewer for the *New York Times* and thus one of the world's most influential literary gatekeepers, praised *Blue Highways* as a "wonderful" book—"on finishing [it], one can be forgiven a little flush of national pride"—did he praise the work as one passing man suspecting and celebrating another, or as a sensitive connoisseur of language and thought appreciating the many passages of eloquence and insight in *Blue Highways*?[28]

NAYLOR'S WHITMAN: REWRITING THE SCRIPT, VOICING THE UNSPEAKABLE

In *Linden Hills*, Gloria Naylor provides an equally intriguing example of a minority writer negotiating with Whitman and exploring the complexities of passing, in this case, a gay man passing for straight. Naylor's treatment of Whitman illuminates her own readiness to take what she will from the literary past, from black or white, male or female. At a more general level, Naylor's novel is suggestive about *why* Whitman has been so enabling for a multiethnic array of writers and *how* they have responded to this predecessor. In *Linden Hills* Naylor enriches her fiction through intertextual engagements with numerous predecessors, with Dante being most central since he provides the general structure for this study of hell on earth. The characters corresponding to the *Inferno*'s Dante and Virgil are two black poets, "White" Willie Mason (nicknamed "White" because he was the blackest kid in school) and Lester Tilson. Lester is a coffeehouse poet more absorbed than Willie into the mainstream of Linden Hills, a wealthy all-black community characterized by a get-ahead mentality and peopled with individuals who have lost the mirrors in their souls.[29] Willie, in contrast, lives outside Linden Hills.

Because Naylor's novel dramatizes horrific consequences of patriarchy, it is especially intriguing to see how she situates herself with regard to male precursors. That is, because the novel so powerfully condemns male dominance, Naylor's own relationship to potentially dominating male predecessors becomes of central importance. In this regard, Whitman is a special case because of his liminality, his fluid sexuality. From the start, sexual identity is at issue for both Willie and Lester. They worry that they will be seen as "fruits" for liking verse. And while both pursue women rather than men, their ongoing banter about same-sex love and their sharing a bed one night keeps their homosocial bond always shimmering in the neighborhood of homosexuality. More than Lester, Willie is willing to recognize his own homoerotic drives: he does not deny the curious ache he felt in his stomach when watching Hank Aaron swivel in the batter's box while hitting a home run or the equally unsettling effects of staring too long at the thighs of a New York Knicks center.

Willie distrusts white-controlled media and thus refuses to write down his poems: "The written word dulls the mind, and since most of what's written is by white men, it's positively poisonous."[30] Willie has the "respect of [his acquaintances] because he was a 'deep' dude."[31] His link to Whitman is emphasized in his own comment to Lester: "You know I have six hundred and sixty-five poems memorized . . . and lots of 'em ain't mine. I have all of Baraka, Soyinka, Hughes, and most of Coleridge. And Whitman—that was one together dude."[32] Willie, Whitman, Malcolm X, and Shakespeare are all described within a few pages as heavy "dudes," and all stand as common cultural resources.

In the exclusive black neighborhood of Linden Hills (owned, operated, and in fact tyrannized over by Luther Nedeed), Willie and Lester get work taking the garbage out at the wedding reception of Winston and Cassandra Alcott. Whites have been hired to wait tables, and Willie and Lester are expected to stay out of the way, invisible. Over the course of six days in the Christmas season, Lester and Willie take other odd jobs, thereby coming to know the inverted hierarchy of this community where down is up and where the finest homes and most prestigious addresses are found in the lower crescent drives, closest to the base of the hill where the satanic Luther himself resides.

Naylor invokes Whitman in a charged moment early in the novel: the wedding reception of Cassandra and Winston. The best man, David, recites "Whoever You are Holding Me Now in Hand," using this Whitman poem to speak to those with ears to hear. Or, better, he speaks in a polyvalent fashion through Whitman, the poet's words conveying different meanings to different audiences.[33] Willie, for example, gleans much about the relationship between Winston and David and, thus, about the falsity of the wedding.[34] Intriguingly, when David recites the Whitman poem, he doctors the pronouns in a way reminiscent of Whitman himself. David says: "Who is she that would become my follower? / Who would sign herself a candidate for my affections?"[35] The incident is intriguing because of the parallel be-

tween the hypocrisy of Winston and the evasiveness—or resourcefulness—
of Whitman, who changed pronouns on more than one occasion to disguise same-sex affections. For example, the printed forms of "Once I Pass'd
through a Populous City" speak of a heterosexual attachment, though the
manuscript version of the poem originally celebrated love between men.[36]
Naylor's novel as a whole credits Whitman for managing to give voice
to the unspeakable. Winston has been coerced, via an anonymous letter
threatening to reveal his homosexuality, into abandoning his eight-year relationship with his lover David. The wedding reception begins with Luther
Nedeed toasting the groom and welcoming Mr. and Mrs. Winston Alcott,
through the gift of a new lease, to a lower rung in Linden Hills. David follows with the Whitman lines indicating to Winston in this coded fashion
that their love affair will end unless he walks away from his marriage.[37]
David's words, specifically addressed to the bride at one level, implore
Winston at another, and indict the assembled guests, the public that "had
given him no words—and ultimately no way—with which to cherish" the
joys and communion he had shared with Winston, at yet another level.[38]
David asks Cassandra to imagine that his voice is Winston's:

> "The whole past theory of your life, and all conformity to the lives
>   around you, would have to be abandon'd;
> Therefore release me now, before troubling yourself any further—
> . . .
> Put me down and depart on your way.
>
> Or else, by stealth, in some wood for trial,
> Or back of a rock, in the open air,
> (For in any roof'd room of a house I emerge not—nor in company . . .)
> But just possibly with you on a high hill—first watching lest any
>   person, for miles around, approach unawares,
> Or possibly with you sailing at sea, or on the beach of the sea, or some
>   quiet island,
> Here to put your lips upon mine I permit you,
> With the comrade's long-dwelling kiss, or the new husband's kiss,
> For I am the new husband, and I am the comrade."[39]

David manages to criticize Winston for being false to himself while re-
asserting his own sense of dignity, his own sense that, in a profound way, he

is the true "husband" for Winston. In the face of powerful social pressure to conform, David chooses to resist.

Luther Nedeed's opening toast, mentioned before, had erased Cassandra's name. Hardly trivial, this is part of a lethal, century-long pattern of effacing women, carried out by several generations of men all looking like clones of one another and all named Luther Nedeed. The latest Luther Nedeed reasserts, in monologic fashion, a male-oriented, heterosexist "truth"; David, on the other hand, speaking through Winston, points to the importance of marginalized voices who, in subtle ways, provide an effective means of response (given the difference in power) through plural signification. Nedeed, the voice of patriarchy, strives to suppress dissonant voices. As the novel unfolds, it becomes clear that the Nedeeds have all along been erasing their wives once each new generation's Luther Nedeed has been born. Through their texts—cookbooks, diaries, photos— the women resist indirectly, using means that memorialize and assert their identities even as they are threatened with destruction.

David offers a dialogical response to Nedeed's monological performance. David speaks "to the other half, the better half," addressing the hidden life of Winston, the life that cannot be accepted, comprehended, or articulated within the confines of Nedeed's univocal text.[40] David finds in Whitman—as does David's creator, Gloria Naylor—a malleable force that can be used against the shortcomings of a flawed social system. David rejects the false smiles and inner emptiness felt by Winston as he slides into a conventional marriage.

Margaret Homans, in commenting on *Linden Hills*, has asserted that "Whereas for Naylor a female tradition (whether in literary history or among her characters) is not sufficiently powerful to counteract the patrilineal power to erase women, her two heroes do benefit from patrilineage in the form of (primarily white) male literary history."[41] Neither Billie Holiday nor Bessie Smith can help the suicidal Laurel Dumont, but Willie and Lester are enabled, in contrast, by black and white male poets—Whitman, Eliot, and "the great slave poet, Jupiter Hammon," and Malcolm X as well. Significantly, Willie benefits by beginning his own, appropriately balanced, oral epic about the underworld: *There is a man in a house at the bottom of a hill. And his wife has no name.*[42] Willie, the only person who has heard the pitiable moans of the suffering Mrs. Nedeed, makes central the victimized woman in hell. Henry Louis Gates Jr. has argued that the "theme of male homosexuality runs through Naylor's representation of literary creativity."[43] Naylor has depicted Willie's sensitivity to David and Winston and to the women in the novel as related to the fluid nature of his sexual identity and his willingness to acknowledge homoerotic aspects of his personality.

WHITMAN AND WHITE MEN IN ISHMAEL REED'S
FLIGHT TO CANADA

If Heat-Moon and Naylor attempt to balance the multiracial resources that support and energize their work, Ishmael Reed also considers the question of a tangled lineage, but he is much less inclined to celebrate white fathers. In fact, he explicitly predicts and tries to offset claims that a white writer might be fundamentally important to his own text. Reed speaks to this problem when he has escaped slave Raven Quickskill (in conversation with William Wells Brown) say: "I'm sure the critics are going to give me some kind of white master. A white man. They'll say that he gave me the inspiration and that I modeled it after him. But I had you in mind."[44]

In *Flight to Canada*, Quickskill's escape from bondage takes place after emancipation, and it parallels his creator's flight from cultural slavery.[45] Quickskill seeks refuge from slavery by fleeing to Canada, but he discovers that the historical and contemporary actuality of Canada is disappointingly far from ideal. Yet the novel also treats an imaginary Canada, a realm of opportunity and freedom. Reed treats slavery at both the literal and the metaphorical level. In a dazzling way, he presents all of his figures and their contexts as both historical and contemporary. The entire novel interweaves the Civil War period and late twentieth-century life, highlighting the continuities between historical slavery and a more enduring cultural slavery.

Although in the nineteenth century the slave narrative was the most visible form of African American self-articulation, it remained subject to the discourse of the master culture.[46] For his own work, Reed renounces the (arguably, white European) conventions of the slave narrative—its reliance on realism, seriousness, and chronological orderliness. Reed seeks to reclaim his black voice, to gain control of discourse, to liberate it from the hold of the former master-texts. To achieve this revisionary goal, the narrator undertakes the tricky, difficult task of riding "Bareback, backwards through / a wood of words." The typical progressive ascent narrative whose arc always moved "up from slavery" has to be broken so as to overcome progressivist white thinking.[47] Reed situates his novel in a "wood of words," a complex set of textual cross-references that entangles thought and thus mimics the subtle forces of slavery itself.

"Flight"—with its double meaning of a dangerous escape on the historic Underground Railroad and the current ease of an air-flight to Canada—becomes Reed's means of blending the past and the present and of illustrating how, in insidious ways, the present recapitulates the past. Freedom, long since achieved in a bodily sense, remains an incompletely realized goal in a cultural sense. Thus it is not the Canada north of the border but the Canada in the mind that Reed is after.[48] He understands that you cannot really "*cash your way out of history*" or do the "Liza Leap" out of history, but you can gain leverage on history through laughter.[49]

Reed is especially audacious with Stowe, referring to her as "Naughty Harriet" and criticizing her appropriation—outright theft as he presents it—of Josiah Henson's story. "It was all he had. His story."[50] In contrast to Uncle Tom, Reed's Uncle Robin—who runs away by staying put—outsmarts and survives his master, Swille. In fact, Robin poisons his master, alters Swille's will, and takes his master's place. He rewrites the documents that would continue the life of slavery and thus breaks the chain of signifiers, the binding discourse. Reed reverses the problem of literacy by having Master Swille be illiterate while his slave Robin uses the power of literacy to write passes and forge freedom papers. Uncle Robin is an alternative to Uncle Tom, though he is not an alternative Reed's Stowe can understand, for she is blinded by her own view of blacks as being a "childish race" in need of white guidance. At the end of the novel, she asks Robin if she could write a book about his achievement, but he leaves the call unanswered. Instead, Robin grants the former fellow-slave, Raven Quickskill, rights to the story, since Raven's poem, "Flight to Canada," has established his credentials as the "true black amanuensis."[51] Refusing to submit either to white culture or to narrative convention, Reed satirizes white thinkers of the nineteenth century, especially those applauded for their links to emancipation—Stowe, Emerson, Thoreau, Whitman, and Lincoln. He criticizes their waffling, their duplicity, and the way they have become the heritage that serves to enforce what Reed sees as a continuing form of bondage. The exception is Poe, who receives some roundabout, quirky praise as the "principal biographer of that strange war. . . . Poe, prophet of a civilization buried alive, where, according to witnesses, people were often whipped for no reason. . . . Poe got it all down. Poe says more in a few stories than all of the volumes by historians."[52] *Flight to Canada* finds contradictions at the core of American thought. Far from being democratic, Reed argues, Americans hanker after medieval fantasies, yearning to be a happy aristocracy supported by slave sweat.[53]

If black writing has been disparaged, Reed will give blow for blow to white writers and white leaders. Significantly, the only account of love-making in the book reaches a climax to coincide with a particular line in the melodrama *Our American Cousin*, which Abraham Lincoln was watching when he was assassinated. Reed apparently assumes that his readers will know that John Wilkes Booth timed his shot to coincide with the line, "You sockdologizing mantrap." Booth, an actor, knew from previous performances that this line would create an uproar and counted on the cover it would give him. In an extraordinary example of what might be called in-your-face writing—and a calculated violation of American secular religion—Reed coordinates the lovemaking of the Indian Quaw Quaw and Raven so that they reach orgasm at the very moment of the assassination of Lincoln.

Throughout the novel, Reed strives to make every image of white sexuality seem depraved or perverted. Swille is associated with all sorts of exotic sexual tastes—at one point he relays a friend's fantasy of stripping bare before Jeff Davis in order to allow that "Adonis" to abuse him—and there are numerous indications of Swille's sexual liaisons with his dead sister. Moreover, Reed emphasizes Swille's involvement with the whips and chains of sadomasochism (he applies the lash to Queen Victoria after finding *Uncle Tom's Cabin* on her nightstand).

Reed takes Whitman in particular to task, no doubt because of his reputation as the quintessential "democrat." Master Swille finds Whitman's embrace of humanity distasteful, as is clear from remarks he makes to Lincoln about the Republican Party: "A far-out institution if there ever was one. Free Soilers, whacky money people, Abolitionists. Can't you persuade some of those people to wear a tie? Transcendentalists, Free Lovers, Free Farmers, Whigs, Know-Nothings, and those awful Whitmanites always running around hugging things."[54] What should we make of Lincoln calling Quickskill a national institution at the end of the chapter with Whitman in it? Quickskill and his poem "Flight to Canada" become a substitute for and challenge to Whitman by rewriting in a fundamental way the fugitive slave passage in "Song of Myself," a passage that is basic to Whitman's self-presentation, as noted in Chapter One. According to Reed, Whitman's account passes as the depiction of a liberating moment, though it actually participates in an enslaving master discourse. When Whitman hugs "things"—including the runaway slave—they remain "things." Only Quickskill's own self-liberation qualifies as true liberation.

In addition, Whitman appears in the novel when Quickskill is invited to a White House reception "honoring the leading scribes of America."

> Walt Whitman was there. He had written a poem called "Respondez," in which he had recommended all manner of excesses: lunatics running the asylum, jailers running the jail. "Let murderers, bigots, fools, unclean persons offer new propositions!" And now, here he was as Lincoln's guest in the White House.
>
> In the same poem he had written: "Let nothing remain but the ashes of teachers, artists, moralists, lawyers and learned and polite persons." I guess he was talking about himself, Quickskill thought, because there he was, as polite as he could be, grinning, shaking the hands of dignitaries.
>
> Whitman had described Lincoln as "dark brown." Whitman was accurate about that. He stood in the corner for most of the party, sniffing a lilac.[55]

Needless to say, this scene with Whitman at the White House is a fabrication. Interestingly, Reed chooses to quote extensively a poem Whitman excised from *Leaves of Grass*, presumably because of its irony and bitterness. Reed finds appealing the limitless outrage and disgust that Whitman's poem registers in the face of the political corruption of the 1850s and in the face of broken national ideals.

Nonetheless, in *Flight to Canada*, with its familiar figures morphed into unusual but hauntingly recognizable versions of themselves, Whitman is associated not with liberation but with capturing runaway slaves. Raven Quickskill, the runaway slave and author of the poem "Flight to Canada," is having a conversation with two trackers who want to take him back to his master. One of the trackers opens the conversation by declaring:

> "I'm a Whitman man, myself." . . .
> "Really?" Quickskill said. "Isn't it strange? Whitman desires to fuse

with Nature, and here I am, involuntarily, the comrade of the inanimate, but not by choice."

"I don't understand," they said together.

[Quickskill responds:] "I am property. I am a thing. I am in the same species as any other kind of property. We form a class, a family of things. This long black deacon's bench decorated with painted white roses I'm sitting on is worth more than me—five hundred dollars. Superior to me."[56]

These remarks are related to the logic of slavery and freedom. Reed suggests that Whitman's romanticized desire to be one with the entire "family of things"—with the grass, with the runaway slave—is only possible because of a freedom that he does not acknowledge. Reed apparently objects to Whitman's own (flattering) depiction of himself as a generous friend and abettor of the runaway slave. Reed probably finds such a self-characterization especially galling because of what we saw in Chapter 1: Whitman's ambivalence and inconsistency on racial issues. When *PMLA* recently ran a forum on the personal in literature, Nellie McKay remarked: "When I consider the history of black people in America, I wonder how a slave's thoughts at Walden Pond would have differed from Thoreau's or how a slave would have responded to Whitman's song of himself."[57] Reed imagines a contemporaneous response of a slave to *Leaves of Grass*, and though it varies from that of Sojourner Truth—the earliest recorded response of a former slave—it nonetheless provides a compelling, plausible, and troubling account of what the response of many slaves might have been.[58]

McKay notes that one former slave, Frederick Douglass, differed sharply from his New England friends in his reaction to the Fourth of July celebration. Interestingly, however, we can also invoke Douglass to show the dangers of condemning Whitman too quickly and completely. That is, Whitman's effort at imagining the runaway slave, presumptuous and impossible though it may be to some critics, is precisely what Douglass asked of his white audience:

> to understand . . . one must . . . imagine himself in similar circumstances. Let him be a fugitive slave in a strange land—a land given up to be the hunting ground for slaveholders . . . I say, let him place himself in my situation— without home or friends—without money or credit—wanting shelter . . . wanting bread . . . —and at the same time . . . he is pursued by merci-

less men-hunters. . . . *Not till then, will he fully appreciate the hardships of, and know how to sympathize with, the toil worn and whip-scarred fugitive slave.*[59]

Whitman's poetic strategy in "Song of Myself" enacts precisely the process of sympathetic identification Douglass called for.

The references to Lincoln being "dark brown" and to Confederate soldiers who claim that Lincoln must be a "nigger"[60] function as the most overt treatment of "passing" in the novel. However, passing operates at more subtle levels, too. Reed resists the patterns that would make blacks succumb to white patterns of thought. He further indicates that elite liberal white culture "passes," more insidiously, as being sympathetic while actually circumscribing the lives of blacks, and he is determined to "out" these pseudo friends. Reed employs synchronicity and a cyclical voodoo time to replace the linear, ascent-driven, Judeo-Christian pattern of development.[61] By intermingling past and present and conflating figures of the past with those of the present, historical time—and platitudinous attitudes toward it—crumbles. At the end of *Flight*, when Reed mentions "Fat Tuesday March 2, 1976" as the closing date of the action, he emphasizes the carnival atmosphere of the novel, a realm where "dogma, hegemony, and authority are dispersed through ridicule and laughter."[62]

Those who have talked back to Whitman have responded to (and helped construct) different Whitmans, as the ongoing reception of *Leaves of Grass* evolves through its varied and strange history. Whitman appears as a writable, or rewritable, text, as it were. His efforts to give voice to what was both denied and undeniable, his exploration in particular of same-sex love, shaped his image as a poet who managed to be at the center of power without ever truly being an insider. Whitman's malleability, explorations of passing, and centrality as an icon have made him irresistible for writers who, in extraordinarily creative ways, reinvent him for their purposes.

CHAPTER 6

WHITMAN AT THE MOVIES

In 1855, Walt Whitman claimed—bravely if not wisely—that "the proof of a poet is that his country absorbs him as affectionately as he has absorbed it."[1] We have yet to experience what Whitman foresaw, a time when farmers, mechanics, and bus drivers routinely go to work with copies of *Leaves of Grass* in their back pockets. Yet the movie industry has in a sense justified his bold prediction, enabling versions of "Whitman" (ranging from the puerile to the subtle) to reach the vast audiences that eluded him in his lifetime. Whitman's relation to film is a complex, fascinating, and largely neglected topic.[2] This chapter explores three interrelated matters. Initially, I note the affinities between Whitman's poetry and film and observe how his poetry developed concurrently with the earliest attempts at animated photography, coming to fruition in the Philadelphia area as artists and inventors, notably Eadweard Muybridge and Thomas Eakins, were advancing the field of motion studies. Next, I consider how in the silent era the groundbreaking American film theorist, Vachel Lindsay, the leading director, D. W. Griffith, and a pair of pioneering avant-garde filmmakers, Paul Strand and Charles Sheeler, all responded directly to Whitman. Finally, I analyze the appropriation of Whitman in films during the past sixty years, and especially the flurry of interest since 1980, for what it tells us about cultural memory and the politics of desire.[3]

CINEMA, *LEAVES OF GRASS*, AND CELEBRITY CULTURE

Whitman's career coincided with the conceptual and technical breakthroughs that made possible the art of film. Animated photography was attempted as early as 1851, and in 1878 Muybridge published the first series of cinematographic pictures depicting a trotting horse taken on Leland Stanford's farm in Palo Alto, California (see fig. 6). The importance of Muybridge's pictures was immediately perceived by Whitman's friend Eakins. When Muybridge gained an appointment at the University of Pennsylva-

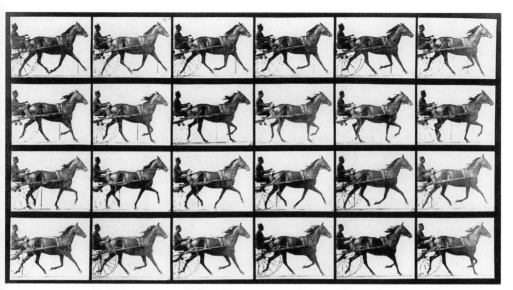

FIGURE 6. *Eadweard Muybridge's serial photographs of a trotting horse on Leland Stanford's farm in California, 1878. These photographs capturing high-speed motion inaugurated a new era in photography. Photograph reproduced courtesy Print and Picture Collection, Free Library of Philadelphia.*

nia in 1884 to continue his study of animal and human locomotion, Eakins served on the commission that supervised his work. In addition, Eakins engaged in his own motion studies and advanced beyond Muybridge in approaching the effect of a motion picture camera by using a single camera instead of a whole battery of cameras. In 1885 Eakins lectured on his photographic motion studies and, the following year, he exhibited one of his works, *History of a Jump* (see fig. 7). In differing ways, Eakins, Muybridge, and Whitman each benefited from the Philadelphia-Camden locale, a center of interest in photography and its new applications for art.[4]

Whitman did not live to experience the nickelodeon (the initial permanent exhibition outlets for films), but his contemporaries imagined cinema before it was realized. As André Bazin has argued, cinema, an "idealistic phenomenon," existed in a well-developed conceptual form long before the "obstinate resistance of matter" was overcome by a series of technical breakthroughs.[5] Whitman kept current about new applications in photography through his dealings with leading photographers and inventors,

FIGURE 7. *Thomas Eakins's* History of a Jump, *1885, with annotations by Eadweard Muybridge. Reproduced courtesy Library Company of Philadelphia.*

including Eakins and James Wallace Black, who was instrumental in the development of the magic lantern, a widely popular means of photographic display.[6] Early film visionaries yearned to advance beyond lantern slide lectures, to portray the world in a seamless fashion combining motion, sound, and color. Thomas Edison (who expressed a desire to "obtain a phonogram from the poet Whitman") sought to link sound and sight by attaching the phonograph to the kinetoscope (an apparatus for viewing recorded images that was widely available in Whitman's time). Like Edison and others, the poet welcomed new technological tools, as is suggested by the wax cylinder of what is apparently Whitman's own voice reciting lines from "America."[7] New inventions enhanced Whitman's toolkit, improving his ability to convey an illusion of presence. As Whitman remarked, "The human expression is so fleeting—so quick—coming and going—all aids are welcome."[8]

Leaves of Grass anticipated many techniques we now associate with filmmakers. When Whitman argued in 1872 that a "modern Image-Making creation is indispensable to fuse and express the modern Political and Scientific creations," he characterized poetry in ways that prefigured film.[9] He once remarked, "I approach nature not to explain but to picture. Who can explain?"[10] As early as the pre-*Leaves* poem "Pictures," Whitman began to develop his mature style that emphasized metonymy rather than metaphor, a style that gloried in the realistic details of life, moved freely across space, and linked images by a private logic. (As Ed Folsom has noted, early photographers were stunned by the clutter and debris in their pictures, since the camera picked up details the eye had not noticed.)[11] "Pictures" stresses the democratic inclusiveness of photography, its capturing of all in its field, in opposition to the selectivity of painting.

> For wherever I have been, has afforded me superb pictures,
> And whatever I have heard has given me perfect pictures,
> And every hour of the day and night has given me copious pictures,
> And every rod of land or sea affords me, as long as I live, inimitable
>   pictures.[12]

The poet strove to give his work the dynamism that marked the best photography of his day, photography that seemed to him magically to catch life "in a flash, as it shifted, moved, evolved."[13] Animated photography, could, even more powerfully, convey both patterns and dynamics of information, the process of seeing, the unfolding of action. Whitman's own fidelity to process in a poem such as "Crossing Brooklyn Ferry" may have led Robert Richardson to the arresting claim that Whitman's example has had "at least as great an impact on film form as it has had on modern poetic practice."[14] I think Richardson overstates his case, but not badly so. Whitman's work was suggestive because of its compelling use of montage as a structural principle (what Sergei Eisenstein called "Walt Whitman's huge montage conception").[15] The poet's catalogues adumbrate the jump cutting, fluent mobility, and surprising juxtapositions frequently seen in films.

It is worth adding that Whitman's fashioning of himself as an artifact, a self-created star, prefigured developments in an industry that would thrive on public relations ingenuity. He set a new precedent for how a literary project could be advanced through photography, demonstrating photography's power to contribute to celebrity status. He included photographic portraits of himself in his books, portraits that contribute to and are inseparable from the meaning of some of his poems. He conceived of *Leaves of Grass* as his "definitive *carte visite* to the coming generations."[16] In England, particularly among those interested in manly love, his photos took on special import, having a type of talismanic function. Recognizable yet elusive, Whitman endures in part because of this star quality. His blending of seeming opposites—intimacy and publicity—is analogous to one of the most powerful effects of film. Through a much commented upon metonymic trick he collapsed the distinction between *Leaves of Grass* and himself, offering the illusion that he and his book were one. Alternately revealing and withholding information, he conveyed a curiously inscrutable familiarity.

"I PASS SO POORLY WITH PAPER AND TYPES": WHITMAN AND SILENT FILMS

Whitman provided more than stylistic hints for early filmmakers. Beginning as early as 1913, filmmakers dramatized him in this new art form. The earliest cinematic treatment of Whitman is *The Carpenter* (see fig. 8), a silent film produced by the Vitagraph Company.[17] This film, apparently no longer extant, was an adaptation of William Douglas O'Connor's short story of the same name. O'Connor's original story did not mention the poet by name, but the bearded visitor to hospitals, caregiver to the Civil War wounded of both North and South, unmistakably referred to Whitman. The emphases of the film are suggested by this review from *The Motion Picture World*:

> Cast in war times and surroundings, the contentions which tore this nation cause severe division in this household; the son is opposed to the father, and espouses the opposite cause and is hated therefor[e] and as was not uncommon in those days, brothers fight against brothers. A second trouble arises in the coming financial ruin of the old home, while a third evil is seen in the advantage being taken of a young wife of one of

FIGURE 8. *A scene from* The Carpenter *(1913), from* Motion Picture World. *Photo courtesy Library of Congress.*

the sons, by a visiting friend of alluring manners; hatred, ruin, and jealousy, are working their insidious way in dreaded canker-like manner, in this once happy and prosperous home.

The review notes that "There is an unknown Christ in the home moulding the control of events and bringing prosperity, peace, and happiness, if allowed to do by a willing yielding to his gracious influences."[18] Neither the review nor an advertisement for the film mentions O'Connor as the author of the original story or Whitman as the prototype of the hero, suggesting that Marguerite Bertsch, the scriptwriter, may have pirated the story. In any event, the film treated one issue, the love triangle, that later would be pivotal in many Whitman films. O'Connor's original story explored the love of comrades, what he called the "love passing the love of women," though it is unclear how this issue figured in the film (an all-male triangle may be suggested by fig. 9). The story associates the poet's hospital work with the

FIGURE 9. *The Whitman figure in* The Carpenter. *Of interest here is the triangulated pattern of relationship and the Carpenter's clothing: the mixed coloring apparently attests to his lack of favoritism to either North or South. Photo courtesy Library of Congress.*

healing powers of Christ and depicts him as uniting a family torn apart by sons fighting for opposing armies. The film version of *The Carpenter* also apparently emphasized the religious aspect of Whitman, an element that later would fade in importance as the dominant threads in Whitman's reception became not the political radical and the religious prophet but the secular poet and spokesman for mainstream liberal American democracy.

Writing two years after *The Carpenter*, Van Wyck Brooks, in *America's Coming of Age* (1915), reinforced the view that Whitman served as an integrating force in American culture. In this vital work in the development of American modernism, Brooks declared Whitman to be part of the "usable past," a middle ground bridging highbrow and lowbrow. "The real significance of Walt Whitman," Brooks asserted, "is that he, for the first time, gave us the sense of something organic in American life. . . . In him the hitherto incompatible extremes of the American temperament were fused."[19] In the same year, Vachel Lindsay, champion of Whitman's legacy in Hollywood, published *The Art of the Moving Picture* (1915), in which he praised film as a new American hieroglyphics. Lindsay, seeking a solution to the problem of Babel, hoped that the hieroglyph of film might be an integrating force on a large scale, that it might provide a universal language because of the ability of narrative and image to cross cultural boundaries. However, in an interesting turn, Lindsay argued that this universal language should have a national inflection: "We must have Whitmanesque scenarios, based on moods akin to that of the poem By Blue Ontario's Shore. The possibility of showing the entire American population its own face in the Mirror Screen has at last come. Whitman brought the idea of democracy to our sophisticated literati, but did not persuade the democracy itself to read his democratic poems. Sooner or later the kinetoscope will do what he could not, bring the nobler side of the equality idea to the people who are so crassly equal." Believing that those in "slums" were most affected by "the photoplay of action," Lindsay underscored the social and political importance of film.[20] Intriguingly, Lindsay does little to mask his own feelings of superiority to those "so crassly equal," despite his advocacy of "Whitmanesque scenarios."

The idea that Whitman could underwrite an approach to filmmaking gained powerful support from D. W. Griffith. Griffith so admired Whitman that he said he "would rather have written one page of *Leaves of Grass* than to have made all the movies for which he received world acclaim."[21] Early in its history, film was associated with inexpensive popular entertainment, poorly educated city dwellers, and the immigrant working classes. As Lindsay's words and Griffith's practices showed, Whitman's ability to achieve high-art standing while retaining populist credentials enabled him to be a resource for a new art form struggling to negotiate class boundaries and the sometimes conflicting claims of commerce and art. When classical film appropriated Whitman, the industry aligned itself with a poet who claimed (oxymoronically) special privilege as a spokesman for democracy.

With *The Birth of a Nation* (1915) Griffith achieved a stunning commercial and artistic success, even as controversy erupted over the film's racism, and Griffith found himself confronting censorship battles. Whitman's own battles with censorship and his reputation as a poet of love increased his appeal for Griffith in the immediate aftermath of *The Birth of a Nation*, a time of both great achievement and great crisis. Griffith attempted mightily to secure middle-class respectability for the fledgling movie industry. Thus he strove to give *Intolerance* (1916), which explicitly invoked Whitman, the status of art, and he succeeded in that the film was greeted as an "epic poem" and "a film fugue."[22] Paradoxically, Griffith attempted to achieve a universal language of cinema *and* to ground cinema, as Lindsay had suggested, in a particular strain of U.S. culture directly related to Whitman, whom he "passionately" admired.[23] One of the central oddities of *Intolerance* is its use of intertitles, which often appear on tablet-like backgrounds displaying various scripts. Viewers encounter English intertitles superimposed upon nonphonetic and non-Western script. The effect is that of a palimpsest, with different systems of graphic notation visible in layered fashion within the same shot.[24] Even as *Intolerance* aspires to overcome textual limitations, the film multiplies textual forms, and if the film privileges any single text it is "Out of the Cradle Endlessly Rocking."

Griffith paralleled the approach of *Leaves of Grass* in his emphasis on the gritty materiality of life, his appreciation of detail, and his grandiose ambition to include seemingly everything. Epic in scope, *Intolerance* features four separate narratives set in radically different places and times. Interwoven by means of parallel montage, these narratives include a modern American story, tracing a young couple's struggle with tenement violence and an unfair legal system; a French narrative treating the Saint Bartholemew's Day Massacre (A.D. 1572); episodes set in Judea focusing on the life of Christ; and a narrative depicting the fall of Babylon to Cyrus (538 B.C.). Whereas the historical episodes all end in bloodshed, the modern story represents a variation in that catastrophe is averted when the young husband escapes execution at the last moment.

The four stories are linked only by a mysterious, mood-setting, shadowy shot of Lillian Gish rocking a cradle accompanied by intertitles that quote —sometimes inexactly—*Leaves of Grass* (see fig. 10). One intertitle reads: "A golden thread binds the four stories—a fairy girl with sunlit hair—her hand on the cradle of humanity—eternally rocking." The rocking cradle image is associated with no particular time (the woman's clothing could be from almost any period), as is true of the mysterious figures, the three

FIGURE 10. *Lillian Gish rocking the cradle in* Intolerance *(1916), with the Fates in the background. Photograph courtesy Museum of Modern Art/Film Stills Archive.*

Fates, visible in the background. The cradle image unifies *Intolerance*, marking transitions and introducing and concluding the film. The image conveys a common humanity linking all people and a view of history that is highly patterned and reiterative, as is suggested by the intertitle "endlessly rocks the cradle, Uniter of here and Hereafter."[25] Critical of this recurrent shot, Sergei Eisenstein noted that "the cradle could not possibly be *abstracted into an image of eternally reborn epochs* and remained inevitably simply a *life-like cradle*, calling forth derision, surprise or vexation in the spectator."[26] The cradle image is a jarring yet curiously powerful feature in this film: perhaps Eisenstein was bothered because the image remains outside the flow of all four narratives. Moreover, because the cradle image is often repeated, the viewer cannot help but notice the laboriousness of the attempt to convey an abstraction by means of a material object. The very oddity of mixing a prominent nonnarrative element in a film notable for its four strong narratives produces a formal complexity that is in keeping with, say, the experimentation of "Song of Myself," with its mini-narratives embedded within a nonnarrative structure.[27] To my way of thinking, Griffith is reasonably successful in achieving a totality of effect when he combines the visual image of the cradle and Whitman's words to suggest "eternally reborn epochs." Through the invocation of "Out of the Cradle Endlessly Rocking," Griffith taps into a poem that is profoundly concerned with problems of "translation" across languages, species, and time, and that, like Griffith's film, reaches far back into western tradition.

While Griffith developed cinema in the direction of narrative and kept his camera focused on actors rather than on the space they inhabited, Charles Sheeler and Paul Strand, more famous for their photography and painting, adopted a starkly different approach. Sheeler and Strand's seven-minute work, *Manhatta* (1921), has been called the first genuine avant-garde film made in the United States.[28] Abandoning classical modes of address and the depiction of heroes and heroines, Sheeler and Strand present no story but instead depict a five-block area in lower Manhattan. Sheeler had proposed to Strand that they might make a kind of "experimental film about New York . . . —a silent film carried along by the titles . . . from Walt Whitman's poem." Shot mainly from the rooftops and streets, the film's disorienting vantage points remind viewers of their subjectivity and emphasize the geometric configurations of the cityscape. Humans, when seen at all, appear antlike, thus making the Whitman invocations strange given the poet's celebration of the larger-than-life "divine average" person.[29] *Manhatta* shifts curiously between a modernism that either shows humans as tiny or as part of well-functioning machines. The incongruity between words and images serves simultaneously as a commentary on the film's own modernist aesthetic and as a commentary on Manhattan itself where, in panoramic shots opening the film, the picturesque waterways jut up against the stark angularity of skyscrapers.[30] The eleven intertitles drawn from various Whitman poems—"A Broadway Pageant," "Mannahatta," "Crossing Brooklyn Ferry"—give structure to the film and serve as a "lyric counter-point to the film's visual imagery."[31] *Manhatta* achieves a compelling and highly original visual style analogous to the pathbreaking nature of Whitman's "language experiment." Interestingly, Griffith, a narrative filmmaker, turns to "Cradle," one of the few narrative poems in Whitman's oeuvre—while Sheeler and Strand turn to Whitman's various nonnarrative lyrics to enable their film to be "carried along," to explore methods of movement and organization in a film that lacks the forward drive of plot development.

WHITMAN FILMS IN THE SOUND ERA

Films through Mid-Century

One of the most intriguing of the early "talkies," *Street Scene* (1931), directed by King Vidor and produced by Samuel Goldwyn, makes use of Whitman in a pivotal scene. This film's origins in a stage play are clear from the static set—the action unfolds on the stoop and on the pavement in front of a three-story brownstone—but Vidor's ingenuity with camera angles maintains visual interest. Elmer Rice, who wrote the Pulitzer Prize-winning play of the same title three years earlier, wrote the screenplay. Like Whitman, Rice valued the rich human variety of New York, and the film weaves together a story of many families of distinct ethnic origins and religious beliefs. The story is made up of several plot lines, but the two key ones are what Rice described as the "central love story: a sort of Romeo and Juliet romance" between Rose Maurrant (Sylvia Sidney) and her Jewish admirer Sam Kaplan (William Collier Jr.). The second significant plot Rice calls the "main dramatic thread of murder," committed by Rose's father when he comes home unexpectedly and finds his wife with her lover. In Act I, Rose tells Sam that she feels blue and discouraged. She takes some solace, though, in having seen a big lilac bush in the park and in recollecting the poem Sam had recently recited for her ("When Lilacs Last in the Dooryard Bloom'd"). However when he repeats for her the opening lines, she corrects him, focusing on her dreams of escaping tenement life, saying, "No, not that part, I mean the part about the farm-house. Say it for me Sam."

> "In the door-yard, fronting an old farm-house, near the white-washed
>   palings,
> Stands the lilac-bush, tall-growing, with heart-shaped leaves of rich
>   green,

> With many a pointed blossom, rising delicate, with the perfume
>   strong I love,
> With every leaf a miracle—and from this bush in the door-yard,
> With delicate-color'd blossoms and heart-shaped leaves of rich green,
> A sprig with its flower I break."[32]

Her eagerness to have him recite these lines underlines her sense that she is trapped in her environment. Rice repeated these lines in his filmscript, but Vidor altered the emphasis by writing "Change" in the margin of his script.[33] He selected instead less profound and tragic lines, a section from "Passage to India" that could conceivably be read as highly romantic:

> Sail forth—steer for the deep waters only,
> Reckless O soul, exploring, I with thee, and thou with me,
> For we are bound where mariner has not yet dared to go,
> And we will risk the ship, ourselves and all.

Interestingly, Whitman serves as a love currency here in ways that prefigure how he will be used in many later films. He mediates a somewhat illicit love. And even when Vidor rejected Rice's selection of particular lines, he concurred with the belief that Whitman was a fitting shorthand for signalling passages across borders of class, religion, and geography.

Two Warner Brothers films, *Now, Voyager* (1942) and *Goodbye, My Fancy* (1951), follow Strand and Sheeler in quoting Whitman in their very titles and follow Griffith's *Intolerance* in making explicit their invocations of the poet and their concern with textuality. *Now, Voyager*, directed by Irving Rapper and based on a novel by Olive Higgins Prouty, pivots on lines from Whitman's "The Untold Want."[34] This much-admired film treats problems of repression and a corresponding yearning for freedom as it traces the maturation of Charlotte Vale (Bette Davis). Charlotte achieves her sense of identity not through an orthodox heterosexual romance but through involvement with a married man, Jerry Durance (Paul Henreid). Moreover, the therapeutic approach of psychiatrist Dr. Jaquith (Claude Rains) hinges on his quoting of Whitman in a key scene with Charlotte in his sanitarium (see fig. 11). Dr. Jaquith turns to Whitman's poem "The Untold Want:" "If old Walt didn't have you in mind when he wrote this, he had hundreds of others like you." He asks her to read for herself the lines: "Untold want, by life and land ne'er granted, / Now, Voyager, sail thou forth, to seek and

FIGURE 11. *An exchange between Dr. Jaquith (Claude Rains) and Charlotte (Bette Davis) in* Now, Voyager *(1942).*

find."[35] (Prouty selected a Whitman text closely echoing that used by Vidor in *Street Scene*; both, intriguingly, transform passages in which Whitman speaks about the journey of "I" and the "soul" into passages about interpersonal relationships.) Whitman opens new possibilities for Charlotte by encouraging freedom from the sexual repression and rigidity of her former days. She finds her way to a new womanhood via a male doctor and a male poet by internalizing their messages and embarking on her own open-ended journey.

Her dilemma is scripted in terms of a rejection of Bostonian conventionalities, pretentiousness, and pieties.[36] The film opens with an image of the Vale name on a house stone and then shifts to a miniature statue of a black jockey, situating Charlotte's personal oppression and repression within a social context based on authority, division, and unequal access to power. The Bostonians depicted here—Charlotte's mother and Eliot Livingston, to whom Charlotte is briefly engaged—view the world very much in hierarchical terms. In opposition to them are Jerry Durance and Dr. Jaquith (and the outré Whitman), figures foreign to the Boston world. Early in the film we see that Charlotte conceals her passionate inner life, disguising racy reading material behind stodgier tomes and hiding a notebook that records an earlier failed romance. Whitman is part of Charlotte's breaking away from the Puritan tradition to embrace a broader range of people and a less repressive outlook. Whitman helps Charlotte embrace her inner life and integrate it with her public personality.

Now, Voyager reconsiders and reconfigures family relations by depicting a woman who reaches full selfhood outside of the nuclear family and outside of marriage.[37] Charlotte cleverly responds to her mother's dim assessment of her marital future by remarking: "I'll get a cat and a parrot and enjoy single blessedness." The film not only explores Charlotte's affair with Jerry, a married man, but also subtly endorses the same-sex affectional bond she develops with Jerry's daughter, Tina, thus making the Whitman aura all the more apt. This film, described by one critic as "blatantly challenging monogamy,"[38] has a subtext of pedophilic lesbianism. In a scene with Tina, Charlotte declares in a voice-over: "This is Jerry's child in my arms. This is Jerry's child clinging to me." Is she making a personal sacrifice to sanctify and sublimate her (heterosexual but illicit) love, or is her emphasis on an even more forbidden love, on the person in her arms? Is she emphasizing the man in her mind or the girl in her arms? Tina later kisses Charlotte's hand after causing a slight burn at a campfire. Even this level of tenderness prompts Tina to wonder over Charlotte's role: is she a friend, asks Tina? A mother figure? Or is she, as the film hints, moving into the role of intimate companion? Charlotte's caring, affectionate, and nurturing role with Tina exceeds typical categories and labels.[39] In this way her affective life is like Whitman's own work in the Civil War hospitals where he was simultaneously mother, father, lover, friend—a powerful and shifting emotional presence, giving and receiving a complicated set of signals in his work with young soldiers.

Like *Now, Voyager* in taking its title from Whitman's poetry, *Goodbye, My Fancy* addresses significant political issues in the immediate aftermath of World War II. The original play *Goodbye, My Fancy* (on which the film was based) was first copyrighted in 1947, one year after Malcolm Cowley's bold treatment of the homosexual Whitman in the *New Republic*[40] and in the same year that forty-three witnesses were subpoenaed in Washington before the House Committee on Un-American Activities investigating "communist" subversion in Hollywood. In 1950, discussions on the floor of the House of Representatives linked homosexuals in government to Russians.[41] The film version of *Goodbye, My Fancy* (directed by Vincent Sherman) appeared in 1951, one year after National Security Council Memorandum 68 inaugurated the Cold War as a problem not only of influence and ideology, but of pressing military threat.[42]

The film adaptation of *Goodbye, My Fancy* also speaks to political issues, including academic freedom, women's rights, and unsanctioned sexuality. In *Goodbye, My Fancy*, when congresswoman Agatha Reed (Joan Crawford) receives an invitation to return to Good Hope College for Women for homecoming, she eagerly accepts.[43] She is motivated by a desire to rekindle an old romance with James Merrill (Robert Young), whom she once knew as her Whitman-quoting history professor and who is now president of the college. Agatha's rise to public success, through an earlier career in journalism, occurred despite a scandal that kept her from graduating: she was dismissed from Good Hope for violating curfew (she was seeing James, then a young professor, whom she protected by disappearing). As they reconsider the broken romance of the past, he tells her that he could never forgive himself for introducing her to the "beauties of Walt Whitman." He still has the departure note she had written him years earlier. Together, they recite "Good-bye My Fancy!" He offers the first two lines: "Good-bye my Fancy! / Farewell dear mate, dear love!" And she follows with the next three lines: "I'm going away, I know not where, / Or to what fortune, or whether I may ever see you again, / So Good-bye my Fancy."[44] Agatha then rips up the old note and says "Hello my Fancy!" before they share a long kiss. This revived romance is doomed, however, because Matt Cole (Frank Lovejoy) arrives on campus intent on renewing his own lost love with Agatha and because she gradually perceives that James, as president, has become a tool of the trustees of Good Hope. The trustees fear the documentary Agatha has made about war-torn Europe. The specific cause of their fear remains unarticulated, but they clearly distrust open thought and debate.[45] Ultimately, Agatha is able to present her documentary, though we get no glimpse of it within the film. Perhaps to the male trustees the documentary's very title, "Command Your Future," makes it something dangerous for women.

In Fay Kanin's original play the documentary was an antiwar film, but the Hollywood scriptwriters switched matters to emphasize the (somewhat) less controversial issue of academic freedom. In the play the admirers of Whitman are Agatha, Ginny (Merrill's daughter), and Dr. Pitt, a physics teacher who is concerned about the destructive capacity of atomic bombs and who encourages critical thinking and urges his students to read *Leaves of Grass*. Kanin's use of Whitman in the original play is more effective than Vincent Sherman's use of him on the screen. In the film, Merrill, stiff yet spineless, seems an unlikely admirer of the controversial, free-thinking Whitman. In the original play, in contrast, Ginny and Agatha exchange the "Goodbye My Fancy" lines, not (as the film giddily has it) James and Agatha. In the early postwar period, Fay Kanin and, to a lesser extent, Vincent Sherman recognized Whitman's power as an icon of alternative thinking and anticipated the way the poet would be employed, more boldly and irreverently, by Jack Kerouac, Allen Ginsberg, and other beat writers.

Representing Whitman in Reagan's America

A flurry of films appearing since 1980 mention, depict, quote, picture, or in some other way make use of Whitman. The poet is invoked in the futuristic films *Until the End of the World* (1991) and *Minority Report* (2002).[46] He is quoted in the psychodrama *Dead Again* (1991) and in the comic drama *Messengers* (forthcoming). He is pictured as the image of devoted love of children in *Blue Lagoon* (1980). He frames the consideration of evil in the horror film *Black Roses* (1988). He supplies an elegiac context in *Bounce* (2000). He serves as a multicultural spokesman in *Fame* (1980), *Working* (1982), *With Honors* (1994), and *Quiz Show* (1994). He represents the quintessential American poet to various Europeans in *Down By Law* (1987), *Little Women* (1994), and *Love and Death on Long Island* (1997). He highlights the contrast between the U.S. dream of freedom and the U.S. nightmare of wide-scale imprisonment in, again, *Down By Law* and *Road Scholar* (1993).[47] He has the most cultural resonance, however, as a poet of love. Alicia Ostriker once remarked that Whitman "permitted love": the "degree and quantity and variety of love in Whitman are simply astonishing."[48] Often he serves as a type of love currency in heterosexual settings. In *Postcards from the Edge* (1990), a speech about Whitman works as the standard pick-up ploy for Jack Faulkner (Dennis Quaid). In *Patch Adams* (1998) a medical student (Robin Williams) takes up reading Whitman instead of his medical books to reorient his education and to woo a female medical student. In *Doc Hollywood* (1991), a character recites "Out of the Cradle Endlessly Rocking" in a scene that first signals ultimate romantic pairings. In *Reds* (1981), just before marrying Jack Reed (Warren Beatty), Louise Bryant (Diane Keaton) hides a love poem written by Eugene O'Neill (Jack Nicholson) in *Leaves of Grass*, a book serving simultaneously as a love intensifier and as an affirmation of their leftist principles.[49]

Somewhat more bold and thus more interesting are filmic treatments of Whitman in connection with same-sex love. James Baldwin once remarked: "men do not kiss each other in American films."[50] This cinematic prohibition on male intimacy held until only recently. In "Gay Love and the Movies" (1969), Ralph Pomeroy discussed the love that had a social life but no screen life:

> Watching love stories on TV,
> watching a movie,
> I wonder where we are.
> I've wondered for a long time.
> I've never seen any of us there,
> straight on, like nouvelle vague lovers,
> like psychedelic dancers.
> I've never seen us, arms akimbo,
> standing in the morning, waiting,
> lying around in grassy meadows . . . .[51]

Here, yearning for a love made visible, Pomeroy exploits the potential of Whitman, whose force as an icon is all the more persuasive in that he need not be named. Instead, Pomeroy calls to mind the poet of *Leaves of Grass*, his famous daguerreotype with arm akimbo, and his key symbol of manly love, the phallic calamus reed found in marshes and grassy meadows. Pomeroy's poem was prescient given the role Whitman has since played in films that have broken through old codes of silence and invisibility about gay life.

Filmmakers have appropriated Whitman as a relatively unthreatening entryway into consideration of same-sex love.[52] Whitman's sexual ambiguity, sanctified status (especially because of his hospital work in the Civil War), and stature as a revered poet have made him a figure granted latitude.[53] But why did this intensified consideration of same-sex love, mediated by Whitman, occur in the 1980s? The timing involves the confluence of the history of Hollywood, the history of sexuality, and the history of Whitman criticism. Between 1930 and 1968 Hollywood production codes precluded overt treatment of homosexuality. The new readiness to invoke Whitman occurred after the lifting of these codes, after the Kinsey report, after Stonewall and the first gay pride marches, and concurrently with post-1980 conservative efforts to curtail the modest advances gays were making within society. In the last two decades of the twentieth century, Whitman's cultural stock was on the rise, while scholars, many of them gay, began to be much more assertive in countering the rather tepid accounts of Whitman's sexuality that had dominated American critical discourse.[54] The early 1980s, the beginning of an intensified interest in Whitman in films, was also a time of anxiety about gay life because of the AIDS crisis. Whitman's treatment of male-male love and his remoteness from the era of AIDS rendered him a safe object of contemplation.

The films discussed below from the 1980s to the present make Whitman "gay" for a popular audience, gay in a way he could only be in a post-Stonewall world, when new terminology contributed to new shapes of psychic lives. Most of these films are market-driven Hollywood productions. Not surprisingly, then, daring is more superficial than real, and while these filmmakers have broken through to new topics they have not shattered old patterns and conceptions. Homosocial films, ranging widely in quality, do not all attempt to construct Whitman as gay.[55] In discussing how these films treat Whitman and gay issues, I move from least direct to most direct, from the homosocial to the homosexual, though not necessarily from the least to the most artful or honest.

One especially effective film, a non-Hollywood production, is Jim Jarmusch's black-and-white *Down By Law*, which turns to Whitman at a pivotal moment in its study of the world of three men in prison and their escape. A concern with comradeship rather than carnal attachment is at the center of this clever, poignant, and thoughtful film. The film contrasts the grand aspirations of poetry with the depressing realities of the down-and-out. It opens by tracing the declining lives of Zack, a New Orleans disc jockey who has been set up to take a murder rap, and Jack, a pimp who, though certainly corrupt, is innocent of the crime he is charged with, soliciting a minor. Jack and Zack mirror one another, as their names imply, though they are unable to work together or sacrifice for one another. The opening scenes depict Zack and Jack in emotionally empty relationships with women, and their ability to interact with others does not improve when they enter the all-male world of the jail. Zack and Jack dislike each

FIGURE 12. *Roberto Benigni in* Down by Law *(1986), on the cot from which he will recite* Leaves of Grass *in Italian translation. Photo courtesy Museum of Modern Art/Film Stills Archive.*

other and barely speak. But with the entrance of Roberto (Roberto Benigni), the dynamic gradually begins to change (see fig. 12). Ostracized by Zack and Jack, Roberto breaks through isolation by conversing with himself. He asserts, "I love Walt Whitman: *Leaves of Glass*! [sic]" Then, in stirring Italian, he recites lines from "The Singer in Prison."[56]

Vision di pietà, di onta e afflizione,
Orribil pensiero, un'alma in prigione.[57]
[O sight of pity, shame and dole!
O fearful thought—a convict soul.][58]

The incongruous humor of the scene underscores a serious matter: Zack and Jack are imprisoned souls not only in their physical incarceration. We never learn why Zack and Jack were set up, but the Whitman lines suggest that the cause is irrelevant, that the real issue is the imprisoned soul: that is, Zack and Jack, especially, were more imprisoned *before* their incarceration than they were during and after it. Jack and Zack have little patience with Roberto and only gradually and grudgingly come to accept him. Yet he is the prisoner who draws a window on the prison wall, who can see, as it were, through the walls toward escape and toward another life. Roberto, against all odds, stumbles upon a café in the Louisiana bayou during their escape and falls in love with the Italian woman who owns it. His example of love and generosity eventually has an effect on Jack and Zack in the final scene when they swap coats as they part ways, their first cooperative action.

Two years later, another homosocial film, *Dead Poets Society*, repressed homosexual content with as much thoroughness as in the days of the Hollywood production codes. Although in this film homosexuality is never discussed as such, it is the submerged topic of concern: the drama of the story hinges on the main student character, Neil Perry (Robert Sean Leonard), who is allied with his teacher John Keating (Robin Williams) against Neil's authoritarian father. Neil's father prohibits him from taking part in a theatrical production (a stereotypical site of homosexual activity), forbidding him to play Puck, a fairy, in *A Midsummer Night's Dream*. Also gratuitously added is a picture of the teacher's girlfriend who is supposedly away in England while he is teaching at a boarding school, a touch apparently meant to reassure the audience that this Whitman-identified teacher in an all-male environment is safely heterosexual.

The film is strangely divided about key issues. *Dead Poets Society* stresses male bonding and invokes a recognizable gay icon. The teacher, Mr. Keating, blurs his own identity with that of Whitman: he urges his students to call him "Captain" (as in Whitman's "O Captain! My Captain!"). Whitman is the patron saint of Keating's classroom: a Whitman photograph from the 1860s hangs directly behind him in numerous shots. Furthermore, "Song of Myself" and specifically Whitman's primal yawp becomes a resource to help a shy and repressed student to find his creativity. Yet the film blinks at a homosexual interpretation of Whitman, emphasizing instead the patriotic poet. Just as curiously, the film calls for independent thought while celebrating a reverential attitude toward a particular teacher and his pseudo-philosophy. As Tania Modleski remarks, because the sexual content of the film has been repressed and excluded from the narrative, it returns to haunt the film through textual inconsistencies and absurdities.[59]

The opportunities and pitfalls of working with Whitman as a film icon are manifest in *Beautiful Dreamers* (1991), a treatment of a romantic triangle that opens up intriguing issues. The combined fascination with and fear of homosexuality that befuddles *Dead Poets Society* also undermines *Beautiful Dreamers*. The film stars Rip Torn, who had broken new ground with his bold treatment of Whitman's love of men in *Song of Myself* (1976), a made-for-television movie produced by CBS in the American Parade series. In *Beautiful Dreamers*, Torn struggles with a script that is deeply flawed. Set in the late 1870s and early 1880s, the film, directly depicting Whitman, focuses on his friendship with his admirer Richard Maurice Bucke (Colm Feore), director of the Asylum for the Insane in Ontario, Canada. The film presents Bucke, who ran the largest asylum in North America at the time, as a gentle, enlightened, forward-thinking man who opposes benighted beliefs about male masturbation and indignantly rejects the practice of removing women's ovaries in order to combat "moral insanity." [60] The film's portrayal of Bucke as unambiguously enlightened distorts his actual role. The historical Bucke was an aggressive intervener, using gynecological surgery to treat mental disorders (at least 200 women had their sexual organs removed while he served as superintendent), and he "approached the insane [male] masturbator with a sense of cleansing vengeance." (A common treatment involved electric shocks applied to the penis.)[61] If anything, then, Bucke was a steadfast enforcer of sexual norms.

Beautiful Dreamers is both inaccurate as history and weak as a story. It fails as a fictional account because it does not pursue the questions it raises. To its credit, the film addresses the erotics of discipleship. The conflict is not between Richard Maurice Bucke and Whitman over Jessie Gurd Bucke (Wendel Meldrum), but between Walt and Jessie over Maurice. Letters between the Buckes indicate that Maurice fell for Whitman so hard that he almost lost his wife. But the film, in treating this triangulated relationship, does not capture the urgency this situation had in life. After raising the idea of Jessie's jealousy of Walt, the film seems to imply—in a scene in which Jessie apparently masturbates while reading *Leaves of Grass* —that her romantic rival is also her savior whose words help her achieve a newly passionate relationship with her husband. By too easily emptying the triangulated conflict of all tension, *Beautiful Dreamers* deprives viewers of a satisfactory resolution of an issue the film itself raises. The key scene, as often in Whitman-related works, involves bathing. At the edge of a pond, Walt and Maurice sing Italian opera in the nude, dangle their legs in the water, and sling mud on one another. When Jessie arrives to witness this scene, she joins the group instead of fleeing. In fact, she strips off her clothes, providing the only full frontal nudity in the film (Walt and Maurice have by this time modestly plunged into the water). She challenges Walt to explain why he never married, asserts that nature intended for men and women to be together, and shifts the dynamic to male-female, restoring a dyadic bond with Maurice. The scene affirms heterosexual bonds and, in the perspective it assumes and the gaze it invites, imagines a heterosexual male audience. Although Walt is not victorious in the romantic competition, his general doctrine of love prevails, or so the film's ending would have it. *Beautiful Dreamers* closes with a celebratory cricket match in which the hospital inmates play against a local club. We are led to believe through a flashing of dates and historical time cards in the final shots that Whitman was the source of the newly loving and gentle treatment of patients at Bucke's asylum. The film highlights a suggestive proximity of dates and events: the visit of the poet to Canada (1880), the lifting by Bucke of restraints on inmates (1882), and the publication of Bucke's biography of Whitman (1883).

The handling of nudity offers a key to the film's shortcomings. Despite his location outside of Hollywood, John Kent Harrison, a Canadian filmmaker, nonetheless adheres to the strict Hollywood prohibition against male frontal nudity. A more daring film would not have repressed the possibility of female fetishization of the male body or of male fetishization of the male body. (The breaking of this taboo would be, arguably, the filmic equivalent of Whitman's own experimental techniques and bold treatment of the body.) As a trope of unregulated desire, the nude male body, open for the scopophilic gaze of the female or the homosexual male, would be a defeat of regulation.[62] Instead, like Bucke himself, *Beautiful Dreamers* only appears to be unconventional but finally reinforces a compulsory heterosexuality.[63]

Much more honest and emotionally convincing are two other films treating Whitman and same-sex attachments by means of triangulated relationships, *Sophie's Choice* (1982) and *Bull Durham* (1988). The striking difference in subject matters between the two films, one treating the Holocaust and the other baseball, should not blind us to a fundamental similarity they share. These two films use Whitman and love triangles—involving two men and a woman—to explore the complexity of erotic desire. Filmmakers tem-

FIGURE 13. *From* Sophie's Choice *(1982). Nathan (Kevin Kline), Sophie (Meryl Streep), and Stingo (Peter MacNicol) on the magic carpet ride at Coney Island. Photo courtesy Museum of Modern Art/Film Stills Archive.*

per courage with caution, managing to treat homosexuality while offering a popular audience multiple possible identifications in considering these relationships. *Sophie's Choice*, set in 1947, involves a love triangle between Sophie (Meryl Streep), her schizophrenic husband Nathan (Kevin Kline), and a writer they befriend, Stingo (Peter MacNicol) (see fig. 13). Alan J. Pakula's script tells the story from Stingo's perspective and adheres fairly closely to the original novel by William Styron. Intriguingly, however, the crucial Whitman material in the film is added by Pakula. The film, unlike the novel, opens with a gift of *Leaves of Grass* to the new writer on his arrival in Brooklyn. Later, in another scene interpolated into the film, the three friends drink champagne on Brooklyn Bridge, toast one another, and pay homage to "the land that gave us Whitman, gave us words." Whitman's prestige as a writer, his Brooklyn roots, and his homoeroticism make him a fitting addition to the storyline. Conveniently, he also reinforces a key aspect of the triadic relationship explored by Styron. However much Stingo lusts for women, he also longs for Nathan. As both film and novel make clear, Stingo finds Nathan to be "utterly, fatally, glamorous."[64] He is smitten with Nathan, loving him with an intensity rivaling his devotion to Sophie. Sophie, a Holocaust survivor from Poland, has faced an unthinkable life choice: to select one of her children for death so that the other might survive. She is a broken woman who can neither forget the past nor forgive herself. Her alliance with the troubled Nathan seems to result from a belief that through him may come punishment and, perhaps, salvation. Stingo's tangled love of Sophie is partly a desire to ease her pain and to rescue her from further tragedy. In Styron's novel Whitman receives only the most brief, passing mention: *Leaves of Grass*, after all, explores a world in which hopefulness and human kindness are dominant forces, in which the central force in the universe, a "kelson of the creation," is love. What can such hopes mean in a world haunted by the grim historical events that frame Styron's almost unbearably painful narrative, a world scarred by the *Shoah*? Pakula's judicious decision to include references to Whitman suits the film, which, though dark, is considerably less bleak than the novel.

The three-sided romance of *Bull Durham* is set in happier circumstances. Early in the film Annie Savoy (Susan Sarandon) reports in a voice-over: "Walt Whitman once said: 'I see great things in baseball. It's our game, the American game. It will repair our losses and be a blessing to us.'" *Bull Durham*, written and directed by Ron Shelton, a former minor league baseball player, explores everything from Whitman to new age metaphysics while analyzing the homoerotic underpinnings of the national pastime. The film explores a three-sided romance involving Ebby Calvin "Nuke" LaLoosh (Tim Robbins), Crash Davis (Kevin Costner), and Annie. In *Bull Durham*, traffic in men serves to cement the bond between Annie and Crash. That is, we have a shifting triangle with Crash and Nuke sometimes competing for Annie, and Annie and Crash sometimes competing for Nuke. The script, with neatly echoing lines, emphasizes the nearly identical roles of Annie and Crash: both are to give Nuke life experience and guide him to the majors. In one scene, Annie ties Nuke, stripped to his underwear, to her bedposts, but instead of engaging in an unusual sexual act; or perhaps *as* a sexual act, she reads to him assorted lines from Whitman's "I Sing the Body Electric" (see fig. 14):

I sing the body electric,
The armies of those I love engirth me and I engirth them,
They will not let me off till I go with them, respond to them,

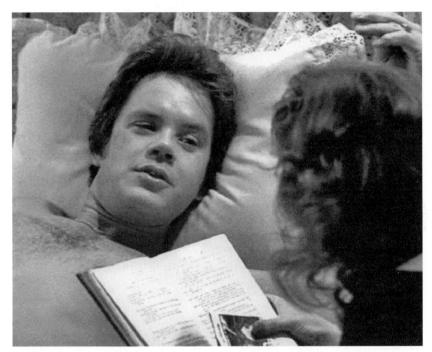

FIGURE 14. *Annie (Susan Sarandon) reading to Nuke (Tim Robbins) from* Leaves of
Grass *in* Bull Durham *(1988).*

> And discorrupt them, and charge them full with the charge of the
>   soul.
>   . . .
> But the expression of a well-made man appears not only in his face,
> It is in his limbs and joints also, it is curiously in the joints of hips and
>   wrists,
>   . . .
> . . . . love-flesh swelling and deliciously aching,
> Limitless limpid jets of love hot and enormous . . . .[65]

In a more subtle use of the poet, Crash announces his credo in strikingly
Whitmanian fashion, through a catalog of parallel items.[66] The film explores what many fans refuse to acknowledge: the homosocial and homoerotic aspects of baseball, a game that depends on the effective wielding
of bats. Fittingly, Annie remarks early in the film that the rivalry between

Nuke and Crash is "really just some redirected homoeroticism." At its best, *Bull Durham* probes the complexity of erotic desire and explores the unstable boundary between homosocial and homoerotic relations.

Other films unmistakably invoke Whitman as a homosexual icon, as for example in the low-budget film *The Incredibly True Adventures of Two Girls in Love* (1995). Writer-director Maria Maggenti's film features one high school girl, Evie (Nicole Parker), who signals her affection for another, Randy (Laurel Holloman), with a gift of *Leaves of Grass*, an illustrated edition once owned by Evie's grandmother. This particular volume is granted a quasi-spiritual force. They swear eternal love—in a besieged hotel room—over *Leaves of Grass*, as if laying hands on a Bible.[67] Interestingly, a volume of Whitman is used rather than other possibilities—Sappho, Emily Dickinson, Adrienne Rich—presumably because he is the most prominent gay icon in the United States and because Maggenti concluded that it was more important to affirm same-sex love in general than to particularize that love as lesbian. In the concluding sequence, the two lovers embrace one another (with ears covered) as the zaniness of society rages on behind them. The film's concluding voice-over quotes "Song of Myself" about "a word unsaid": "It is not in any dictionary, utterance, symbol. / Something it swings on more than the earth I swing on, / To it the creation is the friend whose embracing awakes me."[68] Evie and Randi then agree to change "friend" to "girlfriend."

Love and Death on Long Island (1997), another independent film, also provides an unusually insightful treatment of a love triangle and stands as perhaps the best example of effective treatment of Whitman and gay issues in a widely distributed release. In an earlier chapter, I examined this film in some detail. Here it is useful to note that whereas Gilbert Adair's novel *Love and Death on Long Island* negotiates its relation to fiction and the homosexual past by invoking E. M. Forster, the film negotiates its relation to cinema and previous depictions of homosexuality by invoking a distinguished predecessor, Irving Rapper's *Now, Voyager*. In both films textuality is presented via a slip of paper containing Whitman's poetic lines, and precisely the same lines from "Untold Want" are quoted (see fig. 15). The differences between the films are also instructive. Charlotte in *Now, Voyager* is the object of the audience's gaze, whereas Giles is the gazer through whom we see. Charlotte "learns to be herself under the scrutiny of others' gaze, while Giles learns to accept and understand his own gaze."[69] The film version of

FIGURE 15. *From* Love and Death on Long Island *(1997). Ronnie (Jason Priestly) preparing to quote Whitman at his mother's gravesite. Photo courtesy Museum of Modern Art/Film Stills Archive.*

Love and Death on Long Island makes extensive use of Whitman: Giles quotes *Leaves of Grass* when he arrives on Long Island, and Ronnie Bostock (Jason Priestley) (see fig. 16) quotes *Leaves of Grass* again at the end, suggesting that he has benefited from his encounter with De'Ath, though their relationship never reaches a fully realized romance. The references to Whitman, though they are nowhere to be found in the original novel, are apt. Director Richard Kwietniowski, in creating a fresh work of art guided but not limited by the original source, responds sensitively both to his source text and to the history of the genre in which he works. One can see why Kwietniowski concluded that interjecting Whitman would highlight themes already present in Adair's original novel. Whitman's erotic attachments were with significantly younger men, and Kwietniowski explores precisely this type of bond.[70] This film also considers the question of cultural crossing: Whitman's importance in the development of gay consciousness is directly related to an Atlantic crossing, whereby his ideas were put to use by a group of writers and sex radicals led by John Addington Symonds and Edward Car-

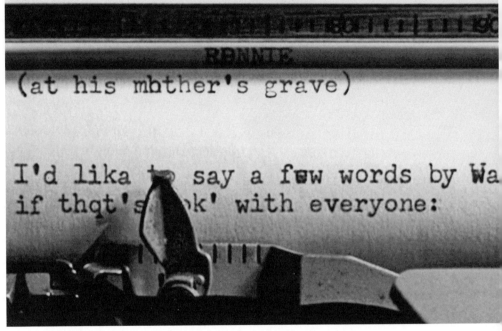

FIGURE 16. *Giles De'Ath scripting Ronnie's graveside speech in* Love and Death on Long Island.

penter who were striving to establish a positive homosexual identity within a hostile British cultural context. The class politics of Whitman's sexuality were key to his reception in Britain, and this film fittingly highlights the class contrast between a stuffy, elegant, and refined upper-class Englishman who reverses the directional flow across the Atlantic in his pursuit of an American B-movie star who, though he is rich, lacks taste and other markers of class. The handling of homoeroticism here avoids the cliches of many films in which older men fall for younger ones, and it also refuses to accept the deathly ending of many of those novels and films, such as *Death in Venice*. In this case, the yearning of an older man for a younger does not

FIGURE 17. *Marilyn Monroe reading* Leaves of Grass *in her apartment. From James Haspiel,* Young Marilyn: Becoming the Legend *(New York: Hyperion, 1994) © 1995 James Haspiel. Reprinted by permission of Hyperion.*

lead to desperation and destruction; on the contrary, Giles, though unsuccessful in his quest, is filled with joy. He has opened himself up to a new life and presumably to a new ability to write novels.[71]

Interestingly, scriptwriters frequently turn to Whitman when he is not in their original source. In the novels *Little Women, Love and Death on Long Island, A Midnight Clear, Postcards from the Edge,* and *The Object of My Affection,* no mention is made of Whitman, and in *Sophie's Choice,* Whitman is mentioned only in passing.[72] In each of the film adaptations, however, he plays a significant role. Whitman has now become a convenient shorthand in American film culture, in a way analogous to his functioning for

British readers at the end of the nineteenth century, when, as Eve Kosofsky Sedgwick has noted, a picture of Whitman or a letter from him served as a homosexual badge of recognition.[73] Despite his crucial role in the construction of Anglo-American gay identities, Whitman's meanings are not limited to a particular type of sexuality. Indeed he is attractive to many filmmakers for his more general aura of being the "tenderest lover." In 1951 in a "candid" shot reproduced in the volume *Young Marilyn*, Marilyn Monroe is seen reading *Leaves of Grass* as she reclines on a bed in her apartment (see fig. 17). What poem was she reading? Perhaps "So Long!" —

> Camerado, this is no book,
> Who touches this touches a man,
> (Is it night? are we here together alone?)
> It is I you hold and who holds you,
> I spring from the pages into your arms . . . .[74]

Walt and Marilyn: two American icons who exude irresistible sexuality. No wonder films found them and they found one another.[75]

NOTES

INTRODUCTION

1. I use the ideologically charged term "American" advisedly here. I choose it over "United States" in part to acknowledge that Whitman did indeed have a significant impact on the full continental spread of the Americas. If the term is implicated in problems of imperialism, that seems to make it all the more appropriate for discussion with Whitman, whose work is complexly related to imperial enterprises.

2. Gay Wilson Allen and Ed Folsom, eds. *Walt Whitman and the World* (Iowa City: University of Iowa Press, 1995), 1–10.

3. Horace Traubel, *With Walt Whitman in Camden*, 9 vols. (editors and publishers vary, 1906–96; vol. 9: ed. Jeanne Chapman and Robert MacIsaac [Oregon House, Cal.: W. L. Bentley, 1996]), 10.

4. Ezra Pound, "What I Feel About Walt Whitman," in *Walt Whitman: The Measure of His Song*, rev. ed., ed. Jim Perlman, Ed Folsom, and Dan Campion (Duluth: Holy Cow! Press, 1998), 112.

5. Malcolm Cowley, "Pascin's America," *Broom* 4 (January 1923): 136.

6. June Jordan, "For the Sake of a People's Poetry: Walt Whitman and the Rest of Us," in *Walt Whitman: The Measure of His Song*, rev. ed., eds Jim Perlman, Ed Folsom, and Dan Campion (Duluth: Holy Cow! Press, 1998), 411.

7. Ed Folsom, "Culturing White Anxiety: Walt Whitman and American Indians," *Études Anglaises* 45 (July–September 1992): 291.

8. The Boston publisher James T. Fields was especially good at promoting the work of Longfellow, Holmes, Emerson, Whittier, and Hawthorne, enabling them to achieve "classic" status even within their lifetimes. See Richard H. Brodhead, *The School of Hawthorne* (New York: Oxford University Press, 1986), 48–66.

9. I echo here the title of Richard Rorty's *Achieving Our Country: Leftist Thought in Twentieth-Century America* (Cambridge: Harvard University Press, 1998). Rorty, in turn, was echoing the conclusion of James Baldwin's *The Fire Next Time* (New York: Dial Press, 1963), 119.

   I have not attempted to track Whitman's impact on twentieth-century poetry because that topic has been admirably treated by others, including Roy Harvey Pearce, *The Continuity of American Poetry* (Princeton, N.J.: Princeton University Press, 1961); James E. Miller Jr., *The American Quest for a Supreme Fiction: Whitman's Legacy in the Personal Epic* (Chicago: University of Chicago Press, 1979); Stephen Tapscott, *American Beauty: William Carlos Williams and the Modernist Whit-*

man (New York: Columbia University Press, 1984); Thomas Gardner, *Discovering Ourselves in Whitman: The Contemporary American Long Poem* (Urbana: University of Illinois Press, 1989); and Ed Folsom, "Talking Back to Whitman: An Introduction," in *Walt Whitman: The Measure of His Song*, rev. ed., ed. Jim Perlman, Ed Folsom, and Dan Campion (Duluth: Holy Cow! Press, 1998), 21–74.

10. George M. Fredrickson, *The Inner Civil War: Northern Intellectuals and the Crisis of the Union* (New York: Harper & Row, 1965), 149.

11. Walt Whitman, *Prose Works 1892*, ed. Floyd Stovall, 2 vols. (New York: New York University Press, 1964) 2:393.

CHAPTER ONE

1. June Jordan, "For the Sake of a People's Poetry: Walt Whitman and the Rest of Us," in *Walt Whitman: The Measure of His Song*, rev. ed., ed. Jim Perlman, Ed Folsom, and Dan Campion (Minneapolis: Holy Cow! Press, 1998), 411.

2. Toni Morrison, "The Talk of the Town," *New Yorker*, 5 October 1998, 31–32. Jabari Asim has commented: "Eleven months after Morrison's essay appeared, Clinton himself resurrected the concept. He told attendees at the Congressional Black Caucus's annual awards dinner that he recently had met with comedian Chris Tucker, who was developing a film project about the nation's first black president. 'I didn't have the heart to tell him that I've already taken the position,' Clinton said. News reports noted that audience members, including various black congressmen, 'cracked up.'" "Bill Clinton Isn't Black!," *Salon.com*, 26 February 2001, <http://dir.salon.com/politics/feature/2001/02/26/black/index.html> (25 April 2003).

3. Clarence Page, "Clinton 'the Outsider' Is Back 'In' Again," *Chicago Tribune*, 8 August 2001, 17.

4. William James, *The Principles of Psychology*, 2 vols. (New York: Henry Holt, 1890), 1: 135.

5. Certainly June Jordan's enthusiasm for Whitman has much to do with her sense that he is an outsider who produced work opposed to "every boring, inaccessible, irrelevant, derivative, and pretentious poem that is glued to the marrow of required readings in American classrooms." See "A People's Poetry," 411.

6. For a description of Whitman as bestial, see for example *New York Times*, 13 November 1856, 2; reprinted in Kenneth M. Price, ed., *Walt Whitman: The Contemporary Reviews* (Cambridge: Cambridge University Press, 1996), 60. The *Critic* wrote that "the man who wrote page 79 of the *Leaves of Grass* deserves nothing so richly as the public executioner's whip." See *Critic* (London) (1 April 1856), 170–71; reprinted in Price, *Contemporary Reviews*, 44. The idea that Whitman was insane can be found in *Frank Leslie's Illustrated Newspaper*, 20 December 1856, 42, and also in *Critic* (London) (14 July 1860): 43–44; reprinted in Price, *Contemporary Reviews*, 99. Calvin Beach, writing under his wife's name, Juliette H. Beach, urged Whitman

to commit suicide. See "Leaves of Grass," *New York Saturday Press*, 2 June 1860, 2. Numerous reviewers described Whitman as a satyr. See the *Times* review cited above; *Christian Examiner* 60 [also numbered as 4th series, 26, no. 3] (November 1856): 471–73; reprinted in Price, *Contemporary Reviews*, 60; *Spectator* 33 (14 July 1860): 669–70; reprinted in Price, *Contemporary Reviews*, 100. Another reviewer remarked that "Walt Whitman reminds us of Caliban flinging down his logs, and setting himself to write a poem. In fact Caliban, and not Walt Whitman, might have written this." See the *Critic* (London) 15 (1 April 1856): 170–71. All of these reviews are also gathered online at *The Walt Whitman Archive*, ed. Ed Folsom and Kenneth M. Price, <http://www.whitmanarchive.org/>.

7. For an interpretation of minstrel shows as antigenteel and possessing potential for progressive racial crossings, see W. T. Lhamon Jr., *Raising Cain: Blackface Performance from Jim Crow to Hip Hop* (Cambridge: Harvard University Press, 1998). By the 1850s the benign elements in minstrel shows had hardened into something more racist. Perhaps sensing this, Whitman took a cue from earlier racial performances in his exploration of racial crossings.

8. This chapter focuses on black-white relations, but it is also true that Whitman identified to some degree with "savages," a term that in nineteenth-century usage overlapped with but did not exactly coincide with Indians.

9. See Eric Lott, *Love and Theft: Blackface Minstrelsy and the American Working Class* (New York: Oxford University Press, 1993), esp. 3–62, and his "White Like Me: Racial Cross-Dressing and the Construction of American Whiteness," in *Cultures of United States Imperialism*, ed. Amy Kaplan and Donald E. Pease (Durham: Duke University Press, 1993), 474–95.

10. Walt Whitman, *Notebooks and Unpublished Prose Manuscripts*, ed. Edward Grier, 6 vols. (New York: New York University Press, 1984), 1:267.

11. Martin Klammer has helped make this clear in *Whitman, Slavery, and the Emergence of* Leaves of Grass (University Park: Pennsylvania State University Press, 1995).

12. Andrew C. Higgins, "Wage Slavery and the Composition of *Leaves of Grass*: The 'Talbot Wilson' Notebook," *Walt Whitman Quarterly Review* 20 (Fall 2002): 53–77.

13. Whitman, *Notebooks and Unpublished Prose Manuscripts*, 1:67. For an image of this document, see also Whitman Notebook #80, 68, Harned-Whitman Collection, Library of Congress, Washington, D.C.; available online, <http://memory.loc.gov/ammem/wwhtml/wwcoll.html> (14 July 2002).

14. Whitman, *Notebooks and Unpublished Prose Manuscripts*, 1:149.

15. The white onlooker inwardly transformed is commonplace in abolitionist literature. One striking example can be found in the account of Listwell overhearing Madison Washington in the woods in Frederick Douglass's *The Heroic Slave*, included in *Three Classic African-American Novels*, ed. William L. Andrews (New York: Penguin, 1990), 26–30.

A similar pattern of entering and understanding, with its suggestion of the violation of bodily boundaries, is found in the 1856 "Sun-Down Poem," ultimately entitled "Crossing Brooklyn Ferry." Whitman remarks:

Curious what is more subtle than this which ties me to the woman or man
    that looks in my face?
Which fuses me into you now, and pours my meaning into you?

We understand then, do we not?"

See Walt Whitman, *Leaves of Grass* (Brooklyn: Fowler & Wells, 1856), 219.

16. Whitman, Notebook #80, 101. The passage is struck through with a vertical line.
17. Ibid., 102.
18. *Critic* (London) 15 (1 April 1856): 170–71; reprinted in Price, *Contemporary Reviews*, 44. William Shakespeare, *The Tempest: A Case Study in Critical Controversy*, ed. Gerald Graff and James Phelan (Boston: Bedford/St. Martin's, 2000), 26–27.
19. Whitman, Notebook #80, 103.
20. Ibid., 104.
21. Ibid., 105.
22. The politics of *Leaves of Grass* were congruent with the antislavery cause, as is clear from the eagerness of Thayer and Eldridge, radical abolitionists, to publish Whitman's work. Thayer's involvement in radical politics intersected directly with his work as a publisher: he instructed Whitman to delay by a week his trip to Boston to oversee the printing of the third edition of *Leaves of Grass* because he was traveling to Pennsylvania to take part in an effort to storm a prison holding men captured in John Brown's raid on Harper's Ferry.
23. For an insightful discussion of the manuscripts relating to "The Sleepers," see Ed Folsom, "Lucifer and Ethiopia: Whitman, Race, and Poetics before the Civil War and After" in *A Historical Guide to Walt Whitman*, ed. David S. Reynolds (New York: Oxford University Press, 2000), 45–53. The particular manuscript I quote is reproduced with permission from the Walt Whitman Collection (#3829-Y), Clifton Waller Barrett Library, Albert H. Small Special Collections Library, University of Virginia Library, Charlottesville.
24. Toni Morrison, *Playing in the Dark: Whiteness and the Literary Imagination* (1992; reprint, New York: Vintage Books, 1993), 38–39.
25. Walt Whitman, *Leaves of Grass* (Brooklyn: [Fowler and Wells], 1855), 29. This volume has been reproduced in facsimile several times, including, most recently, in *Major Authors on CD-Rom: Walt Whitman*, ed. Ed Folsom and Kenneth M. Price (Woodbridge, Conn.: Primary Source Media, 1997).
26. Perhaps the closest Whitman came to this type of direct action was when he attended the trial of Anthony Burns in Boston.
27. Franny Nudelman, "'The Blood of Millions': John Brown's Body, Public Vio-

lence, and Political Community," *American Literary History* 13 (Winter 2001): 645–49; Karen Halttunen, "Humanitarianism and the Pornography of Pain in Anglo-American Culture," *American Historical Review* 100 (April 1995): 303–34.

28. Halttunen, "Humanitarianism"; Laura Hinton, *The Perverse Gaze of Sympathy: Sadomasochistic Sentiments from* Clarissa *to* Rescue 911 (Albany: State University of New York Press, 1999); Marianne Noble, *The Masochistic Pleasures of Sentimental Literature* (Princeton, N.J.: Princeton University Press, 2000).

29. Whitman, *Leaves of Grass* (1855), 74.

30. Folsom, "Lucifer and Ethiopia," 47.

31. "And this black portrait—this head, huge, frowning, sorrowful,—is Lucifer's portrait the denied God's portrait, / (But I do not deny him—though cast out and rebellious, he is my god as much as any;)" See Whitman, *Notebooks and Unpublished Prose Manuscripts*, 4:1300.

32. Christopher Castiglia, "Abolition's Racial Interiors and the Making of White Civic Depth," *American Literary History* 14 (Spring 2002): 43.

33. Whitman, *Notebooks and Unpublished Prose Manuscripts*, 1:115.

34. See Luke Mancuso, *The Strange Sad War Revolving: Walt Whitman, Reconstruction, and the Emergence of Black Citizenship, 1865-1876* (Columbia, S.C.: Camden House, 1997).

35. This manuscript is in the Harry Ransom Humanities Research Center, University of Texas at Austin. See the discussion of this manuscript in Ed Folsom, "Walt Whitman's Working Notes for the First Edition of *Leaves of Grass*," *Walt Whitman Quarterly Review* 16 (Fall 1998): 91. The word "blacks" is badly smudged and could be read as "slaves," as Folsom first saw the word. He has now changed his reading to "blacks" (private conversation with Folsom).

36. Whitman, *Leaves of Grass* (1855), 45, 81. Brett Barney makes a similar point in "Whitman, Race, and Literary History: A Recently Recovered Dialogue," *Walt Whitman Quarterly Review* 20 (Summer 2002): 30–35.

37. Whitman, *Leaves of Grass* (1855), 78–79.

38. Ibid., 81.

39. See Lott, *Love and Theft*, 53–55 and 120–22.

40. Jay Grossman, "Whitman at Auction," a talk delivered at the Modern Language Association meeting, 28 December 2001. For a highly perceptive account of Whitman's experience in New Orleans, see Kirsten Silva Gruesz, *Ambassadors of Culture: The Transamerican Origins of Latino Writing* (Princeton, N.J.: Princeton University Press, 2002), 121–36.

41. Walt Whitman, *Leaves of Grass: Facsimile Edition of the 1860 Text*, ed. Roy Harvey Pearce (Ithaca, N.Y.: Cornell University Press, 1961), 289.

42. Joy S. Kasson, "Narratives of the Female Body: *The Greek Slave*," in *The Culture of Sentiment: Race, Gender, and Sentimentality in Nineteenth-Century America*, ed. Shirley Samuels (New York: Oxford University Press, 1992), 172–90; Christopher

Castiglia, *Bound and Determined: Captivity, Culture-Crossing, and White Woman-hood from Mary Rowlandson to Patty Hearst* (Chicago: University of Chicago Press, 1996).

43. In a recent study of "possession" in Whitman, Mark Maslan quotes Socrates in the *Phaedrus* in explaining that his study is primarily interested in the kind of possession that "'seizes a tender, virgin soul and stimulates it to rapt passion-ate expression, especially in poetry.'" See *Whitman Possessed: Poetry, Sexuality, and Popular Authority* (Baltimore: Johns Hopkins University Press, 2001), 1.

44. Walt Whitman, *Daybooks and Notebooks*, ed. William White, 3 vols. (New York: New York University Press, 1978), 3:761. My transcription of Whitman's punc-tuation differs slightly from that of White.

45. Whitman, *Notebooks and Unpublished Prose Manuscripts*, 1:113.

46. Kenneth M. Price, *Whitman and Tradition* (New Haven, Conn.: Yale University Press, 1990), 41–42.

47. Horace Traubel, *With Walt Whitman in Camden*, 9 vols. (editors and publishers vary, 1906–96; vol. 3 [New York: Mitchell Kennerley, 1914]), 581–82.

48. Whitman's response to Miller has been discussed by many critics, but they tend not to indicate which version of *The Trapper's Bride* they have in mind. It is un-clear which version Whitman knew. He may have seen some of Miller's paintings when they were exhibited for "two or three weeks" at the Apollo Gallery, accord-ing to the *New York Mirror* on 25 May 1839. See Peter Hassrick, *The Way West: Art of Frontier America* (New York: Harry N. Abrams, 1977), 20.

49. Herman J. Viola, "The American Indian Genre Paintings of Catlin, Stanley, Wimar, Eastman, and Miller" in *American Frontier Life: Early Western Painting and Prints*, ed. Alan Axelrod (Fort Worth: Amon Carter Museum, 1987), 156.

50. Hassrick, *The Way West*, 51. James Thomas Flexner also notes the lack of brutality and tragedy in Miller's work, observing that he produced *Running Fight: Sioux and Crows* "without shedding a drop of blood" (quoted in ibid., 51).

51. Mildred Goosman, ed., *Exploration in the West: Catlin, Bodmer, Miller* (Omaha, Ne-braska: Joslyn Art Museum, n.d.), 28.

52. Viola, "American Indian Genre Paintings," 163.

53. Dawn Glanz, *How the West Was Drawn: American Art and the Settling of the Frontier* (Ann Arbor, Mich.: UMI Research Press, 1982), 37.

54. What Miller and other whites regarded as degrading to women and immoral was merely one of a series of customary exchanges between the bride's and groom's families. See Jennifer McLerran, "Trappers' Brides and Country Wives: Native American Women in the Paintings of Alfred Jacob Miller," *American Indian Cul-ture and Research Journal* 18, no. 2 (1994): 10. Sir William George Drummond Stewart, in his novel *Edward Warren*, described his experiences among the trap-pers: "Among the Indians of the Rocky Mountains, a father, or the nearest kin acting as guardian, requires, when the young squaw is married, a compensation

for the loss, which, if he is rich and well disposed towards her, he makes the less, provided the husband to whom she is sold settles handsomely upon her in the way of horses and other property, so as to render her independent in case of death or separation." Quoted in Edgeley W. Todd, "Indian Pictures and Two Whitman Poems," *Huntington Library Quarterly* 19 (November 1955): 4 n. See also Katherine M. Weist, "Beasts of Burden and Menial Slaves: Nineteenth Century Observations of Northern Plains Indian Women" in *The Hidden Half: Studies of Plains Indian Women*, ed. Patricia Albers and Beatrice Medicine (Lanham, Md.: University Press of America, 1983), 44.

55. Marvin C. Ross, *The West of Alfred Jacob Miller*, rev. ed. (Norman: University of Oklahoma Press, 1968), n.p., preceding image 12.

56. McLerran, "Trappers' Brides and Country Wives," 11. Until fairly recently, historians have viewed these marriages simply as "'exploitative' relationships in which mountain men took Indian women as mistresses or 'wives' for a time, out of business, political, or sexual expediency, then abandoned them when they left the mountains and returned to 'civilization.'" See John Mack Faragher, "The Custom of the Country: Cross-Cultural Marriage in the Far Western Fur Trade" in *Western Women: Their Land, Their Lives*, ed. Lillian Schlissel, Vicki L. Ruiz, and Janice Monk (Albuquerque: University of New Mexico Press, 1988), 206. Some recent statistical studies have argued that these relationships were frequently long-lasting and affectionate. William R. Swagerty notes that "overall, marriages seem to have been extremely stable given the circumstances of the multicultural social setting of the fur trade years and the seasonal nature of the industry." "Marriage and Settlement Patterns of Rocky Mountain Trappers and Traders," *Western Historical Quarterly* 11 (1980): 168.

57. Glanz, *How the West Was Drawn*, 37–41. Glanz's reading is endorsed by Joan Carpenter Troccoli, *Alfred Jacob Miller: Watercolors of the American West* (Tulsa, Okla.: Thomas Gilcrease Museum Association, 1990), 9.

58. Susan Prendergast Schoelwer notes that there were generations of intermarriage. See "The Absent Other: Women in the Land and Art of Mountain Men" in *Discovered Lands, Invented Pasts: Transforming Visions of the American West* (New Haven, Conn.: Yale University Press and the Yale University Art Gallery, 1992), 136.

59. Quoted in Glanz, *How the West Was Drawn*, 29. Glanz notes that "fur trade literature effected this reconciliation [between civilization and the wilderness] by describing the trapper as a white (i.e., civilized) man who had learned to live like the Indian and whose values and traits belonged to the wilderness" (*How the West Was Drawn*, 36). McLerran adds that "By most accounts, [participants in the fur trade] demonstrated a much higher degree of tolerance for Indian-white intermarriage (usually according to native custom) than did the majority of early Euro-Americans" ("Trappers' Brides and Country Wives," 2).

60. Ross, *The West of Alfred Jacob Miller*, n.p., preceding image 12.

61. Susan Prendergast Schoelwer notes that the trapper's bride "does occupy center stage, but this seems less to indicate her role in the marriage than to position her as an object of male desire, barefoot and exposed. Perhaps significantly, Miller's patron, Stewart, once called attention to bare feet as a particularly attractive feature of young Indian women." See "The Absent Other," 152.

62. Todd, "Indian Pictures," 2.

63. Yusef Komunyakaa's poem entitled "The Trapper's Bride" appears in *Callaloo* 20.1 (1997): 31.

64. Whitman, *Leaves of Grass* (1855), 18–19.

65. Swagerty, "Marriage and Settlement Patterns," 178–79.

66. Whitman first published the trapper's bride passage in 1855 and kept it in *Leaves* through the "deathbed edition" of 1891–92. In 1867, however, Whitman adopted phrasing with seemingly gentler implications, replacing the trapper's firm grasp of her wrist with the softer phrase "held her by the hand." This description matches no version of Miller's work that I have seen. Their hands barely touch in some versions and are reaching for each other in another, but in no case does he hold her hand, or, as indicated, her wrist. This change is a political step backward since it sentimentalizes the relationship between whites and Indians, throwing a haze of harmony and love over interactions that (despite some cases to the contrary) were fundamentally destructive for Indians. See Mary C. Wright, "Economic Development and Native American Women in the Early Nineteenth Century," *American Quarterly* 33 (Winter 1981): 525–36; Faragher, "The Custom of the Country," 199–215, and Sylvia Van Kirk's "Commentary" on Faragher, in *Western Women: Their Land, Their Lives*, ed. Lillian Schlissel, Vicki L. Ruiz, and Janice Monk (Albuquerque: University of New Mexico Press, 1988), 221–25; and Schoelwer, "The Absent Other," 135–65.

67. Whitman, *Leaves of Grass* (1855), 19.

68. It is impossible to tell if the drayman is, legally speaking, free or enslaved, though clearly at a psychological level he is independent, confident, assured.

69. Shirley Samuels discusses the "fugitive view of marriage" at the time in connection with a pamphlet entitled "Slavery and Marriage: A Dialogue" (1850, attributed to John Humphrey Noyes). See her "The Identity of Slavery," in *The Culture of Sentiment: Race, Gender, and Sentimentality in Nineteenth-Century America*, ed. Shirley Samuels (New York: Oxford University Press, 1992), 166. See also, in the same volume, Karen Sanchez-Eppler, "Bodily Bonds: The Intersecting Rhetorics of Feminism and Abolition," 93.

70. Vivian Pollak, *The Erotic Whitman* (Berkeley: University of California Press, 2000), 89.

71. Price, *Contemporary Reviews*, 248.

72. Walt Whitman, "City Photographs," in *Walt Whitman and the Civil War*, ed. Charles I. Glicksberg (1933; reprint, New York: A. S. Barnes, 1963), 48.

73. For a useful discussion of the gradually changing status of the Bowery, see Robert M. Dowling, "Stephen Crane and the Transformation of the Bowery," forthcoming in *Twisted from the Ordinary: Essays on American Literary Naturalism*, ed. Mary E. Papke (Knoxville: University of Tennessee Press, 2003).

74. Whitman, *Leaves of Grass* (1855), xi.

75. Barrett Wendell and Chester Noyes Greenough, *A History of Literature in America* (New York: Charles Scribner's Sons, 1911), 375.

76. George Woodberry's *America in Literature* (1903), as quoted in Nina Baym, "Early Histories of American Literature: A Chapter in the Institution of New England," *American Literary History* 1 (Fall 1989): 473.

77. Barrett Wendell, *A Literary History of America* (New York: Charles Scribner's Sons, 1901), 465.

78. Werner Sollors, "National Identity and Ethnic Diversity: 'Of Plymouth Rock and Jamestown and Ellis Island'; or, Ethnic Literature and Some Redefinitions of 'America,'" in *History and Memory in African American Culture*, ed. Geneviève Fabre and Robert O'Meally (New York: Oxford University Press, 1994), 105.

79. Wendell, *A Literary History of America*, 471.

80. Baym, "Early Histories of American Literature," 460.

81. See Robert K. Nelson and Kenneth M. Price, "Debating Manliness: Thomas Wentworth Higginson, William Sloane Kennedy, and the Question of Whitman," *American Literature* 73 (September 2001): 497–524.

82. Regarding William Douglas O'Connor's assumptions about Higginson's involvement in the suppression of *Leaves of Grass*, see Whitman, *Daybooks and Notebooks*, 2:289 n. 1515, and Walt Whitman, *The Correspondence*, ed. Edwin Haviland Miller, 6 vols. (New York: New York University Press, 1964), 3:283 n. 74.

83. See Higginson's letter to Kennedy of 7 March 1895, reproduced in part in Nelson and Price, "Debating Manliness," 498; [Higginson], "Walt Whitman: His Death on Saturday Evening—His Life and Literary Place," *New York Evening Post*, 28 March 1892, 11: 1–3; and [Higginson], "Recent Poetry," *Nation*, 15 December 1881, 476–77.

84. Quoted in Mary Thacher Higginson, *Thomas Wentworth Higginson: The Story of His Life* (Boston: Houghton Mifflin, 1914), 126. Higginson further remarked that Hurlbut was "so handsome in his dark beauty that he seemed like a picturesque Oriental." See Thomas Wentworth Higginson, *Cheerful Yesterdays* (Boston: Houghton, Mifflin, 1898), 107. These passages about Hurlbut and other aspects of Higginson's somewhat complex erotic life are further discussed in Christopher Looby, "'As Thoroughly Black as the Most Faithful Philanthropist Could Desire': Erotics of Race in Higginson's *Army Life in a Black Regiment*," in *Race and the Subject of Masculinities*, ed. Harry Stecopoulos and Michael Uebel (Durham: Duke University Press, 1997), 71–115. See also Vivian Pollak, *Dickinson: The Anxiety of Gender* (Ithaca, N.Y.: Cornell University Press, 1984), 225.

85. Thomas Wentworth Higginson, *Army Life in a Black Regiment* (1870; reprint, Williamstown, Mass.: Corner House, 1971), 55.

86. Santayana was never a blind proponent of Whitman, and all of his many comments on the poet were marked by ambivalence. Santayana was too much a part of the genteel culture he attacked to ever fully embrace Whitman's example.

87. Compare the remark by Robert McAlmon about Emanuel Carnevali: "in America he took on idols which I refused to be sold, but in my college days I concluded that it was because he was a foreigner that he so passionately loved Walt Whitman." See Robert McAlmon, *Being Geniuses Together 1920-1930*, revised and with supplementary chapters by Kay Boyle (Berkeley: North Point Press, 1984), 136.

88. George Santayana, *The Last Puritan: A Memoir in the Form of a Novel* (New York: Charles Scribner's Sons, 1936), 178-79.

89. Peter Conn, *The Divided Mind: Ideology and Imagination in America, 1898-1917* (Cambridge: Cambridge University Press, 1983), 278.

90. J. V. Matthews, "'Whig History': The New England Whigs and a Usable Past," *New England Quarterly* 51 (1978): 193-208.

91. Quoted from the documentary *When We Were Kings* (1996), directed by Leon Gast.

92. I would like to thank Robert M. Dowling for drawing the Ali poem to my attention.

93. For an interesting recent discussion of the problems of race and Whitman's bodily representations, see Michael Bennett, "Frances Ellen Watkins Sings the Body Electric," in *Recovering the Black Female Body: Self-Representations by African American Women*, ed. Michael Bennett and Vanessa D. Dickerson (New Brunswick, N.J.: Rutgers University Press, 2001), 19-40. Bennett notes, for example that "Though Watkins works from an understanding of the vexed relationship between the private and public body of the slave, necessitating her efforts to write the black female body into encompassing social bodies while shielding it from harm, the very first lines of 'Song of Myself' make it clear that Whitman assumes a comfortable relation between his own body and that of his compatriots and country" (26).

CHAPTER TWO

1. In a letter dated 1 September [1910] to Morton Fullerton, Wharton remarked about one of his journalistic pieces: "I wish you had relevé the fact that the Temps' saying [William James] is our greatest philosopher since Emerson, is not only—as you have pointed out—absurdly uncritical, but absolutely ignorant, since it leaves Whitman out of consideration; & if 'philosophy' consists not in inventing a system but in thinking—if, in short, Emerson was a philosopher—then Whitman surely comes next to him; & James nowhere!" (Harry Ransom Center, University of Texas at Austin. Throughout this chapter, unpublished items are quoted

with permission of the Watkins Loomis Agency, agents for the estate of Edith Wharton).

Wharton's enthusiasm for Whitman was matched only by her distaste for William James. For analysis of her attitude toward James, see Edith Wharton, *The Letters of Edith Wharton*, ed. R. W. B. Lewis and Nancy Lewis (New York: Scribner's, 1988), 10.

2. See R. W. B. Lewis, *Edith Wharton: A Biography* (1975; reprint, New York: Fromm, 1985), 81, 86. In 1898 Wharton also manifested her interest in Whitman by copying out in her commonplace book a lengthy passage of "Song of Myself" and the entire poem "Life" (see Cynthia Griffin Wolff, *A Feast of Words: The Triumph of Edith Wharton* [New York: Oxford University Press, 1977], 90).

3. Lewis, *Edith Wharton*, 140.

4. Wharton to Bliss Perry, 20 June 1906, Barnard College Library.

5. Although one page of her notes on Whitman bears the words: "Walt Whitman: Plan for an Essay," Wharton's various plans and outlines are sufficiently elaborate that Nancy R. Leach concluded that she meant to publish a book on the poet ("Edith Wharton's Interest in Walt Whitman," *Yale University Library Gazette* 33 [October 1958]: 63–66). It certainly seems that Wharton's outline of her critical study treats so many complex matters that it could not well be contained within an essay (Beinecke Rare Book and Manuscript Library, Yale University). Also worth consulting is Susan Goodman's "Edith Wharton's 'Sketch of an Essay on Walt Whitman'"; she concludes that "Wharton was most drawn to the 'Cosmic Whitman'" (*Walt Whitman Quarterly Review* 10 [1992]: 4).

6. The quoted phrase is attributed to William Crary Brownell, literary consultant for Charles Scribner's Sons, in Wharton, *Letters*, 54–55.

7. See Wolff, *A Feast of Words*, 198. That Wharton had spoken of passion in terms of "triumphant discovery" is clear from her letter to Fullerton of 10 June [1908] (Alan Gribben, "'The Heart is Insatiable': A Selection from Edith Wharton's Letters to Morton Fullerton, 1907–1915," *Library Chronicle of the University of Texas at Austin* n.s., 31 [1985]: 29).

8. Quoted in Clare Colquitt, "Unpacking Her Treasures: Edith Wharton's 'Mysterious Correspondence' with Morton Fullerton," *Library Chronicle of the University of Texas at Austin*, n.s., 31 (1985): 85.

9. Kenneth M. Price and Phyllis McBride, "'The Life Apart': Text and Contexts of Edith Wharton's Love Diary," *American Literature* 66 (1994): 674.

10. See Lewis, *Edith Wharton*, 233, and Candace Waid, *Edith Wharton's Letters from the Underworld* (Chapel Hill: University of North Carolina Press, 1991), 129–30.

11. In "The Life Apart" she remarked: "It is curious how the scraps of verses I wrote from time to time in the past, when a wave of Beauty rushed over me, & I felt *I must tell some one!* —it is curious how they express what I am feeling now, how

they say more than I then understood, & how they go straight to you, like homing birds released long long ago." See Price and McBride, "'The Life Apart,'" 674-75.

12. See Lewis, *Edith Wharton*, 259.

13. Richard Brodhead, *The School of Hawthorne* (New York: Oxford University Press, 1986). Lewis argues persuasively that Wharton's "own emotional agitation in the fall of 1908 was such that what especially interested her in major American writers was their treatment of the emotional life, their investment in their work of their deepest personal feelings. Whitman seemed to her preeminently effective in this regard—and Hawthorne decidedly lacking" (*Edith Wharton*, 237).

14. Edith Wharton, "A Little Girl's New York," *Harper's Magazine*, March 1938, 361.

15. At this time differing "Whitmans" were emerging. There was the radical Whitman developing out of the interests of Horace Traubel, Emma Goldman, and others; the homosexual Whitman, advanced perhaps most effectively by a group of English intellectuals centered around Edward Carpenter; the Whitman of "cosmic consciousness" made famous by R. M. Bucke and his followers; and the Whitman whose comradeship seemed liberating for such women as Wharton, Kate Chopin, Willa Cather, and Charlotte Perkins Gilman.

16. A great deal of material is relevant to the study of the sexual attitudes and practices of these individuals. See, for example, on Lodge: Kenneth M. Price, *Whitman and Tradition: The Poet in His Century* (New Haven, Conn.: Yale University Press, 1990), 136-40. On Berry: Lewis, *Edith Wharton*, 344. On Santayana: his letters to Fullerton of 9 September 1886, 10 July 1887, 31 August 1887, and 28 December 1887, in *The Letters of George Santayana: Book One [1868-1906]*, ed. William G. Holzberger (Cambridge: MIT Press, 2001), 13-14, 83-85, 85-89, and 91-93. On James: Eve Kosofsky Sedgwick, "The Beast in the Closet: James and the Writing of Homosexual Panic" in *Sex, Politics, and Science in the Nineteenth-Century Novel*, ed. Ruth Yeazell (Baltimore: Johns Hopkins University Press, 1986), 148-86. On several of these individuals: Ross Posnock's chapter, "Lifting the Yoke of the Genteel: Henry James, George Santayana, and Howard Sturgis" in *The Trial of Curiosity: Henry James, William James, and the Challenge of Modernity* (New York: Oxford University Press, 1991), 193-220.

17. See Wharton, *Letters*, 121. Since Fullerton rarely gets a positive word from scholars, it should be observed that he was a genuinely useful critic for Wharton— even if his own writing was turgid. Wharton's letters to Fullerton, though they have passages recording beating pulses and offering exquisite testimonials, are more often marked by mention of plans to meet and discuss one or the other's work.

18. Santayana's letters to Fullerton, in subject matter and tone, are unlike any others he wrote. At times, Santayana is flirtatious in a highly mannered way (see, esp., the letter of 9 September 1886). At other times, Santayana is more frank with

Fullerton than anyone else about the range of sexual options open to human beings. Fullerton was also deeply important to Henry James's emotional life. Leon Edel believes that Fullerton liberated James, prompting his growing readiness, in his later years, to cultivate emotionally close attachments to men (*Henry James: The Master: 1901–1916* [New York: Avon, 1978], 412–20).

19. Wharton, *Letters*, 193. Concern about the return of the letters becomes a motif in the correspondence.

20. Wharton, *The Touchstone* (1900; reprint, New York: Harper Collins, 1991), 56.

21. Much of this paragraph is indebted to Gloria Erlich, *The Sexual Education of Edith Wharton* (Berkeley: University of California Press, 1992), 93. Wharton's response to reading Nietzsche is recorded in a letter of 1908: "this is *great* fun—full of wit & originality & poetry—dashes of Meredith & even Whitman. He has no system . . . but wonderful flashes of insight, & a power of breaking through conventions . . . to a wholesome basis of naked instinct" (Wharton, *Letters*, 159). Unfairly and unkindly, Fullerton had called Wharton conventional (Gribben, "'The Heart is Insatiable,'" 30 and 31).

22. Price and McBride, "'The Life Apart,'" 673, 676.

23. Quoted in Lewis, *Edith Wharton*, 193.

24. Wharton, *Letters*, 129. Emerson's phrasing is ultimately traceable to Sophocles.

25. Fullerton's interest in Whitman is indicated by his language, by his exchanging with Wharton a copy of *Leaves of Grass* (see Wharton, *Letters*, 283), and by his quoting of the poem "America" in his *Problems of Power: A Study of International Politics from Sadowa to Kirk-Kilissé* (New York: Charles Scribner's Sons, 1913), 191.

26. Gribben, "'The Heart is Insatiable,'" 56–57.

27. Quoted in Waid, *Letters from the Underworld*, 132. After consulting the manuscript in the Beinecke Library, Yale University, I have changed one word in Waid's transcription: "intimate" should read "intrinsic."

28. Quoted in Judy Simons, *Diaries and Journals of Literary Women from Fanny Burney to Virginia Woolf* (Iowa City: University of Iowa Press, 1990), 139.

29. Wharton, *Letters*, 151.

30. Wharton, *The Touchstone*, 54.

31. See Gribben, "'The Heart is Insatiable,'" 47, and Wharton, *Letters*, 148.

32. Gribben, "'The Heart is Insatiable,'" 28.

33. Quoted in Erlich, *Sexual Education*, 101. Wharton attempted to act on this concept of sharing by helping Fullerton with his writing.

34. This matched "the desire for symmetry," noted in *The Decoration of Houses* (1897), that marked Wharton's thinking from the beginning of her career (Colquitt, "Unpacking Her Treasures," 104).

35. For Wharton's remark, see Gribben, "'The Heart is Insatiable,'" 28. In contrast, it has been hard to grasp Fullerton's thinking about his relationship with Wharton because his letters to her were, apparently, destroyed. A look at the book he

worked on during the affair sheds light on the playfulness and hedonism he advocated. Fullerton first met Wharton at The Mount, her country home in Lenox, Massachusetts; in *Problems of Power* Fullerton makes the following assertions:

> At Lenox . . . the immense extension of the class which possesses the money to buy leisure . . . is a new fact which illustrates once more how useful the economic key may be to open the problems set by history. And these citizens, who can now afford to play, are being imitated by the entire people. . . .
>
> A quarter of a century ago, most Americans doubted whether they had a right to play. None thought it "moral" to play long. This feeling was part . . . of the universally disseminated eleventh commandment: *Thou shalt not like.* Of that commandment not a shred remains. The Americans have issued forth from the dank Puritanism of their old-time places of worship and of study. They have come out into the open. They have treated their moral rheumatism by a bath of sunlight (20–21).

36. This young woman was raised in the mistaken belief that she was Fullerton's sister; only in her graduate years at Bryn Mawr did she learn she was adopted (Wharton, *Letters*, 139 n.)

37. Gloria Erlich observes: "All his life Fullerton had been playing with incestuous feelings in both directions, as a son toward his mother and as a father- and brother-figure toward his cousin. The overheated mother-son relationship was probably the source of his affair with a woman fifteen years older than himself, Margaret Brooke, the Ranee of Sarawak, as well as of the cruel game he played with Katharine's feelings. His engagement to Katharine narrowly skirted acting out his oedipal impulses within his own family" (*Sexual Education*, 100).

38. Wharton, *Letters*, 183 n. 1.

39. Erlich, *Sexual Education*, 101.

40. See Simons, *Diaries and Journals*, 135.

41. Ibid., 136.

42. See Wharton, *Letters*, 15 and 162.

43. Louise J. Kaplan, *Female Perversions: The Temptations of Emma Bovary* (New York: Doubleday, 1991), 231.

44. Wharton, *Letters*, 14. See also ibid., 158.

45. Ibid., 189.

46. Gribben, "'The Heart is Insatiable,'" 35.

47. Gloria Erlich writes that Wharton's "sense of conflict between a masculine professional identity and an ardent but stifled feminine self responded to Fullerton's alternating gender signals. He activated her repertory of repressed possibilities, she affirmed his versatility" (*Sexual Education*, 100–101).

48. David Lodge, *After Bakhtin: Essays on Fiction and Criticism* (London: Routledge, 1990), 21.

49. For Wharton, friendship and love were closely related. She said once (prematurely) when she thought the relationship with Fullerton was over: "My last word is one of tenderness for the friend I love—for the lover I worshipped" (quoted in Wharton, *Letters*, 15). On another occasion she remarked, "I am like one who went out seeking for friendship, & found a kingdom" (ibid., 158). Ironically, Wharton praised Fullerton's love of the clear "line" (see Gribben, "'The Heart is Insatiable,'" 88)—the last trait a relationship with him was likely to enjoy. She wrote on a Sunday night in the winter of 1910, after feeling as if Fullerton was avoiding her: "my friends are free to see me or not see me, think of me or not think of me, as they please! . . . But I do ask something more of the man who asks to be more than my friend; & so must any woman who is proud enough to be worth loving" (Wharton, *Letters*, 198).

50. Whitman, *Leaves of Grass* (1855; reprint in facsimile, New York: Eakins Press, 1966), 27 and 35.

51. Whitman, "America's Mightiest Inheritance," in *New York Dissected*, ed. Emory Holloway and Ralph Adimari (1936; reprint, Folcroft, Penn.: Folcroft Library Editions, 1972), 62.

52. James Perrin Warren, *Walt Whitman's Language Experiment* (University Park: Pennsylvania State University Press, 1990), 49.

53. Wharton, *Letters*, 162.

54. Wolff, *A Feast of Words*, 192.

55. Price and McBride, "'The Life Apart,'" 677.

56. Although Whitman is alluded to in passing in *The Age of Innocence*, his presence is less directly felt than in other Wharton novels. Nonetheless, it should be noted that the marriage between May Welland and Newland Archer is discussed in terms of comradeship. Also significant is Wharton's exploration of May's interweaving of masculine and feminine traits.

Some critics hold that Whitman is a vital presence in *Summer* also. See, for example, Abby Werlock, "Whitman, Wharton, and the Sexuality in *Summer*," in *Speaking the Other Self: American Women Writers*, ed. Jeanne Campbell Reesman (Athens: University of Georgia Press, 1997), 246–62. Carol J. Singley observes that "*Summer* . . . constitutes . . . Wharton's version of American transcendentalism." See *Edith Wharton: Matters of Mind and Spirit* (Cambridge: Cambridge University Press, 1995), 20.

57. On the tendency of women writers to identify with male authors and on the resulting self-conflict, see Elizabeth Ammons, *Conflicting Stories: American Women Writers at the Turn into the Twentieth Century* (New York: Oxford University Press, 1991), 123–27. On Wharton's particular sense of self, see Waid, *Letters from the Underworld*, 7, and Erlich, *Sexual Education*, 14 and 47–48.

58. Edith Wharton, *Hudson River Bracketed* (New York: Charles Scribner's Sons, 1929), 221.

59. Wharton to Bliss Perry, 20 June 1906. Quoted with permission of Barnard College Library.

60. Edith Wharton, "Literature," c. 1914, Beinecke Rare Book and Manuscript Library, Yale University. Quoted with permission.

61. Janet Goodwyn, *Edith Wharton: Traveller in the Land of Letters* (New York: St. Martin's, 1990), 121.

62. Wharton, "Literature."

63. Sigmund Freud, "A Note Upon the 'Mystic Writing-Pad,'" vol. 19 of *The Standard Edition of the Complete Psychological Works of Sigmund Freud*, (London: Hogarth Press and the Institute of Psycho-analysis, 1961), 227–32.

64. Jacques Derrida, *Writing and Difference*, trans. Alan Bass (Chicago: University of Chicago Press, 1978), 224.

65. See also Goodwyn, *Traveller in the Land of Letters*, 121–22.

66. Edith Wharton, *The Custom of the Country* (1913; reprint, New York: Macmillan, 1987), 68.

67. Ibid., 139.

68. Ibid., 402–5.

69. Waid, *Letters from the Underworld*, 131.

70. She turned his own remark against him: "*Do*, cher ami, in your own words, 'adopt a franker idiom'! Such an argument ought to be as bare, as nervous, as manly & energetic as the gamely Sophocles . . . & you've hung it with all the heavy tin draperies of the Times jargon—that most prolix & pedantic of all the dead languages" (Gribben, "'The Heart is Insatiable,'" 50). Wharton failed to see that Fullerton's lack of a frank idiom was part of a larger lack of sincerity in his character. Oscar Wilde, in contrast, seems to have recognized this immediately. Lewis notes "when Wilde came to Paris in 1899, broken and ill after his release from Reading Gaol, he sent Fullerton a copy of his play *The Importance of Being Earnest* and asked him for a loan of a hundred francs. Fullerton wrote so ornate an apology for not being able to come to the aid of so great an artist that Wilde was moved to remonstrate mildly: honest feeling, he said, was never in need of stilts" (Lewis, *Edith Wharton*, 185).

71. Wharton, as quoted in Goodman, "Edith Wharton's 'Sketch of an Essay on Walt Whitman,'" 5.

72. Edith Wharton, *A Son at the Front* (New York: Charles Scribner's Sons, 1923), 40.

73. After his divorce, "Campton settled down to the solitude of his dusty studio at Montmartre, and painted doggedly, all his thoughts on George." He has become a misogynist: "cursèd fools—all women," he remarks later (ibid., 50, 88).

74. Ibid., 53.

75. For speculation about the importance of Jeff to Walt, see Justin Kaplan, *Walt Whitman: A Life* (New York: Simon and Schuster, 1980), 235–36, and *Dear Brother Walt: The Letters of Thomas Jefferson Whitman*, ed. Dennis Berthold and Kenneth M.

Price (Kent, Ohio: Kent State University Press, 1984), xix–xx. Michael Moon contends that an incestuous tie between Walt and his brother Eddie may be suggested by the line "I effuse my flesh in eddies" (unpublished paper delivered at the New York City Museum of History in 1992).

76. See *Specimen Days*: "it was about the best thing I could do to raise their spirits, and show them that somebody cared for them, and practically felt a fatherly or brotherly interest in them" (Walt Whitman, *Prose Works 1892*, ed. Floyd Stovall, 2 vols. [New York: New York University Press, 1963], 1:81). Cf. Whitman's comment in a letter to his mother, Louisa Van Velsor Whitman, that he found the soldiers "appealing to me most profoundly. . . . Often they seem very near to me, even as my own children or younger brothers. I make no bones of petting them just as if they were" (Walt Whitman, vol. 1 of *The Correspondence of Walt Whitman*, ed. Edwin Haviland Miller, [New York: New York University Press, 1961], 125).

77. My interpretation of this novel is indebted to Judith Sensibar's insightful analysis, "'Behind the Lines' in Edith Wharton's *A Son at the Front*: Rewriting a Masculinist Tradition," *Journal of American Studies* 24 (1990): 196.

78. Ibid., 196 n.

79. Ibid., 197.

80. Catherine M. Rae, *Edith Wharton's New York Quartet* (Lanham, Md.: University Press of America, 1984), 45.

81. Edith Wharton, *The Spark*, in *Novellas and Other Writings* (New York: Literary Classics of the United States, 1990), 473.

82. Rae, *Edith Wharton's New York Quartet*, 46.

83. Wharton, *The Spark*, 488.

84. Waid, *Letters from the Underworld*, 197.

85. Abbey Werlock, "Edith Wharton's Subtle Revenge?: Morton Fullerton and the Female Artist in *Hudson River Bracketed* and *The Gods Arrive*," in *Edith Wharton: New Critical Essays*, ed. Alfred Bendixen and Annette Zilversmit (New York: Garland, 1992), 181–99.

86. Wharton, *Hudson River Bracketed*, 96.

87. Wharton, *Letters*, 530.

88. Edith Wharton, *The Gods Arrive* (New York: Charles Scribner's Sons, 1932), 50.

89. Ibid., 152.

90. Ibid., 390.

91. Edith Wharton, *A Backward Glance* in *Novellas and Other Writings*, 856, 873, 895, 909, 975 (the remark about James), and 1061.

92. Wharton, *A Backward Glance*, 873.

93. See Vivian Pollak's discussion of how "Whitman discovers his vocation in 'Out of the Cradle' when he acknowledges the death of his heterosexual aspirations and the birth of his homosexual identity. . . . He discovers his vocation as the 'outsetting bard of love.' But he also discovers that he is to be the poet of unsatis-

fied love" ("Death as Repression, Repression as Death: A Reading of Whitman's 'Calamus' Poems," *Mickle Street Review* 11 [1989]: 64).

94. In works bearing her darkest interpretations of Whitman, for example, *A Son at the Front*, Wharton reached conclusions similar to Robyn Wiegman, who detects a "conflict between [Whitman's] democratic rhetoric and patriarchal culture." Wiegman believes that "Calamus" has at its "core a profound assertion of masculine subjectivity coupled with the exclusion of woman." See "Writing the Male Body: Naked Patriarchy and Whitmanian Democracy," *Literature and Psychology* 33 (1987): 20 and 22–23.

CHAPTER THREE

1. Walt Whitman, *Notebooks and Unpublished Prose Manuscripts*, ed. Edward F. Grier, 6 vols. (New York: New York University Press, 1984), 1:101.

2. These attributes also served Whitman as a way to gender his persona as hypermasculine.

3. Eve Kosofsky Sedgwick, *Between Men: English Literature and Male Homosocial Desire* (New York: Columbia University Press, 1985), esp. 201–17; Richard Dellamora, *Masculine Desire: The Sexual Politics of Victorian Aestheticism* (Chapel Hill: University of North Carolina Press, 1990), esp. 86–93; Ed Folsom, "Whitman's Calamus Photographs" in *Breaking Bounds: Whitman and American Cultural Studies*, ed. Betsy Erkkila and Jay Grossman (New York: Oxford University Press, 1996), 193–219.

4. Michel Foucault has asked if homosexuality existed before that category was invented in the nineteenth century. The question is useful in reminding us that "homosexuality" does not denote a unitary, transhistorical phenomenon. In discussing Whitman, I tend to employ words such as "calamus love" and "comradeship" in an attempt to remain close to his own conceptualization of affection and attachment. When I do employ terms such as homoeroticism and homosexuality, I use them advisedly and nonpejoratively.

5. Byrne R. S. Fone discusses Greece as a signifier of male-male love in *Masculine Landscapes: Walt Whitman and the Homoerotic Text* (Carbondale: Southern Illinois University Press, 1992), 205–7. *Philadelphia Press*, 17 January 1882, as quoted in Richard Ellmann, *Oscar Wilde* (New York: Alfred A. Knopf, 1988), 167.

6. John Addington Symonds, *Studies of the Greek Poets* (London: Smith, 1873), 422 n.

7. Edward Carpenter, *Days with Walt Whitman* (London: George Allen, 1906), 7.

8. Quoted in Emile Delavenay, *D. H. Lawrence and Edward Carpenter: A Study in Edwardian Transition* (New York: Taplinger, 1971), 227.

9. The significant differences between "Live Oak" and "Calamus"—not just in length but in tenor—serve to confirm Hershel Parker's position in his recent controversy with Alan Helms that it is illegitimate to reconstitute the "Live Oak" poems by reconstructing the sequence out of the poems as *later* published in 1860. See Hershel Parker, "The Real 'Live Oak, with Moss': Straight Talk about Whitman's

'Gay Manifesto,'" *Nineteenth-Century Literature* 51 (September 1996): 145–60, and Alan Helms, "Whitman's 'Live Oak with Moss'" in *The Continuing Presence of Walt Whitman: The Life After the Life*, ed. Robert K. Martin (Iowa City: University of Iowa Press, 1992), 185–205.

10. In the 1860 version of the "Calamus" cluster, the poems concerned with death include numbers 2, 17, and 27.

11. Clark Griffith, "Sex and Death: The Significance of Whitman's *Calamus* Themes," *Philological Quarterly* 39 (1960): 36. When I speak of Whitman in 1859 as a poet newly inclined to literary allusiveness, I am excluding from consideration his conventional poetry written in the pre-*Leaves of Grass* period.

12. Louis Crompton notes the possible connection between the Greek story of Carpus and Calamus (recorded by Nonnus in his *Dionysiaca* in 450 C.E.) and Whitman's naming of the "Calamus" poems in *The Gay and Lesbian Literary Heritage: A Reader's Companion to the Writers and Their Works from Antiquity to the Present*, ed. Claude J. Summers (New York: Henry Holt, 1995), 348. See also Byrne R. S. Fone, *Columbia Anthology of Gay Literature* (New York: Columbia University Press, 1998), 57–58. For other useful discussions of the word "calamus," see Ed Folsom, "'Scattering it freely forever': Whitman in a Seminar on Nineteenth-Century American Culture" in *Approaches to Teaching Whitman's Leaves of Grass*, ed. Donald D. Kummings (New York: Modern Language Association, 1990), 143, and Russell Hunt, "Whitman's Poetics and the Unity of 'Calamus,'" *American Literature* 46 (January 1975): 485 n.

13. Vivian Pollak, "Death as Repression, Repression as Death: A Reading of Whitman's 'Calamus' Poems," *Mickle Street Review*, 11 (1989): 61.

14. Michael Moon, *Disseminating Whitman: Revision and Corporeality in Leaves of Grass* (Cambridge: Harvard University Press, 1991), 163. Moon also remarks that "between the range of intense male-homoerotic feelings that the 'Calamus' poems are designed to celebrate and any signs that can be made of this range of feelings in writing—any 'tokens' of it that can be disseminated through writing—there may well be, according to this text, a rupture that can only be figured as the death, burial, and decay of, in some cases, the desiring subject and, in others, its object" (168).

15. "Calamus" number 27 appears in *Leaves of Grass* (Boston: Thayer and Eldridge, 1860), 369–70. This poem was entitled "O Living Always, Always Dying" in the "deathbed edition" of *Leaves*.

16. Moon, *Disseminating Whitman*, 169.

17. Joseph Cady, "Not Happy in the Capitol: Homosexuality and the *Calamus* Poems," *American Studies* 19 (Fall 1978): 5–22.

18. This poem is entitled "Vigil on the Field" in *Poems by Walt Whitman*, ed. William Michael Rossetti (London: John Camden Hotten, 1868).

19. Roden Noel, "A Study of Walt Whitman: The Poet of Modern Democracy," *The*

Dark Blue 2 (October 1871): 251; Symonds, "Love and Death: A Symphony" in *In re Walt Whitman*, ed. Horace L. Traubel et al. (Philadelphia: David McKay, 1893), 1–12; Edward Carpenter, *Towards Democracy: Complete in Four Parts* (New York: Mitchell Kennerley, 1912), 3–110.

20. John Simons, "Edward Carpenter, Whitman and the Radical Aesthetic," in *Gender Roles and Sexuality in Victorian Literature*, ed. Christopher Parker (Aldershot, England: Scolar, 1995), 116.

21. Ibid., 123.

22. "In the 1860s, Karl Ulrichs, the first German writer (and for decades the only openly 'inverted' man) to discuss inversion in a public forum, did not define it in the same terms now used for homosexuality, but characterized the *Urning* (his term for an invert) as representing a 'woman's spirit in a man's body.' " See George Chauncey, *Gay New York: Gender, Urban Culture, and the Making of the Gay Male World 1890–1940* (New York: Basic Books, 1994), 49.

23. From D. H. Lawrence, "Introduction," in *New Poems* (1920), reprinted in *D. H. Lawrence: Selected Literary Criticism*, ed. Anthony Beal (New York: Viking, 1966), 87.

24. M. Wynn Thomas, "Whitman in the British Isles," in *Walt Whitman and the World*, ed. Gay Wilson Allen and Ed Folsom (Iowa City: University of Iowa Press, 1995), 16.

25. Quoted in Jeffrey Meyers, *D. H. Lawrence: A Biography* (New York: Knopf, 1990), 208–9.

26. In this sentence and the preceding one, I follow closely the language and thought of Meyers, *D. H. Lawrence*, 209.

27. Lawrence to Henry Savage, 22 December 1913, reprinted in vol. 1 of *Collected Letters of D. H. Lawrence*, ed. Harry T. Moore (New York: Viking Press, 1962), 257–58.

28. Famously there are three versions of *Lady Chatterley's Lover*.

29. Additional versions that once existed are now thought to be lost.

30. Mark Kinkead-Weekes, *D. H. Lawrence: Triumph to Exile 1912–1922* (Cambridge: Cambridge University Press, 1996), 453.

31. D. H. Lawrence, *Studies in Classic American Literature*, ed. Ezra Greenspan, Lindeth Vasey, and John Worthen (1923; reprint, Cambridge: Cambridge University Press, 2003), 358.

32. D. H. Lawrence, "Whitman," in *The Nation and the Athenæum* 29 (23 July 1921): 618; Lawrence, *Studies in Classic American Literature*, 154–55.

33. Lawrence, "Whitman," 617.

34. Ibid., 617–18.

35. Quoted in Delavenay, *D. H. Lawrence and Edward Carpenter*, 227.

36. Lawrence, *Studies*, 153–54 and 150.

37. Lawrence, "Introduction," 89.

38. E. M. Forster, "Terminal Note," in *Maurice: A Novel* (New York: W. W. Norton, 1971), 249.
39. Robert K. Martin, "Edward Carpenter and the Double Structure of *Maurice*," *Journal of Homosexuality* 8, nos. 3/4 (1983): 38.
40. Forster, *Maurice*, 219, 225, 238, and 250.
41. *The Gay and Lesbian Literary Heritage*, ed. Claude J. Summers (New York: Henry Holt, 1995), 282.
42. Forster, *Maurice*, 239.
43. Whitman, *Leaves of Grass: Comprehensive Reader's Edition* (New York: New York University Press, 1965), 159.
44. Martin, "Edward Carpenter," 44.
45. Roger Ebert, review of *Love and Death on Long Island*, <http://www.suntimes.com/ebert/ebert_reviews/1998/03/061302.html> (31 January 2000).
46. Gilbert Adair, *Love and Death on Long Island* (New York: Grove Press, 1990), 138.

CHAPTER FOUR

1. The 1938 Whitman controversy in the *Boston Globe* has not previously been noted in Whitman criticism or bibliographies. See "The "Good Gray Poet' Again," *Boston Globe*, 22 August 1938, evening edition, 12; A. Maurice Farrell, "Whitman Also a Red?," ibid., 25 August 1938, morning edition, 16; F. F. Hill, "Red Paint on Whitman," ibid., 29 August 1938, morning edition, 12; Evan Amageen, "He Also Wore Whiskers," ibid., 12; W. D. Q., "Whitman's Own Answer," ibid., 31 August 1938, morning edition, 14. Regarding the controversy over Shahn's mural, see "Protest Halts Whitman's 'Irreligious' Verse for Postoffice Mural," *New York Herald Tribune*, 12 December 1938, late city edition, 1, 7.
2. Farrell, "Whitman Also a Red?"
3. Mike Gold, "Ode to Walt Whitman," in *Walt Whitman: The Measure of His Song*, rev. ed., ed. Jim Perlman, Ed Folsom, and Dan Campion (Duluth: Holy Cow! Press, 1998), 171.
4. And with slightly more wit, Evan Amageen of Norfolk also responded: "Walt Whitman was a dangerous Communist. 'Leaves of Grass' is circulated through hidden channels in a deliberate attempt to corrupt American youth and destroy our government by the insidious processes of boring in and undermining our institutions. Walt Whitman also wore whiskers. I should suggest to Mr. Farrell that he handle carefully all volumes of Whitman's works, since the larger ones may well have diabolical machines hidden within the bindings. And look out no one says 'Boo.'" See Hill, "Red Paint on Whitman," and Amageen, "He Also Wore Whiskers."
5. Werner Sollors, "National Identity and Ethnic Diversity: 'Of Plymouth Rock and Jamestown and Ellis Island'; or, Ethnic Literature and Some Redefinitions of

'America,'" in *History and Memory in African American Culture*, ed. Geneviève Fabre and Robert O'Meally (New York: Oxford University Press, 1994), 101. For discussion of Plymouth Rock as African in its origins see John Seelye, *Memory's Nation: The Place of Plymouth Rock* (Chapel Hill: University of North Carolina Press, 1998), 641, and John McPhee's delightful essay "Travels of the Rock" in his *Irons in the Fire* (New York: Farrar, Straus & Giroux, 1997), 205.

6. Walt Whitman, "A Backward Glance o'er Travel'd Roads," in *Leaves of Grass: Comprehensive Reader's Edition* (New York: New York University Press, 1965), 566.

7. John Dos Passos, *The Major Nonfictional Prose*, ed. Donald Pizer (Detroit: Wayne State University Press, 1988), 37.

8. John Dos Passos, *The 42nd Parallel* (1930; reprint, New York: New American Library, 1969), 50. For a discussion of this passage, see John H. Wrenn, *John Dos Passos* (New York: Twayne, 1961), 22–23.

9. Daniel Aaron, "The Riddle of John Dos Passos," *Harper's Magazine* 224 (March 1962): 59.

10. Dos Passos, *The 42nd Parallel*, 240.

11. Blanche Gelfant, "The Search for Identity in the Novels of John Dos Passos," *PMLA* 76 (March 1961): 134.

12. See Charles W. Bernardin, "John Dos Passos' Harvard Years," *New England Quarterly* 27 (1954): 22, and Linda W. Wagner, *Dos Passos: Artist as American* (Austin: University of Texas Press, 1979), xiii.

13. All quotations are drawn from Aaron, "The Riddle of John Dos Passos," 56.

14. Ibid., 57.

15. Gelfant, "The Search for Identity," 138.

16. See the discussion in Lois Hughson, "In Search of the True America: Dos Passos' Debt to Whitman in *U.S.A.*," *Modern Fiction Studies* 19 (Summer 1973): 183–84 and 190.

17. Dos Passos, *The 42nd Parallel*, 30.

18. Hughson, "In Search of the True America," 191.

19. John Dos Passos, "Whither the American Writer," *Modern Quarterly* (1932); reprinted in Dos Passos, *The Major Nonfictional Prose*, 150.

20. John Dos Passos, *The Big Money* (1933; reprint, New York: New American Library, 1969), 167–68.

21. Hughson, "In Search of the True America," 183.

22. Dos Passos, *The Big Money*, 173.

23. John P. Diggins, "Visions of Chaos and Visions of Order: Dos Passos as Historian," *American Literature* 46 (November 1974): 331.

24. Hughson, "In Search of the True America," 192.

25. Dos Passos felt a personal connection: "In college and out I had . . . felt the frustrations that came from being considered a wop or a guinea or a greaser." See

John Dos Passos, *The Best Times: An Informal Memoir* (New York: New American Library, 1966), 166.

26. Donald Pizer, *Dos Passos' U.S.A.* (Charlottesville: University Press of Virginia, 1988), 27.

27. Dos Passos, *The Big Money*, 468–69.

28. He was an editor of *Art Front*. Kate Sampsell notes that "Ben Shahn was so active in these organizations that after World War II, his friend [Walker] Evans steered clear of him, fearing guilt by association in the repressive Cold War McCarthy-era." See Sampsell, "The Testifying Eye: Ben Shahn's New York," *American Quarterly* 53 (March 2001): 106.

29. There were 189 entries in the competition. Shahn won in conjunction with his wife Bernarda Bryson, though she fell into a secondary role in the actual design and painting of the mural once the work began. Bryson explained her role to Carl Baldwin: "Since the designs which won the award were her husband's . . . her own work consisted in collaboration on the execution, in 'painting details all around,' and in spending many hours 'mulling colors'—making finely ground dry colors and grinding them still finer, prior to mixing them with egg and distilled water." Carl Baldwin, "Shahn's Bronx P.O. Murals: The Perils of Public Art," *Art in America* (May/June 1977): 15.

30. Quoted in Diana L. Linden, "Ben Shahn's Murals for the Bronx Central Post Office," *Antiques*, November 1996, 710.

31. Quoted in Linden, "Ben Shahn's Murals," 713.

32. Bernarda Bryson Shahn notes that her husband rejected "all personal identification with sect or creed. He deeply appreciated the observances, the ritual and lore of his inherited Judaism but also was profoundly moved by the sonorous Masses of Catholicism and, again, by the tough spirit of early Protestantism." See Bernarda Bryson Shahn, *Ben Shahn* (New York: Harry N. Abrams, [1972]), 257.

33. Diana L. Linden, "Ben Shahn's New Deal Murals: Jewish Identity in the American Scene," in *Common Man, Mythic Vision: The Paintings of Ben Shahn*, ed. Susan Chevlowe (Princeton, N.J.: Princeton University Press, 1998), 45.

34. Howard Greenfeld, *Ben Shahn: An Artist's Life* (New York: Random House, 1998), 152. After the mural incident, Shahn moved to Jersey Homestead, New Jersey, where he found a cohesive Jewish culture and a community interested in social reform.

35. James Weschler, "The Coughlin Terror," *The Nation*, 22 July 1939, 97. The claim was not outlandish because much on the landscape was disturbing. For example, the German-American Bund, supported with funds from Hitler's government, attracted nearly 20,000 people to Madison Square Garden on 20 February 1939, ostensibly to celebrate George Washington's birthday, though swastikas were more in evidence than flags. "After taking power in Germany, the Nazis allocated funds

to pro-Hitler movements around the world. One of the prime recipients of this assistance was the German-American Bund." See Sheldon Marcus, *Father Coughlin: The Tumultuous Life of the Priest of the Little Flower* (Boston: Little Brown, 1973), 148–49.

36. Ibid., 155.

37. Ibid.

38. Ibid., 156–57. Fortunately, some Catholics, especially the Committee of Catholics for Human Rights, objected to Coughlinism (158).

39. Ibid., 162.

40. Diana L. Linden writes: "In 1938 in New York City, the primary destination of most refugees and immigrants, opponents of open immigration found support from Father Charles Coughlin. At a rally to picket radio station WMCA, which had refused to air Coughlin's broadcasts, they carried signs with such slogans as 'Refugees Get Jobs in This Country! Why Don't 100% Americans?'" See "Ben Shahn, The Four Freedoms, and the S.S. *St. Louis*," *American Jewish History* 86, no. 4 (1998): 427.

41. Greenfeld, *Ben Shahn*, 157. On 11 December 1938, Chancellor J. Francis A. McIntyre of the Archbishopric of New York asserted that the notions expressed by Whitman were "far distant from American ideals" and were instead "suggestive of Asiatic philosophy." Another person protested that the Whitman lines advanced a "strictly pagan philosophy." Yet another individual complained that the inscription constituted an "insult to all religious-minded men and to all established forms of religion, inasmuch as it propagates atheism and irreligion" (ibid., 158). Papers on the controversy are in the National Archives.

42. See Greenfeld, *Ben Shahn*, 155–56. It may be, too, that the mural was meant to conjure up thoughts of Marx. Linden remarks: "With his flowing beard, Whitman resembles a composite of Karl Marx and Moses" (Linden, "Ben Shahn's Murals," 713). Shahn came from a family of socialists. In her study of her husband's art written many years later Bernarda recorded that "ideologically Ben was at that time more under the influence of Walt Whitman than of [Diego] Rivera, an orientation strongly supported by his travels in America" when he served as a photographer for the Resettlement Administration (1935–37), including a stint in the rural South (Greenfeld, *Ben Shahn*, 160–61).

43. Robert Edmondson, director of the Economic Research Service, was a contributor to publications widely circulated in both Nazi Germany and the United States. He wrote these words for recitation at most meetings he conducted:

> The Only People Who Want War Are . . . THE JEWS. Will the Jews do the Fighting? No, They will make the profits.
> But hundreds of thousands of Christian American Boys are to be killed and crippled for life, or blinded on the Altar of Jewish Communism because Ger-

many in Europe and Japan in Asia ARE THE ENEMIES OF JEWISH BOLSHEVISM. If Germany chooses to get rid of Jews that is HER business . . . not ours. We exclude OTHER ASIATICS. . . . The Chinese and Japs.

Quoted in Marcus, *Father Coughlin*, 152.

44. "Protest Halts Whitman's 'Irreligious' Verse for Postoffice Mural," 7.

45. When the *New York Times* ran the story on 13 December 1938, it created irony through juxtaposition: the story appeared next to another one about Catholic youths protesting intolerance toward Jews.

46. Quoted in Greenfeld, *Ben Shahn*, 156.

47. Linden, "Ben Shahn's New Deal Murals," 48.

48. I quote from the lines as Shahn presented them on the mural itself, though his lineation and punctuation do not follow exactly any of Whitman's versions. Shahn slightly misquotes from the 1860 version of these lines. The lines, first published in 1860, were reprinted by Whitman, with minor variations in punctuation, under the title "As I Walk Solitary, Unattended" (1867) and under the title "As I Walk these Broad Majestic Days" (1871).

   As Diana L. Linden has noted, Shahn's depiction of Whitman is "flanked by two small panels showing mine workers—one operating a pneumatic drill . . . and the other pushing a handcar on rails. The result is a twentieth-century version of a Renaissance triptych" ("Ben Shahn's Murals," 712). In Shahn's conception, Whitman, famous as the uniter of here and hereafter, becomes the nineteenth-century poet who joins twentieth-century workers in glimpsing the twenty-first century via the futuristic industrial structure. The triptych suggests that the nation will follow Whitman's lead and will be infused with the strength of working people. Despite the controversy, work proceeded well on other panels and Shahn was gratified by the public response: "People seem to like the mural very much . . . and, needless to say, this sort of daily approval is about the most pleasing experience one can have" (quoted in Greenfeld, *Ben Shahn*, 158).

49. Greenfeld, *Ben Shahn*, 156.

50. Ibid., 157.

51. When one woman responded to his mural by sneering that the figures listening to Whitman appeared to be communist workers and thus offended her as a descendant of those who fought in the American Revolutionary War, he became so angry he kicked over his paint bucket and said that his ancestors fought in the battle of Jericho. Ibid., 159.

52. Linden, "Ben Shahn, The Four Freedoms," 426; Selden Rodman, *Portrait of the Artist as an American; Ben Shahn: A Biography With Pictures* (New York: Harper & Brothers, 1951), 78–79.

53. Linden, "Ben Shahn's New Deal Murals," 50.

54. Quoted in Linden, "Ben Shahn, The Four Freedoms," 439.

55. It is quite possible that Malamud knew of Shahn's troubles, since he might have been inclined to sympathize with him as a fellow Jew of Russian ancestry from Brooklyn.

56. Quoted from *Der Weltkampf* in Linden, "Ben Shahn, The Four Freedoms," 431.

57. Bernard Malamud, "The German Refugee," in *The Stories of Bernard Malamud* (New York: Penguin, 1984), 95.

58. Bernard Malamud, *The Stories of Bernard Malamud*, 107. Whitman had actually written *a* kelson of the creation (i.e., one of the things that holds the universe together—not the only thing). Whitman's wording is slightly less open to attack as wishful thinking.

59. Elie Wiesel, as quoted in Alvin H. Rosenfeld, "The Problematics of Holocaust Literature," in *Confronting the Holocaust: The Impact of Elie Wiesel*, ed. Alvin H. Rosenfeld and Irving Greenberg (Bloomington: Indiana University Press, 1978), 22.

60. Rosenfeld, "The Problematics of Holocaust Literature," 22.

61. Malamud, *The Stories of Bernard Malamud*, 107–08.

62. Lawrence M. Lasher, "Narrative Strategy in Malamud's 'The German Refugee,'" *Studies in Jewish American Literature* 9 (Spring 1990): 81.

63. Ibid., 78.

64. Whitman, *Leaves of Grass: Comprehensive Reader's Edition*, 33.

CHAPTER FIVE

1. The meaning of the name *Whitman* is discussed in William Swinton's *Rambles Among Words*, a book Whitman himself may have contributed to. See Ed Folsom, "Culturing White Anxiety: Walt Whitman and American Indians," *Études Anglaises* 45 (July–September 1992): 291.

2. Henry Louis Gates Jr., "White Like Me," *New Yorker*, 17 June 1996, 67–68.

3. George Hutchinson, "Jean Toomer and American Racial Discourse," *Texas Studies in Literature and Language* 35 (1993): 229; Werner Sollors, "'Never was Born': The Mulatto, an American Tragedy?," *The Massachusetts Review* 27 (1986): 293–316; "Differences in Subject-Matter Content between the 1990 and 2000 Census Questionnaires," at <http://www.census.gov/population/www/cen2000/90vs00.html> (27 January 2003).

4. Fortunately, recent criticism is beginning to correct such oversimplifications. See, for example, George Hutchinson, *The Harlem Renaissance in Black and White* (Cambridge: Harvard University Press, 1995) and Ann Douglas, *Terrible Honesty: Mongrel Manhattan in the 1920s* (New York: Farrar, Straus & Giroux, 1995).

5. George B. Hutchinson, "Jean Toomer and the 'New Negroes' of Washington," *American Literature* 63 (December 1991): 688.

6. Quoted in Cynthia Earl Kerman and Richard Eldridge, *The Lives of Jean Toomer: A Hunger for Wholeness* (Baton Rouge: Louisiana State University Press, 1987), 80–81.

7. George Hutchinson, "Jean Toomer and American Racial Discourse," 227. Hutch-

inson argues that the "difficulty of speaking or writing from outside the dominant discourse of race is a pervasive motif throughout *Cane*, and it has been matched by the difficulty of reading the text *against* the boundaries of that discourse." He adds, the "belief in unified, coherent 'black' and 'white' American 'racial' identities depends formally and ethically upon the sacrifice of the identity that is *both* 'black' and 'white,' just as American racial discourse depends upon maintaining the emphatic silence of the interracial subject at the heart of Toomer's project" (227).

8. James Kaufmann, review of *Blue Highways*, by William Least Heat-Moon, *Christian Science Monitor*, 2 March 1989, B12.

9. For the controversy over Keri Hulme, see Margery Fee, "Who Can Write as Other?," in *The Post-Colonial Studies Reader*, ed. Bill Ashcroft, Gareth Griffiths, and Helen Tiffin (London: Routledge, 1995), 242–45.

10. Rayna Green, "The Tribe Called Wannabee: Playing Indian in America and Europe," *Folklore* 99, no. 1 (1988): 45; Gerald Vizenor, *Manifest Manners: Postindian Warriors of Survivance* (Hanover, N.H.: Wesleyan University Press, 1994), 24; Jim Crace, "Sticking to the Backroads," *Times Literary Supplement*, 26 August 1983, 902.

11. Wendy Rose, "The Great Pretenders: Further Reflections on Whiteshamanism," in *The State of Native America: Genocide, Colonization, and Resistance*, ed. Annette Jaimes (Boston: South End Press, 1992), 404.

12. David J. Ward, E-mail to author, 12 April 1997. Quoted with permission.

13. Michael Elliott, "The Next-To-Last Lecture: 'Wannabe Indians,' Gerald Vizenor, and *Indian Country Today*." Quoted with permission.

14. Jerry Reynolds's three articles all appear in *Indian Country Today*. Part 1: "Indian Writers: Real or Imagined," 8 September 1993, 13: A1, A3; Part 2: "Indian Writers: The Good, the Bad, and the Could Be," 15 September 1993, 13: A1, A3; Part 3: "Indian Writers: The Good, the Bad, and the Could Be," 6 October 1993, 13: A1, A2.

15. Ward Churchill, as quoted in "Indian Writers: The Good, the Bad, and the Could Be," 6 October 1993, 13: A1. Jimmie Durham, as quoted in "Indian Writers: The Good, the Bad, and the Could Be," 15 September 1993, 13: A1, A3.

16. Walt Whitman, *The Correspondence*, ed. Edwin Haviland Miller, 6 vols. (New York: New York University Press, 1961–77), 2:170.

17. William Least Heat-Moon as interviewed by Walter W. Ross, in vol. 119 of *Contemporary Authors*, ed. Hal May et al. (Detroit: Gale Research, 1987), 384.

18. John Updike, "A Long Way Home," *New Yorker*, 2 May 1983, 121. Again the comparison with Broyard is illuminating. When Broyard started to write his long-awaited memoirs he was told by a friend, "You can do many things if you're writing a memoir. But if you squelch stuff that seems to be crucial about you, and pretend it doesn't exist. . . ." (Gates, "White Like Me," 78).

19. William Least Heat-Moon, *Blue Highways* (Boston: Little Brown, 1982), 5.

20. Ibid., 219.

21. Ibid., 5.

22. Heat-Moon in Ross, *Contemporary Authors*, 383.

23. Ibid., 384; and Heat-Moon, *Blue Highways*, 5.

24. Heat-Moon, *Blue Highways*, 64.

25. Folsom, "Culturing White Anxiety," 288–89.

26. Jonathan Yardley, "Seeing America from the Roads Less Traveled," *Washington Post Book World*, 26 December 1982, 3, 7.

27. Allen Ginsberg, "A Supermarket in California," in *Walt Whitman: The Measure of His Song*, rev. ed., ed. Jim Perlman, Ed Folsom, and Dan Campion (Duluth: Holy Cow! Press, 1998), 213.

28. Anatole Broyard, "Books of the Times," *New York Times*, 13 January 1983, late city final edition, sec. C, 20:3.

29. The phrase is from Lester's grandmother, who was famous for defying an ancestor of the novel's central villian, Luther Nedeed.

30. Gloria Naylor, *Linden Hills* (1985; reprint, New York: Penguin, 1986), 29. Yet where is the authentic Willie? — "When he got drunk enough he dropped his street language and totally bewildered [his acquaintances] with long recitations in perfect iambic pentameter about the state of American society" (29).

31. Ibid.

32. Ibid., 44–45.

33. A similar point is made by both Sharon Felton in "Surface, Subtext, and Beyond: Gloria Naylor and Walt Whitman," *Tennessee Philological Bulletin*, 34 (1977): 30, and by Christine G. Berg, "'giving sound to the bruised places in their hearts': Gloria Naylor and Walt Whitman," in *The Critical Response to Gloria Naylor*, ed. Sharon Felton and Michelle C. Loris (Westport, Conn.: Greenwood Press, 1997), 101.

34. For a discussion of this point, see Luke Bouvier, "Reading in Black and White: Space and Race in *Linden Hills*," in *Gloria Naylor: Critical Perspectives Past and Present*, ed. Henry Louis Gates Jr. and K. A. Appiah (New York: Amistad, 1993), 149.

35. Naylor, *Linden Hills*, 88.

36. In fact, using this poem as evidence, early biographers fabricated the so-called New Orleans romance in which Whitman supposedly fathered one or more children. In the manuscript draft, however, Whitman had said in the second line: "But now of all that city I remember only the man who wandered with me, there, for love of me," and the fourth line observes: "I remember, I say, only one rude and ignorant man." Whitman's self-censoring affected other poems, including "A Noiseless Patient Spider," which in an early notebook version originally expressed the calamus theme of same-sex love.

37. Catherine C. Ward argues that "David and Winston are Naylor's version of Dante's Paolo and Francesca, the lovers who were tempted to passionate indul-

gence after reading an Arthurian romance. The medieval lovers are punished by being locked in an eternal embrace while they fly around in a perpetual whirl-wind. . . . David's and Winston's punishment is not the eternal embrace . . . but a lifelong separation." See "Gloria Naylor's *Linden Hills*: A Modern *Inferno*," *Contemporary Literature* 28 (1987): 74.

38. Naylor, *Linden Hills*, 79–80.

39. Ibid., 88–89.

40. Keith Sandiford, "Gothic and Intertextual Constructions in *Linden Hills*," in *Gloria Naylor: Critical Perspectives*, 210–11.

41. Margaret Homans, "The Woman in the Cave: Recent Feminist Fictions and the Classical Underworld," *Contemporary Literature* 29 (1988): 397.

42. Naylor, *Linden Hills*, 291.

43. Henry Louis Gates Jr., "Significant Others," *Contemporary Literature* 29 (1988): 613–14.

44. Ishmael Reed, *Flight to Canada* (1976; reprint, New York: Macmillan, 1989), 121. Robert Levine has pointed out to me the oddity of Reed's celebration of William Wells Brown in a book so concerned with passing: at the end of *Clotel*, Brown has one of his characters happily passing.

45. Reed is involved less with evasion than with what Ralph Ellison calls a "techni-cal assault against the styles which have gone before." For a useful discussion of this point, see Joseph C. Schöpp, " 'Riding Bareback, Backwards through a Wood of Words': Ishmael Reed's Revision of the Slave Narrative," *Historiographic Meta-fiction in Modern American and Canadian Literature* (Paderborn: Ferdinand Schön-ingh, 1994), 270–71.

46. Jennifer Fleischner, *Mastering Slavery: Memory, Family, and Identity in Women's Slave Narratives* (New York: New York University Press, 1996), 1–22.

47. Reed, *Flight to Canada*, 123, and Schöpp, " 'Riding Bareback,' " 269.

48. Schöpp, *Riding Bareback*, 270.

49. Reed, *Flight to Canada*, 10.

50. Ibid., 8.

51. Schöpp, " 'Riding Bareback,' " 273.

52. Reed, *Flight to Canada*, 10.

53. Kathryn Hume, "Ishmael Reed and the Problematics of Control," *PMLA* 108 (May 1993): 508.

54. Reed, *Flight to Canada*, 28.

55. Ibid., 83.

56. Ibid., 63–64.

57. Nellie Y. McKay, untitled forum contribution, *PMLA* 111 (October 1996): 1155.

58. Elisa Seaman Leggett, in an 1881 letter to Whitman (recording an anecdote from 1864), notes the reaction of the former slave Sojourner Truth upon hearing part of *Leaves of Grass* read aloud: " 'Who wrote that?' I turned, and there in the door-

way she stood, her tall figure, with a white turban on her head, her figure and every feature full of expression. Immediately, she added: 'Never mind the man's name. It was God who wrote it. He chose the man to give his message.' After that I often read it to her. Her great brain accepts the highest truths." See Joann P. Krieg, "Whitman and Sojourner Truth," *Walt Whitman Quarterly Review* 16 (Summer 1998): 32–33.

59. Douglass, as quoted in Martin Klammer, *Whitman, Slavery, and the Emergence of* Leaves of Grass (University Park: Pennsylvania State University Press, 1995), 134.

60. Reed also explores the idea of presidents who may have been passing in *Mumbo Jumbo*.

61. Schöpp, "'Riding Bareback,'" 276.

62. Ibid., 277. Renate Lachmann, as quoted in Elliott, "The Next-To-Last Lecture."

CHAPTER SIX

1. Walt Whitman, *Leaves of Grass: Comprehensive Reader's Edition*, ed. Harold W. Blodgett and Sculley Bradley (New York: New York University Press, 1965), 729. All subsequent citations of *Leaves of Grass* in this chapter refer to this edition.

2. Whitman's relationship to film is only beginning to receive sustained treatment. After this chapter was completed, an overview was published by Kenn Pierson, "Reaching 'The Audience Beyond': Whitman's Poetry on Stage and Screen," *Mickle Street Review* 15 (Summer 2002): <http://www.micklestreet.rutgers.edu/> (13 April 2003). Pierson chronicles more than 120 "Whitman dramas" in an "odd assortment of plays, films, radio and television dramas, and other performance pieces." Because Pierson studies so much material, his essay is often reduced to listing items rather than analyzing them. Other critics have pursued particular questions and topics effectively: Alice Ahlers, "Cinematographic Technique in *Leaves of Grass*," *Walt Whitman Review* 12 (December 1966): 93–97; Robert Richardson, *Literature and Film* (Bloomington: Indiana University Press, 1969); Ben Singer, "Connoisseurs of Chaos: Whitman, Vertov, and the 'Poetic Survey,'" *Literature / Film Quarterly* 15 (1987): 247–58; Barry K. Grant, "Whitman and Eisenstein," *Literature / Film Quarterly* 4 (1976): 264–70; Michael Lynch, "Putting Whitman Back in the Closet," *Globe and Mail* (Toronto), 17 April 1990, A7. Additional commentary on Whitman and film is noted below.

   Special thanks go to Brett Barney for help in locating illustrations for this chapter.

3. This study makes no attempt to examine the many documentaries treating Whitman.

4. Philadelphia was home to the country's oldest photographic society and to the journal *Philadelphia Photographer* (see Kathleen A. Foster, *Thomas Eakins Rediscovered: Charles Bregler's Thomas Eakins Collection at the Pennsylvania Academy of Fine Arts* [New Haven: Yale University Press, 1997], 110). Susan Danly notes that "in

Philadelphia there was an active group of photographers and publishers who ardently believed that photography also had an aesthetic component" ("Thomas Eakins and the Art of Photography," in *Thomas Eakins* [Washington, D.C.: Smithsonian Institution Press, 1993], 180). Eakins even offered suggestions to Muybridge, which were ignored (Foster, *Thomas Eakins Rediscovered*, 112). Meanwhile, during their collaboration, Eakins and Muybridge both experimented with the Marey wheel technique, a means of recording a sequence of images on a single plate, requiring the use of a perforated disk that rotated at a constant speed behind the camera lens (see ibid., 330).

5. André Bazin, *What is Cinema?*, as reproduced in part in *Film Theory and Criticism: Introductory Readings*, 2nd ed., ed. Gerald Mast and Marshall Cohen (New York: Oxford University Press, 1979), 23.

6. It is commonly thought that Whitman and Eakins met in 1887, though they may have met earlier, perhaps in 1883. See Ed Folsom, "Whitman's Calamus Photographs," in *Breaking Bounds: Whitman and American Cultural Studies*, ed. Betsy Erkkila and Jay Grossman (New York: Oxford University Press, 1996), 215. Lantern slide lectures were available to Whitman. In the early 1880s, the Pennsylvania Academy of the Fine Arts hosted a series of such lectures and photographic exhibitions (Danly, "Thomas Eakins," 180).

7. For a discussion of this wax cylinder recording and the reasons for concluding that it is probably authentic, see Ed Folsom, "The Whitman Recording," *Walt Whitman Quarterly Review* 9 (Spring 1992): 214–16. Folsom quotes Edison's letter about wanting to "obtain a phonogram" from Whitman.

Interestingly, in *Gangs of New York* (2002), Daniel Day-Lewis supposedly based his voice on the Whitman wax cylinder recording. See Roger Ebert, "Ebert's Oscar Picks," *Chicago Sun-Times*, 16 March 2003, http://www.suntimes.com/output /oscars/sho-sunday-oscar16.html (24 March 2003).

8. Horace Traubel, *With Walt Whitman in Camden*, 9 vols. (editors and publishers vary, 1906–96; vol. 5: ed. Gertrude Traubel [Carbondale: Southern Illinois University Press, 1964]), 479.

9. Whitman, *Leaves of Grass*, 744. Ben Singer also makes this point in "Connoisseurs of Chaos," 247. Singer goes on to note remarkable parallels in the works and rhetoric of Whitman and Dziga Vertov and suggests "a direct influence on Vertov by Whitman." Whitman had a powerful impact on Russian letters, especially during the 1910s and 1920s. Kornei Chukovsky's translation of *Leaves of Grass* went through multiple printings, including one edition of 50,000 copies issued shortly after the revolution by the Petrograd Soviet of Workers and Red Army Deputies. Vertov's brother, Mikhail Kaufman, confirmed in a 1976 interview that Vertov's intertitles were directly indebted to Whitman's poems. Singer argues that the clearest example is *One Sixth of the World* (1926) with its repetition of "I see" (248).

10. Whitman made this remark to Horace Traubel (quoted in Milton Hindus, ed.,

"Leaves of Grass": One Hundred Years After [Stanford, Cal.: Stanford University Press, 1955], 7).

11. See Ed Folsom, *Walt Whitman's Native Representations* (Cambridge: Cambridge University Press, 1994), Chapter 4.

12. Whitman, *Leaves of Grass*, 648–49.

13. Traubel, *With Walt Whitman in Camden*, 9 vols. (editors and publishers vary, 1906–96; vol. 3 [New York: Mitchell Kennerley, 1914]), 23. That Whitman was successful is suggested by a remark of a student: "Whitman's poetry is like a film on fast forward" (Whitman session at the British Association of American Studies, Swansea, Wales, April 2000).

14. Richardson, *Literature and Film*, 24.

15. Quoted (from Eisenstein's *Film Form*) in Grant, "Whitman and Eisenstein," 264.

16. Whitman, *Leaves of Grass*, 562.

17. For discussion of the film (based on advertising copy and letters), see Florence B. Freedman, "A Motion Picture 'First' for Whitman: O'Connor's 'The Carpenter,'" *Walt Whitman Review* 9 (June 1963): 31–33. *The Carpenter* was commissioned by J. H. Johnston, a friend of Whitman, who some decades earlier arranged for a series of photos that depicted him as a paternal or grandfatherly figure.

18. Review of *The Carpenter* by Rev. W. H. Jackson, *Motion Picture World*, 9 August 1913, 616–17. Whitman's connection to the Civil War continues to be invoked in films. The recent *Gods and Generals* (2003) closes, as the credits roll, with Bob Dylan singing "Cross the Green Mountain," a song that unmistakably echoes "Come Up from the Fields Father."

19. Van Wyck Brooks, *America's Coming-of-Age* (1915; reprint, New York: Octagon Books, 1975), 112.

20. Vachel Lindsay, *The Art of the Moving Picture* (New York: Macmillan, 1916), 93–94 and 36. Interest in hieroglyphics had been intense in nineteenth-century America, and Whitman in particular was fascinated by the new discoveries of Egyptology, including the discovery of the Rosetta stone and the decipherment of Egyptian hieroglyphics. In the early 1850s Whitman was a frequent visitor to Dr. Henry Abbott's Egyptian museum in New York. For Whitman, hieroglyphics held appeal as a communication system escaping the customary limits of language.

21. Quoted in Kenneth Joseph Pierson, "Dramatizing Whitman: A Doctoral Dissertation with a Creative Component" (Ph.D. diss., University of Minnesota, 1994), 176. Further evidence of Griffith's admiration for Whitman is provided by the recollections of cameraman Karl Brown: "When we ran out of things to do with the Assyrian army, we went back to the studio and did some shots of Lillian Gish rocking a cradle, all to the tune of Walt Whitman's poetry, which Griffith recited with great feeling and surprisingly good delivery, considering how outstandingly lousy he was as an actor." See Karl Brown, *Adventures with D. W. Griffith* (New York: Farrar, Straus & Giroux, 1973), 166.

22. Miriam Hansen, *Babel and Babylon: Spectatorship in American Silent Film* (Cambridge: Harvard University Press, 1991), 165. Despite the film's initial reception—first warm, than chilly—it is now regarded as an extraordinary achievement.

23. Ibid., 169.

24. Ibid., 190.

25. Richard J. Meyer, "The Films of David Wark Griffith: The Development of Themes and Techniques in Forty-two of His Films," in *Focus on D. W. Griffith*, ed. Harry M. Geduld (Englewood Cliffs, N.J.: Prentice-Hall, 1971), 118.

26. Sergei Eisenstein, *Film Form: Essays in Film Theory*, ed. and trans. Jay Leyda (New York: Harcourt, Brace, 1949), 241.

27. Similar formal complexity is found of course in *Moby-Dick*, a novel that constantly tests and disrupts typical definitions of genre.

28. The original title of the film is a matter of some debate. When reminiscing about the film, Strand alternately called it *Manhatta* and *Mannahatta*. The Rialto Theatre probably chose the title used when the film was first released commercially: *New York the Magnificent*. See Jan-Christopher Horak, "Paul Strand and Charles Sheeler's *Manhatta*," in *Lovers of Cinema: The First American Film Avant-Garde 1919–1945*, ed. Jan-Christopher Horak (Madison: University of Wisconsin Press, 1995), 269. With regard to the title, I would add that the very use of the words Manhatta or Mannahatta is a poeticizing of the more literal choices also available: Manhattan or, perhaps, even less poetically, New York. Sheeler and Strand follow Whitman's preference for the original Algonquin term for the "'place encircled by many swift tides and sparkling waters.'" See Walt Whitman, *Prose Works 1892*, ed. Floyd Stovall, 2 vols. (New York: New York University Press, 1964), 2:683.

29. Jan-Christopher Horak writes: "Another difference separating *Manhatta* from films like *Berlin, Symphony of a City* and *Man with a Movie Camera* is its lack of interest in human subjects. Considering the humanist impulse inherent in Strand's 'Photography and the New God,' it seems ironic than *Manhatta* would almost totally exclude images of city dwellers in its portrait of the urban environment .... *Manhatta*'s view remains distanced, perching the spectator on skyscrapers, away from any day-to-day activity." See "Modernist Perspectives and Romantic Desire in *Manhatta*," *AfterImage* 15 (November 1987): 14.

30. The same experimentation, a comparable emphasis on the city, and a similar interest in Whitman underlie Vertov's *Man with a Movie Camera* and *One Sixth of the World*. The latter film uses catalogues in the intertitles and a type of parallel structure that is quite similar to Whitman. For more on the Vertov-Whitman connection, see Singer, "Connoisseurs of Chaos," 247–58.

31. Jan-Christopher Horak, "Paul Strand," 277–78.

32. Elmer Rice, *Street Scene: A Play in Three Acts* (New York: Samuel French, 1928), 106–7.

33. Raymond Durgnat and Scott Simmon, *King Vidor, American* (Berkeley: University of California Press, 1988), 119.

34. Olive Higgins Prouty, *Now, Voyager* (Boston: Houghton Mifflin, 1941). Prouty's title page includes the following epigraph: "Untold want, by life and land ne'er granted, / Now, Voyager, sail thou forth, to seek and find." These lines are quoted again within the body of the text. The expression "Now, Voyager" also appears in Whitman's poem "Now Finalè to the Shore." See M. Lynda Ely, "The Untold Want: Representation and Transformation, Echoes of Walt Whitman's *Passage to India* in *Now, Voyager*," *Literature / Film Quarterly* 29 (2001): 43–52, for another view of how Whitman's poetry, Prouty's novel, and Rapper's film interrelate; Ely's article appeared after this chapter was completed.

35. Jeanne Thomas Allen, ed., *Now, Voyager* (Madison: University of Wisconsin Press, 1984), 84–85.

36. The film makes this point when Jerry is reintroduced to Charlotte and is described as a "nice chap . . . not Boston, you know." In Prouty's novel, however, Jerry has a stronger association with Boston and New England (he was a student at MIT and lives in New Hampshire). The film, vaguer about Jerry's background, makes him seem non-Bostonian and even a bit exotic because of Henreid's accent.

37. Jeanne Thomas Allen argues that "Charlotte turns her new-found energies to parenting Jerry's child, applying the knowledge Jaquith offered her to become the mother she needed as a child. And since it is one of Jaquith's patients she is caring for, she implicitly becomes a partner to Jaquith. Although the novel ends with Charlotte's insistence that caring for Tina unites her with Jerry through a sublimation of their love affair, character development suggests that Charlotte has outgrown the father-lover she met on the boat and become the peer of the father-doctor, joining in his work and supporting it" (Allen, *Now, Voyager*, 17).

38. Ibid., 24.

39. Lea Jacobs notes: "The question of how, and through whom, Charlotte Vale's desire will express itself engenders a dizzying chain of displacement and counter-displacement which never comes to rest. . . . Tina, the stars, they all serve as replacements for the man, yet the fact remains that Charlotte refuses the man. In a gloriously perverse gesture the narrative does not bring Charlotte's desire to fruition and an even more perverse sub-text would lead one to suspect that she likes it that way." See Jacobs, "*Now, Voyager*: Some Problems of Enunciation and Sexual Difference," *Camera Obscura* 7 (Spring 1981): 103.

40. Malcolm Cowley, "Walt Whitman: The Secret," *New Republic*, 8 April 1946, 481–84.

41. See <http://www.english.upenn.edu/%7Eafilreis/50s/gays-in-govt.html> and *Congressional Record*, 81st Cong., 2nd sess., March 29–April 24, 1950, 96, pt. 4:4527–28.

42. Mark Goble, "'Our Country's Black and White Past': Film and the Figures of

History in Frank O'Hara," *American Literature* 71 (March 1999): 76. At this time Warner Brothers was speaking in contradictory fashion politically. In the same year that the company brought forth the liberalism of *Goodbye, My Fancy*, it also produced *I Was a Communist for the FBI*, a film suggesting that any labor meeting or race riot stemmed from communists.

43. Fay Kanin's original play makes clear that the college is set in Massachusetts. Thus, like Prouty, Kanin turns to Whitman to reconstruct the United States on more egalitarian lines and away from what each author sees as a more narrow and patriarchal mode associated with New England.

44. Whitman, *Leaves of Grass*, 557.

45. Anticommunist fervor led to distrust of open, lively discussion in the academy. For an interesting discussion of this point shedding indirect light on *Goodbye, My Fancy*, see Alan Filreis, " 'Conflict Seems Vaguely Un-American': Teaching the Conflicts and the Legacy of Cold War," *Review* 17 (1995): 155–69.

46. A paperback copy of *Leaves of Grass* is present on a table at the key moment of *Until the End of the World*, the attempt to restore vision to a woman who has been blind for years. In *Minority Report*, a somewhat highfalutin account of murder and its special status in breaking human bonds is greeted by the one-liner: "Somehow I don't think that was Walt Whitman." Clearly, the poet is expected to remain a touchstone of cogent expression even in 2054.

47. Two other uses of Whitman in film can be noted here. In *Sub Down* (1997) a character quotes *Leaves of Grass* at a moment of great crisis, perhaps because the filmmaker wanted to add a touch of culture to a film of little value. Much more interesting and challenging is D. W. Harper's award-winning alternative film, *Delicate Art of the Rifle* (1996), based on a story by Stephen Grant, which makes haunting use of Whitman. This student-made film is loosely based on the 1966 University of Texas sniper shootings by Charles Whitman. The filmmakers have rechristened Charles Whitman "Walt Whitman," a move that has both resonance and disorienting effects.

48. Alicia Ostriker, "Loving Walt Whitman and the Problem of America," in *Walt Whitman: The Measure of His Song*, rev. ed., ed. Jim Perlman, Ed Folsom, and Dan Campion, (Duluth: Holy Cow! Press, 1998), 458.

49. *Reds* is a rare U.S. film treating Whitman's appeal for leftist groups.

50. Baldwin, *The Devil Finds Work* (1976; reprint, New York: Dell, 1990), 67.

51. Ray Pomeroy, "Gay Love and the Movies," in *The Columbia Anthology of Gay Literature: Readings from Western Antiquity to the Present Day*, ed. Byrne R. S. Fone (New York: Columbia University Press, 1998), 732–33.

52. Threatening and scandalous in his own time, Whitman's relatively tame current status is seen in the frequent use of him in television programs, including the 5 April 1997 episode of the CBS-TV series, "Dr. Quinn, Medicine Woman." The episode treats the Peter Doyle-Whitman relationship. For discussion of this pro-

gram, see Joann P. Krieg, "Walt and Pete in the Family Hour," *Walt Whitman Quarterly Review* 14 (Spring 1997): 201–2, and Desirée Henderson, "*Dr. Quinn, Medicine Woman* and the Prime-Time 'Outing' of Walt Whitman," *Walt Whitman Quarterly Review* 17 (Summer/Fall 1999): 69–76. The entire matter of the representation of Whitman in television shows deserves thoughtful treatment. Some of the key shows for study include: a *Twilight Zone* (old series) adaptation of Ray Bradbury's "I Sing The Body Electric" and a *Northern Exposure* episode in which the disc jockey, Chris, is fired by his boss (the superpatriotic ex-astronaut) for mentioning on the air that Whitman was gay.

53. Whitman sent ambiguous and shifting signals to many soldiers in the Civil War: he could seem like a father, mother, uncle, brother, friend, and lover. The drama of the war and the drama of these personal interactions have fascinated poets, novelists, short story writers, and filmmakers. Andy Warhol planned at one time to do a film about Whitman in the war with Allen Ginsberg playing Whitman and Joe Dellasandro playing a wounded soldier. Ginsberg backed out of the film, apparently because he feared it would be disrespectful of the memory of Whitman. See Michael Ferguson, "Short Cuts: On and Off the Cutting Room Floor," <http://www.joedallesandro.com/html/short_cuts.htm> (13 April 2003).

54. Robert K. Martin's *The Homosexual Tradition in American Poetry* (Austin: University of Texas Press, 1979), was an especially important critical and cultural intervention.

55. Of this group, one of the more interesting films is the non-Hollywood production *Urinal*. Though it makes only passing reference to Whitman, the film is more daring aesthetically and politically than most of the films discussed here, popular films that reached a broad audience but challenged that audience only minimally.

56. "The Road Not Taken" is also quoted in Italian translation.

57. Benigni seems to quote from the standard Italian translation of *Leaves of Grass*. See *Foglie d'erba e Prose di Walt Whitman*, ed. Giulio Einaudi (Turin, Italy: Francesco Toso, 1950), 459.

58. Whitman, *Leaves of Grass*, 376.

59. Tania Modleski, *Feminism Without Women: Culture and Criticism in a "Postfeminist" Age* (New York: Routledge, 1991), 139.

60. One irony is that Bucke's asylum held that the "solitary vice" (masturbation) caused insanity, but the film provides a glimpse of his wife apparently masturbating while reading *Leaves of Grass*.

61. Lynch, "Putting Whitman Back," A7; S. E. D. Shortt, *Victorian Lunacy: Richard M. Bucke and the Practice of Late Nineteenth-Century Psychiatry* (Cambridge: Cambridge University Press, 1986), 125–26.

62. Gwendolyn Audrey Foster, "No Male Frontal Nudity: The Denial of Female Fetishism in Hollywood Cinema," *Mid-Atlantic Almanack* 4 (1995): 37. Consideration of male nudity is explored in Sarah Dunham's *Realism and Lilacs*, a film that fo-

cuses on Thoma Eakins but that also includes a murder mystery involving Walt Whitman. As of August 2003, the film exists in a rough cut. For the script, see <http://bailiwick.lib.uiowa.edu/realism&lilacs/script.html> (13 April 2003).

63. I am indebted to Ed Folsom for this idea.

64. This remark is made in the film *Sophie's Choice*, but comparable sentiments can be found in the novel.

65. Whitman, *Leaves of Grass*, 93–94, 96.

66. Crash's speech, if lineated in the style of *Leaves of Grass*, would break into parallel units reminiscent of Whitman's own work. When Annie asks, "What do you believe in then?" he responds:

> Well, I believe in the soul, the cock, the pussy, the small of a woman's back, the hanging curve ball, high fiber, good scotch, that the novels of Susan Sontag are self-indulgent, overrated crap; I believe Lee Harvey Oswald acted alone; I believe there ought to be a constitutional amendment outlawing astroturf and the designated hitter; I believe in the sweet spot, softcore pornography, opening your presents Christmas morning rather than Christmas eve; and I believe in long slow deep soft wet kisses that last three days.

Few would mistake Crash for Whitman, of course, yet his fondness for lists and rough parallelism shows a rhetorical affinity with the poet who was also willing to announce a credo:

> I believe a leaf of grass is no less than the journey-work of the stars,
> And the pismire is equally perfect, and a grain of sand, and the egg of the wren,
> And the tree-toad is a chef-d'œuvre for the highest,
> And the running blackberry would adorn the parlors of heaven,
> And the narrowest hinge in my hand puts to scorn all machinery,
> And the cow crunching with depress'd head surpasses any statue,
> And a mouse is miracle enough to stagger sextillions of infidels. (Whitman, *Leaves of Grass*, 59)

67. The film is both a celebration of lesbianism and an acknowledgment that lesbianism is under siege. Randy's lesbian family gives thanks at night routinely for getting through another day.

68. Whitman, *Leaves of Grass*, 88.

69. Nicole Cloeren, "Whitman as Signpost to Self-Discovery in *Now, Voyager* and *Love and Death on Long Island*." Quoted with permission.

70. After this chapter was drafted, another film was released, *L.I.E.* (2001), directed by Michael Cuesta, that explores man-boy attachment. In one section of the film, the teenage boy quotes "Out of the Cradle Endlessly Rocking" about the "unknown want," the "destiny of me."

71. With regard to Ronnie, the novel is much bleaker in its ending than is the film.

72. I refer to the most recent film adaptation of *Little Women* (1994).

73. A recent film, *Town and Country* (2001), issued after this chapter was first written, confirms that Whitman retains this shorthand function as a homosexual icon as we enter the new millennium. In this film, Griffin (Garry Shandling) can not quite bring himself to tell his equally affluent friend Porter (Warren Beatty) that he is gay. Instead, while riding in a taxi cab, Griffin, after struggling for words, begins to quote without explanation lines from Whitman's "O Tan-Faced Prairie Boy," leaving Porter unenlightened. But the cabbie immediately breaks into their private conversation, identifies the poet as Whitman and continues by quoting the next lines. Here, again, Whitman's ability to function as a type of love currency and to cross class lines is reinforced.

74. Whitman, *Leaves of Grass*, 505.

75. Those interested in Monroe-Whitman connections may wish to read "Give me Librium or give me Meth!," a poem about the two icons appearing in Lewis MacAdams's *Africa and the Marriage of Walt Whitman and Marilyn Monroe* (Los Angeles: Little Caesar Press, 1982), 38–42.

Abolitionists: and Whitman, 11, 13, 17, 142 (n. 22); in *Flight to Canada*, 103

Adair, Gilbert, 67–69, 134

African Americans: reactions to Whitman, 4–5, 9–10, 98, 104–7; and Bill Clinton, 9, 140 (n. 2); Whitman associated with, 10, 11; in Whitman's works, 11–21, 27–28, 95, 104–5, 148 (n. 93); Thomas W. Higginson and, 31–33, 147 (n. 84); Muhammad Ali on, 34–36; and racial passing, 91–92, 95, 98, 164–65 (n. 7); in *Linden Hills*, 98–102; in *Flight to Canada*, 102–7, 167 (n. 44)

"Against American Literature" (John Dos Passos), 72

Ali, Muhammad, 34–36

America's Coming of Age (Brooks), 114–15

Anglo-Saxon Century, The (J. Randolph Dos Passos), 72, 74

Anti-Semitism, 78–79, 80, 85, 162–63 (n. 43); in "The German Refugee," 86–87

Art of the Moving Picture, The (Lindsay), 115

Backward Glance, A (Wharton), 47, 49, 51, 54

"Beatrice Palmato" (Wharton), 52

Beautiful Dreamers, 128–30

Birth of a Nation, The, 115–16

Black Elk Speaks (Neihardt), 96

Blood quantum, 94

Blue Highways (Heat-Moon), 92–98

Boston, Mass., 29–30, 31, 33, 40, 41; in *Now, Voyager*, 121–22, 172 (n. 36). *See also* New England

Brooks, Van Wyck, 114–15

Bucke, Richard Maurice, 129, 130

Bull Durham, 130, 132–34, *133*, 175 (n. 66)

Burns, Ken, 3

Burns, Ric, 3

Calamus (plant), 58–59

Caliban, 10, 14, 140–41 (n. 6)

Carpenter, Edward, 57, 60–61, 65, 66, 67; *The Intermediate Sex*, 61

Carpenter, The (film), 112–14, *113*, *114*, 170 (n. 17)

"Carpenter, The" (O'Connor short story), 112, 113–14, 170 (n. 17)

Churchill, Ward, 94

Civil liberties: Shahn and, 82, 83–85

Civil War (Ken Burns), 3

Clinton, Bill, 3, 9, 140 (n. 2)

Coughlin, Charles E., 79, 82, 162 (n. 40)

Cowley, Malcolm, 4, 122

Cox, Ignatius W., 80–81, 82

Custom of the Country, The (Wharton), 50–51

Dead Poets Society, 128

Dos Passos, John, 160–61 (n. 25); "Against American Literature," 72; parentage and childhood, 72–73; rejection of upper class, 73; invocation of Whitman, 73–75; nostalgic populism in *U.S.A.*, 75–76

Dos Passos, John Randolph, 72, 74
Douglass, Frederick, 106–7
Down by Law, 126–28
Durham, Jimmie, 94

Eakins, Thomas, 108–10
Edison, Thomas, 110
Enrollment (tribal), 93–94
Erickson, Peter, 8

Father Coughlin (Shahn), 82, *84*
Flight to Canada (Reed), 102–7
Forster, E. M., 65–67
Four Freedoms (Shahn), 82–83
Fredrickson, George, 8
Fullerton, William Morton, 38–39, 41, 42–47, 50, 51, 54, 55, 150 (n. 17), 151 (n. 18), 153 (n. 49), 154 (n. 70)

Gender roles, 41; in *The Trapper's Bride*, 22–26; in "Song of Myself," 26–29, 146 (n. 69); in *Linden Hills*, 101
"German Refugee, The" (Malamud), 85–89
Gods Arrive, The (Wharton), 53–54
Goodbye, My Fancy (film), 122–24
Goodbye, My Fancy (play), 122, 173 (n. 43)
Green, Rayna, 92–93, 95
Griffith, D. W., 115–19

Hawthorne, Nathaniel, 40
Heat-Moon, William Least, 92–98
Higginson, Thomas Wentworth, 31–33, 147 (n. 84)
History of a Jump (Eakins), 109, *110*
Holocaust, 85–89, 132
Homoeroticism. *See* Same-sex love; Whitman, Walt: homoeroticism in works of
Homosexuality. *See* Same-sex love

House of Mirth, The (Wharton), 38
Hudson River Bracketed (Wharton), 53–54

Immigrants and immigration, 162 (n. 40); Whitman linked to, 29, 32, 33, 71, 72; in *U.S.A.*, 76; and "The German Refugee," 85–87
Incredibly True Adventures of Two Girls in Love, The, 134, 175 (n. 67)
Indian Arts and Crafts Act, 94
Intermediate Sex, The (Carpenter), 61
Intolerance, 116–18, *117*, 119

James, William, 9–10
Jordan, June, 4, 9, 140 (n. 5)
Judaism: Shahn and, 78, 161 (nn. 32, 34). *See also* Anti-Semitism

Komunyakaa, Yusef, 26

Lawrence, D. H., 57, 61–65
"Life Apart, The" (Wharton), 39, 42–43, 45, 149–50 (n. 11)
Linden Hills (Naylor), 98–102
Lindsay, Vachel, 115
"Literature" (Wharton), 48–49
Love and Death on Long Island (Adair novel), 67–69, 134, 176 (n. 71)
Love and Death on Long Island (film), 68–69, 134–37, *135*, *136*, 176 (n. 71)

Malamud, Bernard, 85–89
Man at the Crossroads (Rivera), 77
Manhatta (Sheeler and Strand), 118–19, 171 (nn. 28, 29)
Maurice (Forster), 66–67
Miller, Alfred Jacob, 22–27, 144 (n. 48), 146 (n. 66)
Monroe, Marilyn, *137*, 138, 176 (n. 75)
Morrison, Toni, 9, 19
Motion studies: development of, 108–

11, 168–69 (n. 4); analogues in Whitman's work, 111–12

Multiracial identity, 91, 95, 96, 164–65 (n. 7)

Muybridge, Eadweard, 108–9; trotting horse series, *109*

Native American identity, 92–95; in *Blue Highways*, 96, 97–98

Native Americans: marriage customs of, 22–23, 144–45 (nn. 54, 56, 59)

Neihardt, John G., 96

New England: literary and cultural bias toward, 6, 30–34, 40–41, 71, 139 (n. 8); associated with social conservatism, 173 (n. 43). *See also* Boston, Mass.

New York: A Documentary Film (Ric Burns), 3

New York, N.Y.: Bowery, 29–30; as center of fascism, 78–79, 161–62 (n. 35); in *Manhatta*, 118–19; in *Street Scene*, 119

Noel, Roden, 60

Now, Voyager (film), 120–22, *121*, 134, 172 (nn. 34, 36, 37, 39)

Now, Voyager (Prouty novel), 120, 172 (nn. 34, 36)

Nudity in film, 129–30, 174–75 (n. 62)

O'Connor, William Douglas, 112, 113–14

Page, Clarence, 9

Passing, racial, 5, 90–91; and *Blue Highways*, 92–98; in *Flight to Canada*, 105, 107, 167 (n. 44)

Passing, sexual, 5, 98–101

Past: merged with present in *Flight to Canada*, 102–3

Photography: Whitman's interest in, 109–11. *See also* Motion studies

Plymouth Rock, 29, 71

Poe, Edgar Allan: treatment of, in *Flight to Canada*, 103–4

Pound, Ezra, 4

Prouty, Olive Higgins, 120, 172 (nn. 34, 36)

Puritan tradition, 33, 122

Radical politics: Shahn's associations with, 77, 78, 161 (n. 28), 162 (n. 42). *See also* Whitman, Walt: as Leftist icon

Rambles among Words (Swinton), 5

Resources of America (Shahn), 70, 77–78, 80–81, *83*, 163 (nn. 48, 51)

Reynolds, Jerry, 94, 95

Rice, Elmer, 119–20

Rivera, Diego, 77

Romanticism in *Blue Highways*, 97

Sacco and Vanzetti, 75–76

Same-sex love: Thomas W. Higginson and, 32–33; changes in attitudes and terminology concerning, 41–42, 57, 60, 61, 66, 67, 69, 125–26, 156 (n. 4), 158 (n. 22); in *A Son at the Front*, 52; in *Specimen Days*, 52, 155 (n. 76); and British society, 56, 60–61, 66; in "Calamus" poems, 57–60, 157 (n. 14); and death, 57–69 passim; in "Drum-Taps" poems, 60; Edward Carpenter and, 60–61, 66, 67; D. H. Lawrence and, 61–65; E. M. Forster and, 65–67; in *Linden Hills*, 98–99, 101–2; in films, 113, 122, 125–38

Santayana, George, 33–34

Shahn, Ben: *Resources of America*, 70, 77–78, 80–81, *83*, 162 (n. 42), 163 (nn. 48, 51); and left-wing politics, 77, 161 (n. 28); *The Passion of Sacco and Vanzetti*, 77; transformative changes in personal life of, 78; and anti-Semitism, 78–81; and *Man at the*

Crossroads, 81–82; *Father Coughlin*, 82, 84; *Four Freedoms*, 82–83, 85

Sheeler, Charles, 118–19, 171 (nn. 28, 29)

Slave narratives: and *Flight to Canada*, 102

Slavery: Whitman and, 11–21, 22, 27–28; and tribal marriage, 23; in *Flight to Canada*, 102–7; and responses to Whitman, 106, 167–68 (n. 58). *See also* Abolitionists

Son at the Front, A (Wharton), 51–52

Sophie's Choice, 130–32, *131*

Spark, The (Wharton), 52–53

Stowe, Harriet Beecher: treatment of, in *Flight to Canada*, 103

Strand, Paul, 118–19, 171 (nn. 28, 29)

Street Scene, 119–20

Swinton, William. See *Rambles among Words*

Symonds, John Addington, 57, 60

Takaki, Ronald, 10

Thayer and Eldridge, 17, 142 (n. 22)

Toomer, Jean, 91–92, 164–65 (n. 7)

Touchstone, The (Wharton), 42, 44

Trapper's Bride, The (Miller), 22–27, *24*, *25*, 144 (n. 49), 146 (nn. 61, 66)

Trogdon, William. See *Blue Highways*

U.S.A. (John Dos Passos), 72, 74–76

Vidor, King, 119–20

Ward, David J., 93

Wharton, Edith, 28–29; on Whitman, 37, 43, 48, 148–49 (n. 1); *The House of Mirth*, 38; projected critical work on Whitman, 38, 51, 149 (n. 5); affair with William Morton Fullerton, 38–39, 42–47, 50, 51, 54, 55, 150 (n. 17), 151 (n. 35), 153 (n. 49), 154 (n. 70); letters of, 38–39, 42, 51; "The Life Apart" (love diary), 39, 42–43, 45, 149–50 (n. 11); poetry of, 39–40; Boston connections of, 41; marriage to Edward Wharton, 41; associations with sexually ambiguous writers, 41–42, 55; *The Touchstone*, 42, 44; affinities with Whitman, 44, 46–48, 55, 150 (n. 13); and "comradeship," 44–47, 50, 51, 53–55, 150 (n. 15), 153 (n. 56); *A Backward Glance*, 47, 49, 51, 54; and masculinity, 47; "Literature," 48–49; on artistic creation, 49–50; and aesthetics, 50–51; *The Custom of the Country*, 50–51; and incest, 51–52; *A Son at the Front*, 51–52, 156 (n. 94); "Beatrice Palmato" fragment, 52; *The Spark*, 52–53; and suicide, 53; *The Gods Arrive*, 53–54; *Hudson River Bracketed*, 53–54

Whitman, Walt: and American nationalism, 3, 4, 11–12, 30–31, 33, 56, 70, 89; absorption into popular culture, 3–4; international appeal of, 3–4, 56, 86, 135–36, 169 (n. 9); and metonymy, 4, 36, 112; and African American writers, 4–5, 9–10, 36; name, meaning of, 4–5, 90, 164 (n. 1); ambiguous cultural status of, 5, 10, 40, 107, 115; rumored heterosexual relationships of, 5, 166 (n. 36); and cultural appropriation, 8, 11, 16–17, 90, 105; and egalitarianism, 8, 9, 10, 11, 17, 18, 30, 34, 57, 75; appeal of, to marginalized groups, 9–10, 90, 92, 98; and racism, 9–19 passim, 105; attacks on, 10, 29–31, 32, 70, 80, 104–6, 140–41 (n. 6), 162 (n. 41); and abolitionists, 11, 13, 17, 142 (n. 22); associated with working-class culture, 11, 29–31, 32, 33, 90; and trans-racial identification,

11, 12–19, 30, 106–7; and slavery, 11–21, 22, 27–28; homoeroticism in works of, 20–21, 32; attraction to drivers, 28; gender constructions in works of, 28–29, 156 (n. 94); paralellism in works of, 34, 133, 175 (n. 66); and genteel tradition, 37, 72, 136; as free thinker, 42, 124; and gender crossing, 46, 98; and incest, 52, 154–55 (n. 75); hospital nursing of, 52–53; associated with Greece, 56–57; as homosexual icon, 56–57, 60, 125–38 passim, 176 (n. 73); death in works of, 57–60, 63, 64–65; as Leftist icon, 70–71, 74, 124–25; use of, in *Resources of America*, 77–82; use of, in "The German Refugee," 86, 87–89; and racial passing, 90; and Native American writers, 97; treatment of, in *Flight to Canada*, 104–6; interest in photography, 109–11, 112, 169 (n. 6); cinematic techniques in works of, 111; as portrayed in *The Carpenter*, 112–14; D. W. Griffith's admiration of, 115, 116, 170 (n. 21); as mediating figure, 120, 122; as love poet, 124–26, 138
—works
  "Broadway Pageant, A," 118
  "By Blue Ontario's Shore," 115
  "Calamus," 57–60, 64–65, 156–57 (nn. 9, 12, 14); death in, 57–60
  "Calamus" number 27, 59–60, 157 (n. 15)
  "Chants Democratic" number 21, 81
  "Crossing Brooklyn Ferry" ("Sun-Down Poem"), 111, 118, 141–42 (n. 15)
  "Drum-Taps," 60
  "Enfans d'Adam" number 2 ("From Pent-up Aching Rivers"), 20–21
  "Good-bye My Fancy!," 123–24

  "I Sing the Body Electric," 18–20, 132–33
Leaves of Grass: slavery and central image of, 15, 21; in *Blue Highways*, 96, 97
Leaves of Grass (1855), 11, 17, 18–20, 22–29
Leaves of Grass (1856), 11
Leaves of Grass (1860), 19, 20, 57
Leaves of Grass (1881–82), 81
  "Live Oak, with Moss," 57–58, 156–57 (n. 9); death in, 57–60
  "Mannahatta," 118
  "Noiseless Patient Spider, A," 166 (n. 36)
  "Now, Voyager," 69
  "O Captain! My Captain!," 128
  "Once I Pass'd through a Populous City," 5, 100
  "Out of the Cradle Endlessly Rocking" ("A Child's Reminiscence"), 58, 64, 116–18, 119, 175 (n. 70)
  "Passage to India," 120
  "Pictures," 18, 111, 143 (n. 31)
  "Respondez!," 105
  "Scented Herbage of My Breast," 59
  "Singer in Prison, The," 127
  "Sleepers, The," 13, 15–17
  "So Long!," 138
  "Song of Myself," 11, 22–29, 87, 88–89, 90, 104–5, 106, 118, 128, 134, 146 (n. 66)
  "Song of the Open Road," 67
Specimen Days, 52, 155 (n. 76)
  "Talbot Wilson" notebook, 12–15
  "Thou Mother with Thy Equal Brood," 70, 78, 80
  "Untold Want, The," 120, 134
  "When Lilacs Last in the Dooryard Bloom'd," 119–20

"Whoever You are Holding Me Now in Hand," 99–100

Women: and nineteenth-century gynecological treatments, 129

Wright, Frank Lloyd, 3

Wright, Richard, 34